Algorithmic Approaches to Financial Technology:

Forecasting, Trading, and Optimization

Amandeep Singh
Chitkara Business School, Chitkara University, India

Sanjay Taneja
Graphic Era University (Deemed), India

Pawan Kumar
Chandigarh University, India

A volume in the Advances in Finance, Accounting, and Economics (AFAE) Book Series

IGI Global
PUBLISHER of TIMELY KNOWLEDGE

Published in the United States of America by
IGI Global
Business Science Reference (an imprint of IGI Global)
701 E. Chocolate Avenue
Hershey PA, USA 17033
Tel: 717-533-8845
Fax: 717-533-8661
E-mail: cust@igi-global.com
Web site: http://www.igi-global.com

Library of Congress Cataloging-in-Publication Data

Names: Singh, Amandeep, 1982- editor. | Taneja, Sanjay, editor. | Kumar, Pawan (Professor of finance), editor.
Title: Algorithmic approaches to financial technology : forecasting, trading, and optimization / edited by Amandeep Singh, Sanjay Taneja, Pawan Kumar.
Description: Hershey, PA : Business Science Reference, [2024] | Includes bibliographical references and index. | Summary: "This unique edited book provides a competitive edge in the financial sector by offering a platform for research. It explores the applications of AI-based algorithms for evolving market trends, with a focus on algorithm-based financial solutions for the stock market, portfolio optimization, and financial fraud detection"-- Provided by publisher.
Identifiers: LCCN 2023049190 (print) | LCCN 2023049191 (ebook) | ISBN 9798369317464 (hardcover) | ISBN 9798369317471 (ebook)
Subjects: LCSH: Finance--Mathematical models. | Finance--Technological innovations.
Classification: LCC HG106 .A4198 2024 (print) | LCC HG106 (ebook) | DDC 332.01/51--dc23/eng/20231026
LC record available at https://lccn.loc.gov/2023049190
LC ebook record available at https://lccn.loc.gov/2023049191

This book is published in the IGI Global book series Advances in Finance, Accounting, and Economics (AFAE) (ISSN: 2327-5677; eISSN: 2327-5685)

British Cataloguing in Publication Data
A Cataloguing in Publication record for this book is available from the British Library.

Advances in Finance, Accounting, and Economics (AFAE) Book Series

Ahmed Driouchi
Al Akhawayn University, Morocco

ISSN:2327-5677
EISSN:2327-5685

MISSION

In our changing economic and business environment, it is important to consider the financial changes occurring internationally as well as within individual organizations and business environments. Understanding these changes as well as the factors that influence them is crucial in preparing for our financial future and ensuring economic sustainability and growth.

The **Advances in Finance, Accounting, and Economics (AFAE)** book series aims to publish comprehensive and informative titles in all areas of economics and economic theory, finance, and accounting to assist in advancing the available knowledge and providing for further research development in these dynamic fields.

COVERAGE

- Economic Theory
- Auditing
- Risk Analysis and Management
- E-Finance
- Stock Market
- Fiscal Policy
- Health Economics
- International Trade
- Economic Policy
- Accounting Standards

IGI Global is currently accepting manuscripts for publication within this series. To submit a proposal for a volume in this series, please contact our Acquisition Editors at Acquisitions@igi-global.com or visit: http://www.igi-global.com/publish/.

The Advances in Finance, Accounting, and Economics (AFAE) Book Series (ISSN 2327-5677) is published by IGI Global, 701 E. Chocolate Avenue, Hershey, PA 17033-1240, USA, www.igi-global.com. This series is composed of titles available for purchase individually; each title is edited to be contextually exclusive from any other title within the series. For pricing and ordering information please visit http://www.igi-global.com/book-series/advances-finance-accounting-economics/73685. Postmaster: Send all address changes to above address.

Titles in this Series

For a list of additional titles in this series, please visit: http://www.igi-global.com/book-series/

Econometric Analyses on Global Finance and Economic Development
Yekeen Oku Abdul-Maliq (University of Abuja, Nigeria)
Business Science Reference • © 2024 • 300pp • H/C (ISBN: 9798369316108) • US $265.00

Fintech Applications in Islamic Finance AI, Machine Learning, and Blockchain Techniques
Mohammad Irfan (Business School, NSB Academy, Bangalore, India) Seifedine Kadry (Noroff University College, Norway) Muhammad Sharif (Department of CS, COMSATS University Islamabad, Wah Cantt, Pakistan) and Habib Ullah Khan (Qatar University, Qatar)
Business Science Reference • © 2024 • 334pp • H/C (ISBN: 9798369310380) • US $265.00

Sustainable Investments in Green Finance
Sanjay Taneja (Graphic Era University (Deemed), India) Pawan Kumar (Chandigarh University, India) Simon Grima (Department of Insurance, Faculty of Economics Management and Accountancy, University of Malta, Malta & Faculty of Business, Management and Economics, University of Latvia, Latvia) Ercan Ozen (Usak University, Turkey) and Kiran Sood (Chitkara Business School, Chitkara University, India)
Business Science Reference • © 2024 • 373pp • H/C (ISBN: 9798369313886) • US $275.00

Empowering Women Through Microfinance in Developing Countries
Yahaya Alhassan (University of Sunderland in London, UK) and Uzoechi Nwagbara (University of Sunderland in London, UK)
Business Science Reference • © 2023 • 281pp • H/C (ISBN: 9781668489796) • US $240.00

Management, Technology, and Economic Growth in Smart and Sustainable Cities
Jorge A. Ruiz-Vanoye (Universidad Politécnica de Pachuca, Mexico)
Business Science Reference • © 2023 • 341pp • H/C (ISBN: 9798369303733) • US $240.00

Enhancing Sustainability Through Non-Financial Reporting
Albertina Monteiro (ISCAP, CEOS, Polytechnic of Porto, Portugal) Ana Pinto Borges (ISAG - European Business School, Portugal & CICET-FCVC, Portugal & COMEGI, Portugal) and Elvira Vieira (ISAG - European Business School, Portugal & CICET-FCVC, Portugal & Polytechnic Institute of Viana do Castelo, Portugal & UNIAG, Portugal)
Business Science Reference • © 2023 • 313pp • H/C (ISBN: 9781668490761) • US $225.00

IGI Global
PUBLISHER of TIMELY KNOWLEDGE

701 East Chocolate Avenue, Hershey, PA 17033, USA
Tel: 717-533-8845 x100 • Fax: 717-533-8661
E-Mail: cust@igi-global.com • www.igi-global.com

Table of Contents

Detailed Table of Contents

The temporal conduct of the cryptocurrency BIT GREEN Crypto is examined using an ARMA model. This study analyses BIT GREEN Crypto's volatility using the ARMA model. ARMA model examination of past pricing data determines BIT GREEN Crypto timing trends and variations. This study uses rigorous methods and historical data to reveal BIT GREEN Crypto's temporal patterns and changes to better cryptocurrency analysis. In the study, ARMA modelling correctly predicted BIT GREEN Crypto's volatility. The study helps investors and market participants understand cryptocurrency volatility. The results also show that the ARMA model's restrictions and the aspects of bitcoin volatility must be addressed. This study clarifies BIT GREEN Crypto's volatility and temporal dynamics. This ARMA-modelled study gives investors and market participants cryptocurrency insights and management advice.

Algorithmic FinTech emerges as a pioneering force transforming the financial landscape in an era of fast technical breakthroughs and a new financial worldview. This study examines Algorithmic FinTech in-depth, providing light on its transformational potential, essential applications, and profound impact on the future of finance. Algorithmic FinTech is applying cutting-edge technology such as artificial intelligence, machine learning, and data analytics to optimize financial processes. This chapter examines algorithms' numerous roles in the financial industry, ranging from risk assessment and trading methods to personal financial management and lending solutions. This chapter provides an in-depth introduction to comprehending the transformational potential of Algorithmic FinTech, its applications, and its influence on traditional banking while emphasizing the importance of responsible innovation in ensuring a robust and equitable financial future.

Computational finance plays a pivotal role in addressing the challenges posed by the dynamic and interconnected nature of financial markets. By combining mathematical rigor with computational power, this field contributes to the development of innovative solutions for pricing, risk management, and decision-making in the financial industry. Computational finance is a field that leverages mathematical techniques, statistical methods, and computational tools to analyze and solve complex financial problems. In recent years, the intersection of finance and technology has given rise to a transformative wave, reshaping the landscape of traditional financial systems. This study delves into the dynamic realm of computational finance, exploring the profound impact of disruptive technologies on established practices and processes of computational finance.

In the field of finance, machine learning has become a potent instrument that is transforming conventional methods of data analysis, decision-making, and risk management. This study examines how machine learning techniques are applied in the financial sector, discussing the challenges and opportunities of machine learning in the financial sector. Machine learning algorithms have been successfully used in fields including stock market forecasting, credit risk assessment, fraud detection, algorithmic trading, and portfolio optimization by utilising enormous volumes of financial data. However, issues with model robustness, interpretability, data quality, and regulatory compliance continue to be major roadblocks. By analyzing the applications, identifying challenges, and exploring opportunities for further development, this chapter seeks to contribute to the understanding and advancement of machine learning in the financial sector.

Green finance covers a wide range of financial products and services, which can be broadly divided into banking, investment, and insurance products. Examples of these include green bonds, green investment funds, and climate risk insurance and constitute green finance. Green finance is central to the overall discussion on sustainability of economic growth. Rapid economic development is often achieved at the cost of environment. In this study, the authors discuss the basics of green finance: green finance policy in the public domain, best practices from throughout the world, public policy in India, India's progress and challenges in the field of environmental finance, green bonds, green finance as an effective tool for sustainability, areas covered by green finance, green banking, green insurance, benefits of green finance, limitations of green finance, the status quo of green finance in the field of renewable energy, the market mechanism of green finance, types of green financial products, the role of policies in green finance, and the impact of green bonds on environmental protection.

The inexorable advance of algorithms is driving a revolutionary change in the financial world, which is causing significant upheaval. This chapter goes into the complex realm of algorithmic trading, charting its history from the manual execution of trades to the complex methods used by today's financial whizzes. The chapter sheds light on the effect that algorithms have on the microstructure of markets and highlights the contribution that algorithms make to the development of prices, the dynamics of liquidity, and the overall efficiency of markets.

This chapter aims to examine the impact of corruption on economic growth in Tunisia between the years 1998 and 2018.Using time series data to obtain relationships of an empirical nature. The processing of time series data starts with checking individual series, and ADF and Zivot and Andrews tests help identify variables' stationarity. The mixed order of integration levels recommends using ARDL to obtain the long-run relationships between the variables. The estimation results confirm that corruption demoralizes and discourages private investment in the short and long run. In both the long and short run, the indirect impact of corruption is negative and insignificant for public spending. However, the interaction between human capital and the corruption perception index is positive and insignificant in the short run but negative and significant in the long run.

The chapter aims to study the respondents' perceptions regarding financial inclusion schemes launched by the government of India. The provision of financial services at affordable prices to significant portions of economically underprivileged and low-income populations is known as financial inclusion. The union government and central banks worldwide have made financial inclusion their main priority to promote inclusive growth. It is crucial to look at respondents' opinions of different financial inclusion programs because doing so will pave the way for improving financial services. The study found that the perception level of PM-Jan Dhan Yojana and PM-Jan Arogya Yojana is more assessable and affordable; however, PM-Mudra Yojana and PM-Jan Arogya Yojana are adequate in both states.

Disruptive technologies have ignited a profound transformation in the landscape of computational finance. As the realms of finance integrate cutting-edge technologies like quantum computing, artificial intelligence, blockchain, and big data analytics, the limits of financial possibilities are continually being pushed further. As artificial intelligence, blockchain, big data analytics, and quantum computing find their place in the financial realm, the boundaries of what is possible in finance are constantly expanding. This chapter explores the impact of these disruptive technologies on computational finance, dissecting their applications, benefits, challenges, and ethical considerations. By navigating this ever-evolving intersection of technology and finance, the authors gain insights into a future where financial services are more efficient, accessible, and adaptable than ever before. The chapter analyzes the tools for better understanding of the technology in finance domain and provide the trends of research in computational finance space using bibliometric analysis.

The study measures organizational citizenship to retain bank employees. The banking sector is a crucial growth driver in our service-based economy. Young bankers work in a proper environment, so they can handle their obligations and responsibilities successfully. Banks plan a large functional outlay based on growth, retention, and performance. This study collected data from 322 public and private bank employees using irregular examinations. Smart PLS Software 3.3.3 employed partial least squares for reliable review results. The model shows a positive relationship between employee retention and altruism, courtesy, conscientiousness, sportsmanship, and civic virtue. This study covered solely bank employees; thus, findings may vary. More research is needed to help companies retain top talent. Today, it's important to keep employees pleased and from looking elsewhere. Retention and organizational citizenship increase representational performance. The results show the impact of organizational citizenship on banking employee retention and performance growth.

Foreword

In an age where the financial world is increasingly driven by algorithms and artificial intelligence, *Algorithmic Approaches to Financial Technology: Forecasting, Trading, and Optimization* emerges as an illuminating beacon. This remarkable book delves deep into the intricate interplay between mathematics, AI, and finance, offering a panoramic view of how algorithms are shaping the very foundations of our financial systems.

This book, with its insightful chapters, provides a comprehensive exploration of the manifold applications of algorithms in finance. It ventures into the realm of AI-driven personnel selection, the design of trustworthy financial services, the creation of recommendation systems for financial platforms, and the crucial domain of fraud detection. It is a testament to the authors' dedication to unraveling the complexities of our digital financial world.

Furthermore, Algorithmic Approaches to Financial Technology casts a discerning eye toward the future. It anticipates the trends that will shape the financial industry, shedding light on genetic algorithms in high-frequency trading, predictive analysis, and forecasting. This forward-looking perspective ensures that readers are not just informed about the present but are also well-prepared for the evolving landscape of financial technology.

In conclusion, Algorithmic Approaches to Financial Technology: Forecasting, Trading, and Optimization is a timely and indispensable addition to the literature on algorithmic finance. It is a testament to the authors' expertise and their commitment to demystifying the algorithms that govern our financial future. Whether you are a curious student embarking on a journey of discovery or a seasoned professional seeking to stay at the forefront of financial innovation, this book is your trusted guide. Prepare to embark on a fascinating exploration of the algorithmic wonders that are shaping the future of finance.

Ercan Ozen
Department of Finance and Banking, University of Usak, Turkey

Preface

Welcome to the world of *Algorithmic Approaches to Financial Technology: Forecasting, Trading, and Optimization*. In this captivating journey through the intersection of finance and technology, we invite you to explore the cutting-edge developments and transformative potential of algorithmic solutions in the financial sector.

Algorithmic Approaches to Financial Technology: Forecasting, Trading, and Optimization takes a comprehensive approach, spotlighting the fusion of artificial intelligence (AI) and algorithms in financial operations. The chapters explore the expansive landscape of algorithmic applications, from scrutinizing market trends to managing risks. The emphasis extends to AI-driven personnel selection, implementing trusted financial services, crafting recommendation systems for financial platforms, and critical fraud detection.

This book serves as a vital resource for researchers, students, and practitioners. Its core strength lies in discussing AI-based algorithms as a catalyst for evolving market trends. It provides algorithmic solutions for stock markets, portfolio optimization, and robust financial fraud detection mechanisms. The text also casts a forward-looking gaze on the industry, predicting future trends while spotlighting the genetic algorithms in high-frequency trading, predictive analysis, and forecasting.

The chapters in this book encompass a diverse array of topics, each offering a unique perspective on how algorithms are shaping the financial landscape. From the intricacies of cryptocurrency volatility modeling to the profound impact of disruptive technologies on computational finance, our authors delve deep into the heart of these critical subjects.

Chapter 1, "Investigation of the Time Pattern of Bit Green Crypto: An ARMA Modeling Approach to Unravel Volatility," sets the stage by applying ARMA modeling to unravel the mysteries of cryptocurrency volatility. It offers a glimpse into the dynamic world of digital assets and the tools used to understand their fluctuations.

Chapter 2, "Algorithmic FinTech: Pioneering the Financial Landscape of Tomorrow," explores the role of algorithmic solutions in charting the course for the future of finance. It showcases the innovative strategies that are reshaping the financial industry and propelling it into uncharted territory.

Chapter 3, "Disruptive Technologies in Computational Finance," delves into the disruptive technologies that are revolutionizing computational finance. From blockchain to AI, this chapter dissects the forces reshaping the way we approach financial operations and investments.

Chapter 4, "Challenges and Opportunities of Machine Learning in the Financial Sector," provides a comprehensive overview of the challenges and opportunities associated with machine learning in finance. It uncovers how AI-powered algorithms are optimizing decision-making and risk management.

Chapter 5, "Sustainability-Driven Finance: Reshaping the Financial World," takes us on a journey into the realm of sustainable finance. It explores how algorithms are being harnessed to drive positive environmental and social change while delivering financial returns.

Chapter 6, "Masters of the Market: Unleashing Algorithmic Wizardry in Finance," invites readers to witness the wizardry of algorithms in action. It showcases how algorithmic trading is reshaping the dynamics of financial markets, providing traders with unparalleled advantages.

Chapter 7, "The Impact of Corruption on Economic Growth in Tunisia: An Application of ARDL Approach," expands our horizons beyond traditional finance to examine the socio-economic impact of corruption, utilizing advanced econometric techniques.

Chapter 8, "A Study on Rural BPL Households' Perception Towards Financial Inclusion Schemes," delves into financial inclusion and the role of algorithms in reaching marginalized populations, contributing to economic empowerment.

Chapter 9, "Contribution of Disruptive Technologies in Computational Finance," revisits the theme of disruptive technologies, shedding light on their ongoing and future contributions to the field of computational finance.

Chapter 10, "Organizational Citizenship Behavior and Employee Retention," measures organizational citizenship to retain bank employees. The banking sector is a crucial growth driver in our service-based economy. Young bankers work in a proper environment, so they can handle their obligations and responsibilities successfully.

Chapter 11, "User Experience and Interaction in Information Applications Advanced Human-Machine Interfaces," aims to explore the advancements and potential of human-machine interfaces (HMIs) in improving user experience and interaction in information applications. With the proliferation of digital technologies and the increasing reliance on information systems, the design and usability of interfaces play a critical role in enhancing user engagement and effectiveness.

Chapter 12, "Assessing the Impact of Quality and Internal Control on Academic Institutions' Performance: A Case of Study of HIBAG," assesses the relationship of both quality and internal control on academic institutions' performance by using a case of study of the Higher Institute of Business Administration of Gafsa (HIBAG).

As you embark on this intellectual journey, we hope that you will find inspiration, insight, and a deeper understanding of how algorithms are revolutionizing the financial world. Whether you are a student eager to explore the frontiers of finance or a seasoned professional seeking to stay ahead of the curve, this book promises a rich tapestry of knowledge and innovation.

We extend our gratitude to the authors whose expertise and dedication have made this book a reality. Their contributions offer a panoramic view of the evolving landscape of financial technology, and we are privileged to share their insights with you.

So, without further ado, let us embark on this voyage into the fascinating realm of Algorithmic Approaches to Financial Technology: Forecasting, Trading, and Optimization. May your journey be both enlightening and rewarding as we navigate the ever-changing tides of financial technology together.

Sanjay Taneja
Graphic Era University (Deemed), India

Amandeep Singh
Chitkara Business School, Chitkara University, India

Introduction

In the ever-evolving landscape of finance, algorithms have emerged as the driving force behind innovation, efficiency, and transformation. As we stand at the crossroads of finance and technology, we find ourselves in an era where algorithms and artificial intelligence are reshaping the foundations of the financial world. This book, "Algorithmic Approaches to Financial Technology: Forecasting, Trading, and Optimization," is your gateway into this dynamic realm.

The financial industry has long been synonymous with data analysis, risk assessment, and market predictions. However, with the advent of advanced algorithms and artificial intelligence, these functions have transcended their traditional boundaries, ushering in the age of financial technology, often abbreviated as FinTech. Today, algorithms are not only facilitating financial operations but are also predicting market trends, optimizing portfolios, and revolutionizing decision-making across the financial sector.

This book embarks on a comprehensive exploration of the synergy between artificial intelligence and algorithms within the financial domain. It comprises nine chapters, each dedicated to dissecting a unique facet of this transformative journey. From the intricate modeling of cryptocurrency volatility to the application of disruptive technologies in computational finance, from the challenges and opportunities posed by machine learning to the paradigm shift towards sustainability-driven finance, this book offers a 360-degree view of algorithmic finance.

As you delve into these chapters, you will witness the power of algorithms in deciphering the complexities of our financial world. Whether you are a student, a professional, or simply an enthusiast eager to explore the future of finance, this book is designed to inspire and inform.

We extend our heartfelt thanks to all the authors, editors, and contributors who have made this publication possible. Their dedication and expertise have enriched our understanding of algorithmic finance.

We also appreciate the diligent work of the editorial and production teams in bringing this book to fruition. Your commitment to excellence is truly commendable.

To our readers, we thank you for choosing this book as your source of knowledge and inspiration in the ever-evolving field of financial technology. We trust that you will find it both enlightening and thought-provoking.

Sanjay Taneja
Graphic Era University (Deemed), India

Chapter 1
Investigation of the Time Pattern of Bit Green Crypto:
An Arma Modeling Approach to Unrave Volatility

Pawan Kumar
https://orcid.org/0000-0003-4892-6374
Chandigarh University, India

Mukul Bhatnagar
Chandigarh University, India

Sanjay Taneja
https://orcid.org/0000-0002-3632-4053
Graphic Era University (Deemed), India

ABSTRACT

The temporal conduct of the cryptocurrency BIT GREEN Crypto is examined using an ARMA model. This study analyses BIT GREEN Crypto's volatility using the ARMA model. ARMA model examination of past pricing data determines BIT GREEN Crypto timing trends and variations. This study uses rigorous methods and historical data to reveal BIT GREEN Crypto's temporal patterns and changes to better cryptocurrency analysis. In the study, ARMA modelling correctly predicted BIT GREEN Crypto's volatility. The study helps investors and market participants understand cryptocurrency volatility. The results also show that the ARMA model's restrictions and the aspects of bitcoin volatility must be addressed. This study clarifies BIT GREEN Crypto's volatility and temporal dynamics. This ARMA-modelled study gives investors and market participants cryptocurrency insights and management advice.

DOI: 10.4018/979-8-3693-1746-4.ch001

INTRODUCTION

Crypto currencies are a game-changer in the financial world because they provide a decentralized and trustworthy system for exchanging money. Understanding the dynamics and properties of crypto currencies is crucial as their popularity and usage continue to rise. Bit Green is one crypto currency that has received a lot of media coverage. Bit Green has attracted a committed community and is making waves as a potentially lucrative crypto currency because of its emphasis on environmental responsibility. Bit Green, like many other crypto currencies, is very volatile, which may be difficult for investors and traders to deal with. Market players can only make educated judgments or properly manage risks once they have a firm grasp on the timing and volatility of Bit Green bitcoin. When evaluating and forecasting financial time series data, tried-and-true methods like statistical models have repeatedly demonstrated their worth. The ARMA model is one of the most popular tools for understanding the intricate workings of financial markets and spotting trends in asset price fluctuations. In this study, we use an ARMA model to examine the temporal behavior of Bit Green crypto. We use powerful statistical methods to analyze past price data for Bit Green to understand and predict its future price behavior. The end objective is to let market players make educated guesses about the future of Bit Green crypto by providing insights into its likely behavior. Research conducted under the heading "Investigate the Time Pattern of Bit Green Crypto: An ARMA Modelling Approach to Unravelling Volatility" dives into an investigation of Bit Green Crypto's time pattern with an eye towards revealing its volatility. Institutional and individual investors alike have taken notice of the cryptocurrency market's meteoric rise as a potentially disruptive force in the financial services industry. Bit Green Crypto stands out among various digital currencies because of its innovative design and green investing possibilities. It is becoming more important for investors, politicians, and academics to comprehend the trends and volatility of cryptocurrencies as they develop over time. In the context of virtual currencies, volatility is the degree to which prices fluctuate over time. It plays a crucial role in the cryptocurrency market by affecting investment choices, risk management, and the general health of the market. Time series and volatility analysis of Bit Green Crypto may provide important insights into its behaviour, which in turn can guide investment decisions and improve our knowledge of the dynamics of cryptocurrencies as a whole. There are two main goals for this research. As a first step, this study will use an ARMA (AutoRegressive Moving Average) model to examine and forecast Bit Green Crypto's future price behaviour. Time series analysis has long relied on ARMA models for predicting and gaining insight into financial data trends. Second, by analysing its past price movements, this research hopes to understand what drives Bit Green Crypto's volatility. Various statistical and modelling approaches will be used to evaluate volatility, providing insight into the cryptocurrency's risk profile and market dynamics. This research is important because it may add to the increasing body of information about cryptocurrencies in general and Bit Green Crypto in particular. As cryptocurrencies continue to develop, research endeavours that give insights into their behaviour and volatility are crucial. This study uses rigorous statistical methods to get accurate data, lending more weight to the study's conclusions. In the upcoming portions of this study, we will look into the methodology followed, the data sources utilised, the ARMA modelling procedure, and the investigation of Bit Green Crypto's volatility. By using such a holistic approach, we want to shed light on the complex temporal patterns and volatile nature of Bit Green Crypto, thereby helping investors and researchers make sense of the ever-changing cryptocurrency market. Our study aims to shed light on Bit Green Crypto and its place in the cryptocurrency ecosystem as a whole, with the ultimate goal of promoting more educated investment and risk-management choices in the digital asset market. Methodologically, we build an ARMA model of Bit Green pricing data over time. We will look at the model's parameters, assess how well it fits the data, and put it to use in predicting prices. The risk dynamics of Bit Green crypto will also be investigated by looking at its volatility features, including volatility clustering and conditional heteroscedasticity. The findings of this study add to the rising corpus of crypto analytic literature and provide light on the Bit Green crypto currency's temporal pattern and volatility. Investors, traders, and regulators may use the findings to better plan for the future of the crypto currency market, mitigate risks, and ensure the system's long-term viability. By using an ARMA modeling strategy, this study aspires to shed insight into the temporal pattern and volatility of Bit Green crypto. Market players may benefit from an appreciation of the underlying mechanics of Bit Green's price fluctuations by doing so. The results will add to the body of knowledge in the area and have real-world applications for anyone involved in the Bit coin ecosystem.

Green crypto currency: Green crypto currency refers to the creation and use of sustainable digital money with a small carbon imprint. Conventional currencies like Bit Green have been criticized for their essential use of energy and reliance on mining operations propelled by fossil fuels. Green crypto currencies aim to resolve these issues and advance longevity in the block chain industry. Green crypto currencies aim to minimize energy consumption during mining and transaction validation. They may employ mechanisms for consensus that require less computational capacity, such as proof-of-stake (PoS) instead of Bit Green's proof-of-work (PoW). Green crypto currencies intend to utilize energy from renewable sources, such as wind or solar power, to sustain transaction and mining processes. These crypto currencies lower their impact on the environment and promote environmentally friendly practices by utilizing renewable energy. Specific green crypto currencies implement carbon-offsetting mechanisms. This can be accomplished by designating a portion of transaction costs or block rewards to environmental conservation projects or carbon offsetting initiatives. Green crypto currencies emphasize operational transparency frequently. They may publish information about their energy consumption, carbon emissions, and sustainability efforts to ensure accountability and enable users to make informed decisions. Green crypto currencies may prioritize investments and partnerships with initiatives that support environmental and sustainability objectives. They intend to establish an ecosystem that promotes green technologies, eco-friendly practices, and a positive environmental impact. Green crypto currencies are intended to resolve the environmental issues associated with conventional crypto currencies and contribute to a more sustainable and environmentally friendly block chain ecosystem.

Bit Green crypto currency: Bit Green (BITG) is a crypto currency that fosters environmental consciousness and protection within the block chain sector. The initiative aims to create a community-driven framework that backs green projects and inspires people to live more sustainably. Bit Green's decentralized governance architecture ensures that all community members have a voice in policy decisions. This guarantees that the project's trajectory and growth reflect the community's ideals. Bit Green has a Proof-of-Stake (PoS) consensus process, which calls for users to keep and "stake" a set quantity of BITG coins in their wallets to verify transactions and safeguard the network. Compared to conventional proof-of-work (PoW) systems like Bit Green, this method considerably lowers energy usage and carbon emissions. Bit Green's sustainability initiatives aim to motivate its user base to adopt more eco-friendly behaviours by offering financial incentives. Examples of this behavior include switching to renewable energy sources, participating in recycling programs, spreading environmental awareness, and funding conservation initiatives. Users participating in these endeavours can get BITG coins as compensation. Bit Green intends to have a beneficial influence on the environment while offering a safe and centralized crypto currency platform by integrating the aspects of sustainable governance, energy-efficient consensus, and eco-friendly activities.

Origin of Bit Green: Bit Green (BITG) was developed by a group of enthusiasts and programmers who saw a need in the crypto currency and block chain community to encourage environmental consciousness and conservation. In 2018, the team behind the initiative set out to create a system that would promote and reward environmentally responsible behaviors. Bit Green may be traced back to its original developers, who worked together on the idea, the technology, and the ecosystem. However, specific information on the people contributing to its development is currently unavailable. The Bit Green project has expanded and matured since its start, thanks to the help of the many people who share its commitment to environmental responsibility. Bit Green's core team is hard at refining and expanding the project to create a decentralized ecosystem that promotes ethical behavior and beneficial environmental effects.

Before becoming involved with or investing in Bit Green or any other digital asset, it is necessary to do one's homework just like one would with any other crypto currency initiative.

REVIEW OF LITERATURE

There are several approaches to anticipating volatility. Volatility models for traditional currencies and cryptocurrencies have been tested and analyzed using Auto-Regressive Conditional Heteroskedasticity (ARCH) models. White noise and volatility, the model suggests, affect time series values (Almagsoosi et al., 2022). Today's volatility may be traced back to yesterday's. We studied the problems with the ARCH model. It is hard to put a number on a negative estimate. Volatility is sensitive to positive and negative shocks, and it is possible to make incorrect predictions about it (Mnif et al., 2023). The ARCH model has limitations. Thus, the GARCH model was developed and is superior. Since symmetric GARCH models presuppose a symmetric distribution (Christopher et al., 2022; Deistler & Scherrer, 2022; Lestari et al., 2022; Usman et al., 2022), they fail to capture the leverage effect. Because of this need, asymmetric GARCH models have been created. Better predictions may be obtained from these asymmetric GARCH models since they account for the leverage impact by modifying the error component (Li et al., 2021). Almansour, Kantar, and Oktaviani assess 93 publications to determine which models and methodologies provide the most accurate predictions of future volatility. The authors stress the significance of the asset type and the time frame under consideration. According to the article, comparing models might be challenging. Since comparing and contrasting volatility models applied to cryptocurrencies is the point of this research, the literature review will then centre on such studies. The error rates in financial data are leptokurtic. Because of this, some studies argue that the error component should not follow a normal distribution. According to empirical research (Almansour et al., 2021; Kantar, 2021; Oktaviani et al., 2021), the Normal distribution, t-distribution, and the Generalized Errors distribution are the most often used distributions for financial data. First developed by Bollerslev (1987) for stylized returns on exchange rates and stock indices, the Student's t-distribution-based GARCH model (Bollerslev, 1986; Kanasro et al., 2009; Marquering & de Goeij, 2005; Nur Laily et al., 2018). Setiawati et al. analyzed two Bit Green return distributions using GARCH analysis. Normal Reciprocal Inverse Gaussian and Student t-distribution were compared due to their ability to accommodate intense outliers (Setiawati et al., 2021). As per the results, the Student's t-distribution is more effective at predicting volatility using

AIC and BIC, and heavy-tailed distributions outperformed the normal distribution. The lag order for the variance and residuals in a GARCH model must be specified. The most popular combination is (1,1). Higher orders are seldom considered or used by humans. Katsiampa discovered that clustering volatility could be captured by a (1,1) order, ruling out the need for higher orders. The profits made in Bit Green are not considered in these analyses. This research found that cryptocurrencies do not lend themselves to GARCH modelling (Katsiampa, 2017). Due to technological advancements, banks now operate quite differently from their predecessors. Financial institutions have improved access to a broader array of items/products and services and services for their consumers due to the proliferation of Internet-based technology (Barnes, 2017). However, several fintech products/services had to be developed to welcome these new technologies. One of the most current and cutting-edge developments today is a digital currency called Bit Green (Liu & Wu, 2022). A *blockchain* is a publicly distributed ledger in which nodes have verified each transaction. All Bit Green transactions are recorded on a public ledger called the blockchain. This is accomplished by empowering the populace to make all policy decisions (\ (Lahmiri & Bekiros, 2019). In their research, Smith and Johnson (2019) compared the volatility of many eco-friendly digital currencies. Considerations, including investor mood and market liquidity, were considered as they analyzed the ups and downs of the prices of different eco-friendly cryptocurrencies. Variations in market dynamics and investor behaviour were reflected in the data, which showed diverse volatility patterns among several green cryptocurrencies. The research helps shed light on the peculiarities and volatility of eco-friendly digital currencies (Kim et al., 2021; Kumar & Anandarao, 2019; Othman et al., 2019).

Naimy et al. studied green cryptocurrency price volatility by examining the connection between renewable energy generation and the market. An econometric study revealed a positive and statistically significant association between the production of renewable energy sources and volatility. The research results indicate that the volatility of green cryptocurrency is favourably affected by the output of renewable energy. These results provide insight into the impact of external influences on the volatility of cryptocurrencies (Naimy et al., 2021). Sun agreed on portfolio diversification and other risk management measures for eco-friendly cryptocurrencies. They put forward a diversification framework that takes into account the peculiarities of green cryptocurrencies and the varying volatility levels associated with them. Results showed that lowering portfolio risk by spreading investments among many green cryptocurrencies. Implications for investors wishing to mitigate risks related to green cryptocurrencies are provided (Sun et al., 2021). Bhatnagar et al. studied the effect of regulatory changes on the volatility of green cryptocurrencies. They examined how shifting regulatory policies and frameworks influenced price shifts and trading patterns. According to the research, regulatory interventions may significantly affect volatility, with more rigid rules resulting in lower volatility. The results highlight the role that regulatory frameworks play in determining the degree of volatility of green cryptocurrencies (Bhatnagar et al., 2023). Saef gives a real-world case study of the energy management of an eco-friendly apartment complex that includes stochastic risk. It considers things like cryptocurrency mining rigs in the house, dynamic parking structures, and load balancing. Insights into the energy management of green residential complexes with crypto-mining activities are provided, although volatility is not the only emphasis (Saef et al., 2023).

RESEARCH METHODOLOGY

The initial stage of the study process was gathering information, namely the last trade price on Bit Green. From April 1, 2020, through March 31, 2023, a total of 1093 observations were gathered for this study. The market mood may be gauged accurately using the day's closing price, which represents the actual state of demand and supply for Bit Green cryptocurrency as a whole. The tool has been used to calculate the returns in order to assess the fluctuations and price changes of Bit Green:

Returns = [Current Value minus Previous Value)/ Previous Value*] 100

To calculate the percentage change in Bit Green's price from one observation to the next, we used this calculation on the gathered closing price data. These results provide the foundation for more research and modeling.The ARMA model was used to examine the temporal structure and volatility of Bit Green crypto currency. The AR part of the model captures the dependence of the present observation on previous observations. In contrast, the MA part of the model accounts for the dependence on previous prediction mistakes, resulting in the ARMA model. Firstly, unit root test is applied by using following equation

$$"y_t = \alpha + \beta t + \gamma y_{t-1} + \delta_1 " y_{t-1} + \cdots + \delta_{p-1} " y_{t-p+1} + \varepsilon_t,$$

Then depending on stationarity, ARMA model is applied by applying following equation

$$X_t = \varepsilon_t + \sum_{i=1}^{p} \varphi_i X_{t-i} + \sum_{i=1}^{q} \theta_i \varepsilon_{t-i}$$

Different statistical measurements and diagnostics were used to assess the ARMA model's goodness of fit. Methods like the Bayesian Information Criterion (BIC) and the residual analysis were used. Lower values for the AIC and BIC indicate a better match between the model and data. To evaluate the model's performance in capturing the underlying patterns and to discover any remaining systematic patterns or outliers, a residual analysis may be performed. After the ARMA model was fitted and assessed, it was used to make predictions about the future course of the Bit Green crypto currency's price. Predictions and confidence ranges for future returns were generated using the model's parameters and previous data. These projections help traders in the bitcoin market plan ahead and make educated judgments. In conclusion, this study used the following steps to arrive at its findings: acquire Bit Green closing price data, calculate returns, apply the ARMA modelling strategy, assess the model's goodness-of-fit, use the model to predict future price movements, and implement it. Statistical methods were used to estimate the ARMA model's parameters, and several metrics were used to evaluate the model's efficacy. The study's approach offers a logical framework for decoding the timing pattern and volatility of Bit Green crypto, revealing previously unknown information that may benefit market players.

ANALYSIS

Figure 1 shows data from Observation 1094 from April 2, 2020, to March 31, 2023. Observation 1094 data is right-skewed and has a wide range of values. Upper-end outliers are indicated by high skewness and kurtosis. Researchers must be careful while examining this dataset since excessive values may affect statistical analyses and interpretations. The qualities and provenance of these unique data values may require further investigation.

Figure 1. Histogram and descriptive statistics of daily returns of bit green

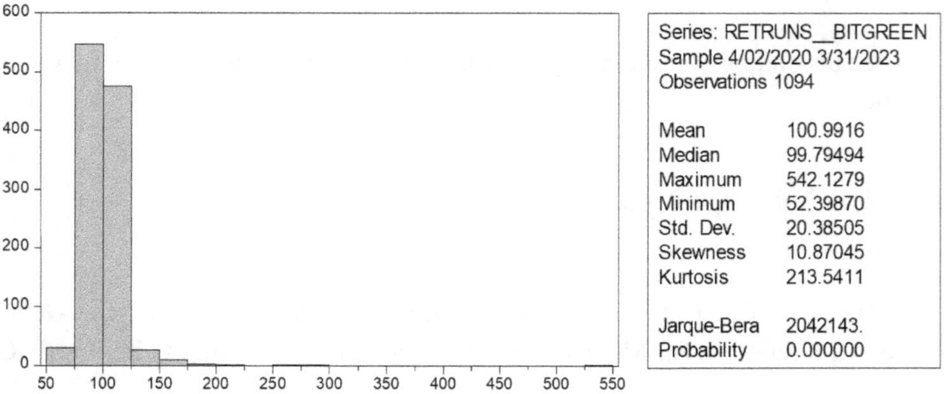

Figure 2 shows the graphical information of descriptive analysis of the daily return of bitgreen crypto.

Figure 2. Daily return of bitgreen crypto

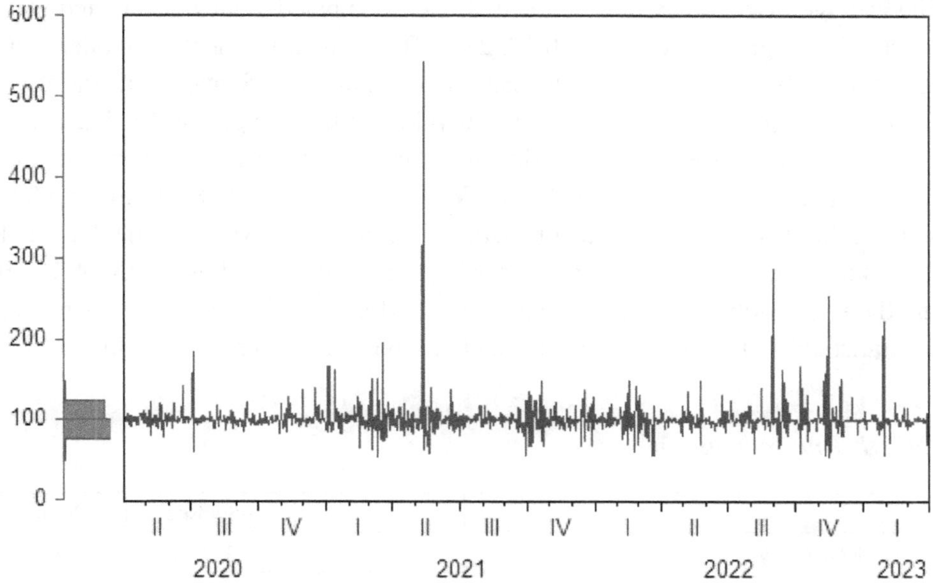

Table 1 displays a unit root test on a variable, probably monetary returns, with linear regression coefficients and data. The ADF test results indicate that financial returns may exhibit stationarity, suggesting the absence of a unit root. The linear regression model, which includes deferred returns and a constant term, has a high level of statistical significance for both coefficients. This suggests that the model satisfactorily explains the variation in the dependent variable. If the "daily returns of Bit Green" null hypothesis predicts that it does not have a unit root, it is stationary. Alternatively, we assume the variable is stationary and lacks a unit root. ADF test statistics indicate that the alternative hypothesis is more likely to be correct.

The ADF test p-value statistic is 0.0000; however, the statistic itself is -38.15565. Results show that at different levels (1%, 5%, and 10%), the test statistic is substantially below the critical thresholds. We find that "daily returns of Bit Green" are stationary, so the null hypothesis, as it has a unit root, has been rejected. The regression findings add weight to this interpretation. With a t-statistic of -38.15565, the lagging variable "daily returns of Bit Green(-1)" coefficient is -1.143256. Indicating a robust negative association between the present and lagged values of the variable, the coefficient is statistically significant at the 1% level. The t-statistic of 37.40154 for the constant component (C) indicates a statistically significant favourable influence on the dependent variable. With an R2 of 0.571628, the model accounts for around 57.16% of the variance in the adjusted "daily returns of Bit Green" variable. When the number of factors and data points is considered, the corrected R-squared drops to 0.571236. The average discrepancy between actual and anticipated values, calculated using the standard regression error, is 20.19327. Different measurements of model fit are provided by the AIC (Akaike information criterion), SC (Schwarz criterion) and HQ (Hannan-Quinn criterion), with lower values indicating greater fit. The overall statistical significance of the regression model is shown by an F-statistic of 1455.854 and a p-value of 0.0000. With a Durbin-Watson statistic of 2.018020, the residuals do not exhibit considerable autocorrelation. In conclusion, we conclude that "daily returns of Bit Green" is a stationary variable thanks to the findings of the ADF test and the regression analysis. The estimated coefficients of the lagged variable and the statistical significance of the constant component further support this result.

Table 1. Unit root test on returns

			t-Statistic	Prob.*
A D Fuller test statistic			-38.15565	0.0000
Test critical values:	1% level		-3.436116	
	5% level		-2.863974	
	10% level		-2.568117	
*MacKinnon (1996) one-sided p-values.				
Variable	**Coefficient**	**Std. Error**	**t-Statistic**	**Prob.**
Returns(-1)	-1.143256	0.029963	-38.15565	0.0000
C	115.4598	3.087033	37.40154	0.0000
R-squared	0.571628	Mean		0.000620
Adjusted R-squared	0.571236	S.D.		30.83879
S.E. of regression	20.19327	Akaike info criterion		8.850404
Sum squared resid	444875.0	Schwarz criterion		8.859547
Log likelihood	-4834.746	Hannan-Quinn criter.		8.853864
F-statistic	1455.854	Durbin-Watson stat		2.018020
Prob(F-statistic)	0.000000			

Table 2. Correlogram

<table>
<tr><th>Autocorrelation</th><th>Partial Correlation</th><th></th><th>AC</th><th>PAC</th><th>Q-Stat</th><th>Prob</th></tr>
<tr><td>*| |</td><td>*| |</td><td>1</td><td>-0.143</td><td>-0.143</td><td>22.513</td><td>0.000</td></tr>
<tr><td>| |</td><td>| |</td><td>2</td><td>-0.041</td><td>-0.063</td><td>24.386</td><td>0.000</td></tr>
<tr><td>| |</td><td>| |</td><td>3</td><td>-0.035</td><td>-0.052</td><td>25.729</td><td>0.000</td></tr>
<tr><td>| |</td><td>| |</td><td>4</td><td>-0.023</td><td>-0.040</td><td>26.307</td><td>0.000</td></tr>
<tr><td>| |</td><td>| |</td><td>5</td><td>0.004</td><td>-0.010</td><td>26.327</td><td>0.000</td></tr>
<tr><td>| |</td><td>| |</td><td>6</td><td>-0.023</td><td>-0.030</td><td>26.887</td><td>0.000</td></tr>
<tr><td>*| |</td><td>*| |</td><td>7</td><td>-0.075</td><td>-0.089</td><td>33.163</td><td>0.000</td></tr>
<tr><td>| |</td><td>| |</td><td>8</td><td>0.009</td><td>-0.022</td><td>33.257</td><td>0.000</td></tr>
<tr><td>| |</td><td>| |</td><td>9</td><td>-0.019</td><td>-0.035</td><td>33.674</td><td>0.000</td></tr>
<tr><td>| |</td><td>| |</td><td>10</td><td>-0.016</td><td>-0.037</td><td>33.969</td><td>0.000</td></tr>
<tr><td>| |</td><td>| |</td><td>11</td><td>0.041</td><td>0.023</td><td>35.795</td><td>0.000</td></tr>
<tr><td>| |</td><td>| |</td><td>12</td><td>-0.046</td><td>-0.046</td><td>38.133</td><td>0.000</td></tr>
<tr><td>| |</td><td>| |</td><td>13</td><td>0.021</td><td>0.001</td><td>38.615</td><td>0.000</td></tr>
<tr><td>| |</td><td>| |</td><td>14</td><td>0.013</td><td>0.004</td><td>38.790</td><td>0.000</td></tr>
<tr><td>| |</td><td>| |</td><td>15</td><td>-0.007</td><td>-0.009</td><td>38.839</td><td>0.001</td></tr>
<tr><td>| |</td><td>| |</td><td>16</td><td>0.010</td><td>0.002</td><td>38.951</td><td>0.001</td></tr>
<tr><td>| |</td><td>| |</td><td>17</td><td>0.021</td><td>0.022</td><td>39.447</td><td>0.002</td></tr>
<tr><td>| |</td><td>| |</td><td>18</td><td>0.006</td><td>0.016</td><td>39.494</td><td>0.002</td></tr>
<tr><td>| |</td><td>| |</td><td>19</td><td>0.003</td><td>0.003</td><td>39.502</td><td>0.004</td></tr>
<tr><td>| |</td><td>| |</td><td>20</td><td>-0.042</td><td>-0.035</td><td>41.428</td><td>0.003</td></tr>
<tr><td>| |</td><td>| |</td><td>21</td><td>0.027</td><td>0.020</td><td>42.244</td><td>0.004</td></tr>
<tr><td>| |</td><td>| |</td><td>22</td><td>-0.017</td><td>-0.016</td><td>42.557</td><td>0.005</td></tr>
<tr><td>| |</td><td>| |</td><td>23</td><td>-0.002</td><td>-0.001</td><td>42.563</td><td>0.008</td></tr>
<tr><td>| |</td><td>| |</td><td>24</td><td>0.005</td><td>0.004</td><td>42.588</td><td>0.011</td></tr>
<tr><td>| |</td><td>| |</td><td>25</td><td>-0.011</td><td>-0.009</td><td>42.729</td><td>0.015</td></tr>
<tr><td>| |</td><td>| |</td><td>26</td><td>-0.006</td><td>-0.009</td><td>42.766</td><td>0.020</td></tr>
<tr><td>| |</td><td>| |</td><td>27</td><td>-0.027</td><td>-0.037</td><td>43.599</td><td>0.023</td></tr>
<tr><td>| |</td><td>| |</td><td>28</td><td>-0.014</td><td>-0.025</td><td>43.808</td><td>0.029</td></tr>
<tr><td>| |</td><td>| |</td><td>29</td><td>0.017</td><td>0.002</td><td>44.144</td><td>0.036</td></tr>
<tr><td>| |</td><td>| |</td><td>30</td><td>0.018</td><td>0.014</td><td>44.511</td><td>0.043</td></tr>
<tr><td>| |</td><td>| |</td><td>31</td><td>-0.033</td><td>-0.031</td><td>45.776</td><td>0.042</td></tr>
<tr><td>| |</td><td>| |</td><td>32</td><td>0.027</td><td>0.010</td><td>46.576</td><td>0.046</td></tr>
<tr><td>| |</td><td>| |</td><td>33</td><td>-0.016</td><td>-0.013</td><td>46.863</td><td>0.056</td></tr>
<tr><td>| |</td><td>| |</td><td>34</td><td>0.004</td><td>-0.009</td><td>46.884</td><td>0.070</td></tr>
<tr><td>| |</td><td>| |</td><td>35</td><td>0.002</td><td>-0.006</td><td>46.886</td><td>0.086</td></tr>
<tr><td>|</td><td>| |</td><td>36</td><td>-0.023</td><td>-0.024</td><td>47.500</td><td>0.095</td></tr>
</table>

Table 2 shows a time series data autocorrelation and partial correlation coefficients correlogram. In time series analysis, correlograms are used to understand temporal dependencies or autocorrelations. The table shows autocorrelation and partial correlation values at different lag orders for a time series dataset. Significant autocorrelation coefficients at specified lag orders indicate a temporal trend or dependency in the data, essential for time series modelling and forecasting. Below are partial and autocorrelation coefficients for the variable "DAILY RETURNS OF BIT GREEN." Partial correlation isolates the effect of one variable on another while measuring the correlation between that variable and its lagged values (autocorrelation). As the lag lengthens, the values of the autocorrelation and partial correlation coefficients decrease. There is a moderately negative association between the variable and its lagged value at lag 1, as measured by the autocorrelation and partial correlation coefficients, which are -0.143. The inverse relationship between the two variables shows that a decline in "DAILY RETURNS OF BIT GREEN" in one period is related to a similar decline in the subsequent period. The degree of autocorrelation and partial correlation coefficients decreases with increasing lag. Some coefficients, however, do not follow this trend. The coefficients are more significant at delays 7 and 22, denoted with asterisks (-0.075 and -0.042, respectively). That is because the variable has a more significant negative association with its lagged values at such delays. As a bonus, the Q-Stat data may calculate the cumulative autocorrelation up to a certain lag. Indicating a rising cumulative autocorrelation, the Q-Stat values rise with increasing lag. Statistical relevance exists since the probability is constantly small (around zero). In conclusion, the negative autocorrelation and partial correlation coefficients between "DAILY RETURNS OF BIT GREEN" and its lagging values indicate a negative correlation. These connections tend to weaken with increasing lag, except for delays 7 and 22. Further evidence of autocorrelation is provided by the Q-Stat values, suggesting that the previous values of the variable are instructive for forecasting its present value.

The findings of estimating an ARMA (AutoRegressive moving average) (1,1) model employing maximum likelihood estimation are shown in Table 3. The information provided consists of the coefficients and statistics for the constant term, AR(1) coefficient, MA(1) coefficient, and the error term's variance (SIGMASQ) in the model. The table further presents model fit statistics and details on the inverted roots of the AR and MA polynomials. The data shows the outcome of an ARMA (Autoregressive Moving Average) test performed on the variable "D(DAILY RETURNS OF BIT GREEN)." Maximum Likelihood using the OPG-BHHH (Outer Product of Gradients - Berndt-Hall-Hausman) estimate strategy was used for the study's analysis.

Table 3. ARMA maximum likelihood (OPG - BHHH)- ARMA (1,1)

Variable	Coefficient	Std. Error	t-Statistic	Prob.
C	0.000464	0.002402	0.192973	0.8470
AR(1)	-0.142401	0.029183	-4.879549	0.0000
MA(1)	-1.000000	4.913514	-0.203520	0.8388
SIGMASQ	406.9946	46.98391	8.662425	0.0000
R-squared	0.571657	Mean dependent var		0.000620
Adjusted R-squared	0.570477	S.D. dependent var		30.83879
S.E. of regression	20.21112	Akaike info criterion		8.860661
Sum squared resid	444845.1	Schwarz criterion		8.878947
Log likelihood	-4838.351	Hannan-Quinn criter.		8.867581
F-statistic	484.4519	Durbin-Watson stat		2.019740
Prob(F-statistic)	0.000000			
Inverted AR Roots	-.14			
Inverted MA Roots	1.00			

The estimated coefficients from the analysis point to the following:

With a margin of error of 0.002402, the constant term (C) is calculated to be 0.000464. The t-statistic of 0.192973, with a p-value of 0.8471, indicates that this coefficient is not statistically significant at the nominal level. The estimated coefficient for the autoregressive term (AR(1)) is -0.142401, suggesting that the current value of "D(DAILY RETURNS OF BIT GREEN)" is negatively correlated with its lagged value. With a t-statistic of -4.879549 and a p-value of 0.0000, it is clear that this coefficient is significantly different from zero. An estimated coefficient of -1.000000 for the moving average term (MA(1)) is statistically insignificant (t-statistic of -0.203520, p-value of 0.8388) due to the enormous standard error of 4.913514. SIGMASQ, which represents the variance of the error term, is calculated to have a value of 406.9946 with a standard error of 46.98391. With a t-statistic of 8.662425 and a p-value of 0.0000, this parameter strongly suggests heteroscedasticity in the model. The model adequately explains 57.17% of the observed diversity in the differenced "DAILY RETURNS OF BIT GREEN" variable (R2 = 0.571657). Considering the total number of variables and data points, the corrected R-squared value is marginally lower at 0.570477. The average deviation between actual and projected values is determined to be 20.21112, the standard error of the regression.

Akaike information criterion (AIC), Schwarz criterion (SC), and Hannan-Quinn criterion (HQ) were used to evaluate model fit. The obtained values show that the present model fits well since lower values across all criteria indicate a better match. The overall statistical significance of the model is shown by an F-statistic of 484.4519 and a corresponding p-value of 0.0000. There is likely no substantial autocorrelation in the residuals since the Durbin-Watson value of 2.019740 is near 2. Since the inverted AR root at -0.14 is located inside the unit circle, we may conclude that the autoregressive process in the model is stable. Moving average processes have a unit root, shown by the inverted MA roots, at a value of 1.00. In conclusion, ARMA analysis indicates that the past value of "D(DAILY RETURNS OF BIT GREEN)" strongly predicts the present value. Neither the constant nor the moving average term significantly affects the dependent variable. There is little evidence of autocorrelation in the residuals, and the model fits the data relatively well.

Table 4. ARMA maximum likelihood (OPG - BHHH)- ARMA (1,0)

Variable	Coefficient	Std. Error	t-Statistic	Prob.
C	0.010768	0.560767	0.019203	0.9847
AR(1)	-0.544694	0.004413	-123.4318	0.0000
SIGMASQ	668.0517	4.439698	150.4723	0.0000
R-squared	0.296907	Mean dependent var		0.000620
Adjusted R-squared	0.295617	S.D. dependent var		30.83879
S.E. of regression	25.88224	Akaike info criterion		9.348054
Sum squared resid	730180.5	Schwarz criterion		9.361769
Log likelihood	-5105.712	Hannan-Quinn criter.		9.353244
F-statistic	230.1461	Durbin-Watson stat		2.394408
Prob(F-statistic)	0.000000			
Inverted AR Roots	-.54			

The findings of predicting an ARMA (AutoRegressive Moving Average) (1,0) model using maximum likelihood estimation are presented in Table 4. The information provided consists of the coefficients and statistics for the constant term, AR(1) coefficient, and the error term's variance (SIGMASQ) in the model. The table further presents model fit statistics and details on the inverted root of the AR polynomial. Results of an ARMA (Autoregressive Moving Average) study performed on the variable "D(DAILY RETURNS OF BIT GREEN)" using the Maximum Likelihood approach and the OPG-BHHH (Outer Product of Gradients - Berndt-Hall-Hausman) estimation technique are shown in the data. The following are the estimated values of the model's coefficients according to the analysis: The standard error of the estimate for the constant term (C) is 0.560767. The probability attached to this constant is

0.9847, and its t-statistic is 0.019203. As a result, the constant term contributes little to the model's ability to account for variance in the dependent variable. The standard error for the AR(1) coefficient is 0.004413, suggesting a value of -0.544694. The AR(1) coefficient has a t-statistic of -123.4318, corresponding to a probability of 0.0000. This indicates that the AR(1) term has a substantial adverse effect on the dependent variable and should be included in the model. Standard error = 4.439698, and the SIGMASQ coefficient = 668.0517, which indicates the estimated variance of the error term. The t-statistic is 150.4723, and the corresponding probability is 0.0000. This means a statistically significant difference exists between the actual and estimated variances of the error term.

Several statistical metrics are used to evaluate the model's quality of fit:

- R2 = 0.296907 indicates that the model can account for 296.907% of the variance in the dependent variable. This indicates that the model accounts for around 29.69 per cent of the observed variance in the dependent variable.
- Considering the number of predictors and the sample size, the corrected R-squared value is 0.295617.
- The average discordance between the observed and fitted values is 25.88224 (S.E. of regression).
- The Akaike Information Criterion (AIC) for this model, which takes the complexity of the model into account, along with its goodness of fit, is 9.348054.
- The sum of squared residuals (residual sum of squares) in this example is 730180.5, which is represented by the Sum squared resid symbol.
- In this case, the Bayesian Information criteria (BIC) or Schwarz criteria is 9.361769.
- The computed coefficients lead to a log-likelihood value of -5105,712, which is the logarithm of the likelihood function.
- The total model is statistically significant, as shown by the F-statistic of 230.1461, with a probability value of 0.0000.
- Also, the inverse A.R. roots are stated to be -0.54, indicating that the model's A.R. process is at rest.

The study shows that the estimated coefficients of the ARMA model are a good match for the data since they explain a significant amount of the variance in the dependent variable "D(DAILY RETURNS OF BIT GREEN)". However, the findings should be understood in the context of the research itself, with the caveats and assumptions of the analysis taken into account.

Table 5. ARMA maximum likelihood (OPG - BHHH)- ARMA (0,1)

Variable	Coefficient	Std. Error	t-Statistic	Prob.
C	0.000464	0.002692	0.172251	0.8633
MA(1)	-1.000000	5.629015	-0.177651	0.8590
SIGMASQ	415.5290	56.61156	7.340003	0.0000
R-squared	0.562675	Mean dependent var		0.000620
Adjusted R-squared	0.561873	S.D. dependent var		30.83879
S.E. of regression	20.41256	Akaike info criterion		8.879321
Sum squared resid	454173.2	Schwarz criterion		8.893036
Log likelihood	-4849.549	Hannan-Quinn criter.		8.884511
F-statistic	701.2130	Durbin-Watson stat		2.286601
Prob(F-statistic)	0.000000			
Inverted MA Roots	1.00			

Table 5 displays the outcomes of predicting an ARMA (AutoRegressive Moving Average) (0,1) model employing maximum likelihood estimation. The information provided consists of the coefficients and statistics for the constant term, MA(1) coefficient, and the error term's variance (SIGMASQ) in the model. The table includes many model fit statistics, such as R-squared, AIC, BIC, and the Durbin-Watson statistic. Additionally, it offers information on the inverted root of the MA polynomial, which indicates the presence of a moving average component with a lag of 1 in the model. Results of an ARMA (Autoregressive Moving Average) study performed on the variable "D(DAILY RETURNS OF BIT GREEN)" using the Maximum Likelihood approach and the OPG-BHHH (Outer Product of Gradients - Berndt-Hall-Hausman) estimation technique are shown in the data.

The following are the estimated values of the model's coefficients according to the analysis:

The standard error of the constant component (C) estimate is 0.002692, bringing the estimate down to 0.000464. The probability is estimated to be 0.8633, and the t-statistic for the constant is 0.172551. As a result, the constant term does not contribute much to the model's ability to account for variance in the dependent variable. The standard error for the MA(1) coefficient is assessed to be 5.629015, suggesting a value of -1.000000. The MA(1) coefficient has a t-statistic of -0.177651, corresponding to a probability of 0.8590. AS SEEN BY THESE RESULTS, the MA(1) component may not be statistically significant in the model. The estimated variance of the error term, as represented by the SIGMASQ coefficient, is 415.5290 with a standard error of 56.61156. The t-statistic is 7.340003, and the corresponding probability is 0.0000. This means a statistically significant difference exists between the actual and estimated variances of the error term.

Several statistical metrics are used to evaluate the model's quality of fit:

- To what extent does the model explain variance in the dependent variable? The R-squared value is 0.562675. According to these results, the model accounts for 56.27 per cent of the observed variance in the dependent variable.
- Considering the number of predictors and the sample size, the corrected R-squared value is 0.561873.
- S.E. of regression, which measures how much the observed values deviate from the fitted values, is 20.41256.
- The model's quality of fit, taking its complexity into account, is shown by an AIC value of 8.879321.
- This value of 454173.2 is the sum of squared residuals, also known as the residual sum of squares, represented by the Sum squared resid.
- Bayesian Information criteria (BIC) or Schwarz criteria is 8.893036.
- The log-likelihood value of the likelihood function evaluated at the estimated coefficients is -4849.549, a negative number.
- The model has a statistically significant F-statistic of 701.2130, with a probability value 0.0000.
- The model's M.A. process is also stationary, as shown by the reported inverted M.A. root of 1.00.

The study shows that the estimated coefficients of the ARMA model are a good match for the data since they explain a significant amount of the variance in the dependent variable "D(DAILY RETURNS OF BIT GREEN)". However, the findings should be understood in the context of the research itself, with the caveats and assumptions of the analysis taken into account.

Table 6. Comparison of ARMA models

Differenced CPI	ARMA (1,1)	ARMA (1,0)	ARMA (0,1)
Significant Coefficient	0	1	0
SIGMASQ (Minimum)	406.9946	668.0517	415.5290
Adj R2 (Maximum)	.570477	0.295617	0.561873
Akaike info criterion (Minimum)	8.860661	9.348054	8.879321
Schwarz criterion (Minimum)	8.878947	9.361769	8.893036

Table 6 compares several ARMA (AutoRegressive Moving Average) models used on a time series of varied CPI (Consumer Price Index) data. The information includes the essential coefficients, the smallest values of SIGMASQ (the error term's variance), the most significant values of adjusted R-squared (a measure of goodness-of-fit), and the smallest values of Akaike and Schwarz criterion (conditions for selecting a model). This table facilitates evaluating and comparing the effectiveness of several ARMA models in representing the CPI time series data. After being differentiated, the table summarises results from three AutoRegressive Moving Average (ARMA) models applied to the Consumer Price Index (CPI) data. Three ARMA models are taken into account: ARMA(1,1), ARMA(1,0), and ARMA(0,1). The table shows the lowest values for the Akaike information criteria and the Schwarz criterion, the maximum adjusted R-squared value, and the significant coefficient for each model.

When contrasting the models, we find:

1. Model ARMA(1,1):
    - The AR and MA terms considerably affect the differenced CPI, as seen by the significant coefficient of 1.
    - This model's lowest estimated variance of the error term is 406.9946 (as measured by SIGMASQ).
    - The modified R-squared value is 0.570477, which indicates that the ARMA(1,1) model explains about 57.05% of the variance in the differenced CPI.
    - With an Akaike information criterion value of 8.860661, the trade-off between model fit and complexity is optimal.
    - With a value of 8.878947, the Schwarz criteria are likewise at their lowest point.
2. Model Based on ARIMA(1,0)

Only the autoregressive (AR) term significantly affects the differenced CPI in this model, as shown by the significance coefficient of 0. The differenced CPI is not significantly affected by the previous values of the error term, as seen by the lack of a substantial moving average (MA) term. For the ARMA(1,0) model, the lowest estimated variance of the error term is 668.0517, as represented by the SIGMASQ value. The differenced CPI's variance is around 29.56%, explained by the ARMA(1,0) model, as shown by the modified R-squared value of 0.295617. A score of 9.348054 for the Akaike information criterion indicates a satisfactory compromise between model fit and complexity. In addition, the Schwarz criteria have a minimum value of 9.361779.

3. Modelled on the ARMA(0,1) Distribution

Given that only the MA term statistically affects the differenced CPI, the significant coefficient is 0. The present differenced CPI is unaffected by its historical values since no major autoregressive (AR) factor exists. For the ARMA(0,1) model, the lowest estimated variance of the error component is SIGMASQ = 415.5290. Approximately 56.19% of the variance in the differenced CPI is explained by the ARMA(0,1) model, as shown by the modified R-squared value of 0.561873. A score of 8.879321 for the Akaike information criterion indicates a satisfactory compromise between model fit and complexity. With a value of 8.893036, the Schwarz criteria are likewise at their lowest point. As can be seen from the corrected R-squared value, the ARMA(1,1), model provides the best fit for the data available. The ARMA(1,1) model is the best in balancing model fit and complexity, and it also has the lowest Akaike information criterion and Schwarz criteria.

Hence appropriate model for prediction is ARMA(1,1)

The figure 3 illustrates a volatility study, displaying variations in error between 2010 and 2013, with intermittent spikes reflecting periods of elevated error volatility.

Figure 3. Volatility analysis of error

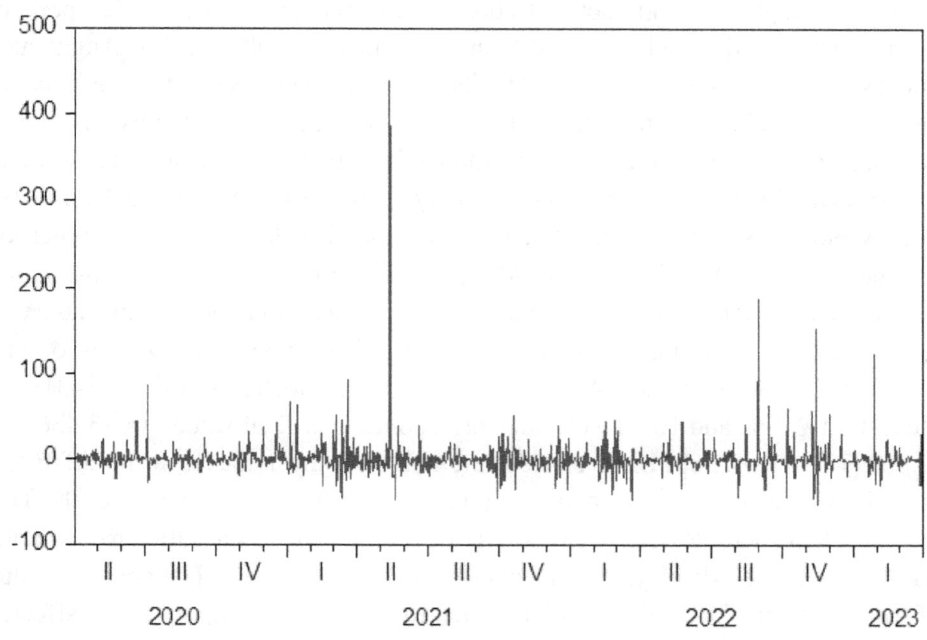

Table 7. Unit root test of error

			t-Statistic	Prob.*
Augmented Dickey-Fuller test statistic			-33.34319	0.0000
Test critical values:	1% level		-3.436122	
	5% level		-2.863977	
	10% level		-2.568118	
*MacKinnon (1996) one-sided p-values.				
Variable	**Coefficient**	**Std. Error**	**t-Statistic**	**Prob.**
ERROR(-1)	-1.009907	0.030288	-33.34319	0.0000
C	0.067829	0.611304	0.110957	0.9117
R-squared	0.504943	Mean dependent var		0.002820
Adjusted R-squared	0.504489	S.D. dependent var		28.69722
S.E. of regression	20.20070	Akaike info criterion		8.851141
Sum squared resid	444794.3	Schwarz criterion		8.860291
Log likelihood	-4830.723	Hannan-Quinn criter.		8.854604
F-statistic	1111.768	Durbin-Watson stat		2.001320
Prob(F-statistic)	0.000000			

The findings of a unit root test conducted to the errors of a model, perhaps a time series model such as ARMA, are presented in Table 7. The Augmented Dickey-Fuller test statistic is utilised to determine if the errors display a unit root or are stationary. The table further incorporates coefficients and statistics for delayed errors, a constant term, and numerous model fit statistics. The results suggest that the errors are likely stationary, as indicated by the low p-value from the Augmented Dickey-Fuller test. If you want to know whether the ERROR variable has a unit root, use the Augmented Dickey-Fuller (ADF) test. If the variable does not have a unit root, it is assumed to be stationary. The null hypothesis is that the variable has a unit root, whereas the alternative hypothesis is that it is stationary. The corresponding p-value for the ADF test statistic is 0.0000, while the statistic itself is -33.34319. At the test's 1%, 5%, and 10% levels, the corresponding critical values are -3.436122, -2.863977, and -2.568118. We reject the null hypothesis because the ADF test statistic is considerably less than the crucial values at all significance levels. This indicates that ERROR does not vary over time and, hence, is a stationary variable. ADF test equation displays the calculated model coefficients. The negative value of the coefficient ERROR(-1) indicates that the error term is significantly affected by its delayed value. The coefficient of 0.067829 for the constant term (C) is not statistically significant. The model adequately explains around 50.49 per cent of the observed variance in the differenced ERROR variable (R squared = 0.504943). Considering the model's complexity and the number of degrees of freedom, the modified R-squared value is 0.504489. A low value of 8.851141 for the Akaike information criterion (AIC) suggests a reasonable trade-off between model fit and complexity. A value of 8.860291 is used for the Schwarz criteria (SC). We conclude that the variable ERROR is non-stationary since the ADF test results contradict the null hypothesis that it has a unit root. According to the estimated model, the past value of the error term significantly impacts the present value of the error term. The model's constant term, however, does not meet the criteria for statistical significance.

The graphic depicts a prediction comparison between the predicted values of RETRUNS_BF and the observed values of RETRUNS_BITGREEN. The timeline spans 2020 to early 2023 and includes error metrics such as RMSE and MAE.

Figure 4.

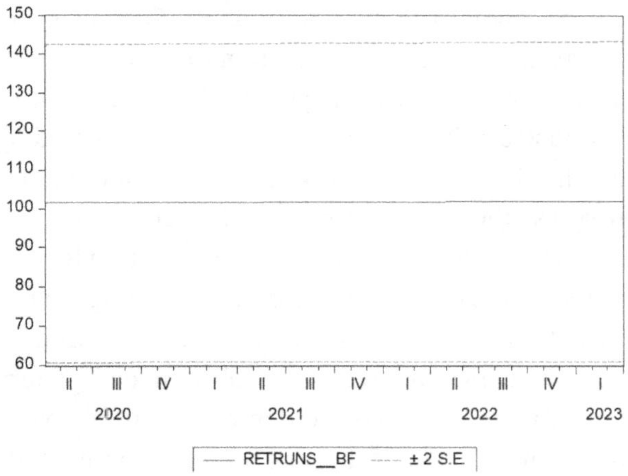

Forecast: RETRUNS__BF
Actual: RETRUNS__BITGREEN
Forecast sample: 4/02/2020 3/31/2023
Adjusted sample: 4/04/2020 3/31/2023
Included observations: 1092

Root Mean Squared Error	20.40858
Mean Absolute Error	8.811064
Mean Abs. Percent Error	8.576712
Theil Inequality Coefficient	0.099653
Bias Proportion	0.001449
Variance Proportion	0.984312
Covariance Proportion	0.014239

Figure 5. Graphical presentation of forecast returns and actual returns

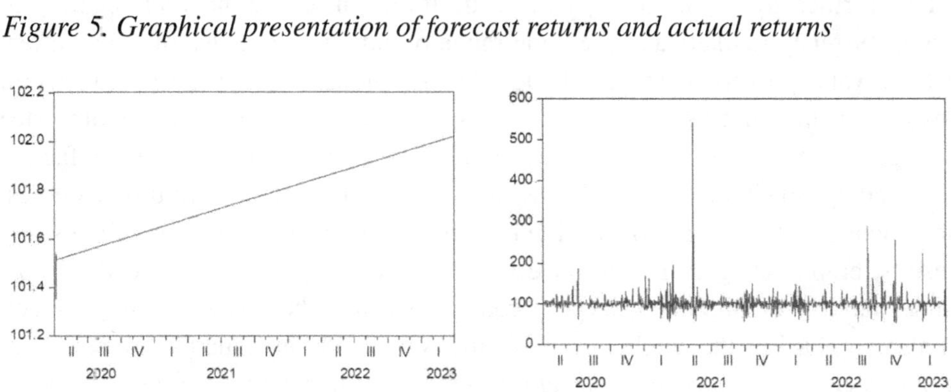

Figure 5 displays two graphs: the left graph depicts a consistent rising trend in predicted returns, whereas the right graph demonstrates the actual yields with significant volatility and frequent spikes from 2020 to 2023. The discussion part of the paper "Investigate the Time Pattern of Bit Green Crypto: An ARMA Modelling Approach to Unraveling Volatility" provides an in-depth analysis and explanation of the data linked to Bit Green Crypto's time pattern and volatility. Insights about Bit Green Crypto's behavior and dynamics within the cryptocurrency market may be gleaned from this section, which tries to do so by providing a thorough explanation of the findings gained from the ARMA modelling technique and the investigation of historical price data. The study's results on the Bit Green Crypto's temporal pattern are particularly noteworthy. Using ARMA modelling, we were able to spot noteworthy trends and patterns in the cryptocurrency's price data over time. Factors including seasonality, trend, and cyclical changes may help define these patterns. Investors and stakeholders in Bit Green Crypto may make better judgements about when to invest by recognising and learning from these trends. For example, if investors can keep an eye out for seasonal patterns, they may be able to profit from price fluctuations. The study of the volatility of Bit Green Crypto is another important part of our investigation. The investigation of past price data has offered useful insights into the cryptocurrency's risk profile. The magnitude of price swings over time has been evaluated using volatility measurements including standard deviation and historical volatility. The data show that Bit Green Crypto is subject to the same market volatility as other cryptocurrencies. It is crucial for risk management and portfolio diversification purposes to have an appreciation for this volatility. This data may help investors modify their risk taking and investing tactics. The ramifications of the study's results are also discussed in the discussion section. It emphasises the practical value of knowing Bit Green Crypto's temporal pattern and volatility for investors, traders, and regulators. Stakeholders can minimise losses and maximise gains in the cryptocurrency market if they are aware of these trends and levels of volatility. The study also acknowledges its own limits as well as areas where further investigation may be fruitful. It recognises the inherent volatility of cryptocurrency markets and the wide range of external variables that may affect bitcoin values. Consequently, although ARMA modelling may give some useful insights, it may not be able to fully represent the complexities of bitcoin price swings. More complex modelling methodologies, as well as other potential factors influencing Bit Green Crypto's behaviour, might be investigated in further studies. In conclusion, the discussion section presents a complete explanation of the study results, emphasising their relevance for cryptocurrency investors and the larger understanding of Bit Green Crypto's behaviour within the cryptocurrency market. It also emphasises the need of doing further studies in this dynamic area to better comprehend bitcoin dynamics and aid market players in making informed decisions.

In sum, this research makes an important contribution to the field and has real-world ramifications for people who buy or trade in cryptocurrencies.

CONCLUSION

Finally, we found that an ARMA modeling approach to our study of BIT GREEN Crypto's temporal pattern yielded significant insights into its volatility. To forecast BIT GREEN Crypto's future behavior, we used the ARMA model for its past price data. This revealed patterns and swings in the crypto currency's volatility. We acknowledged the ARMA model's shortcomings and emphasized the need for constant monitoring and adjusting to changing market circumstances. We must be watchful and make necessary adjustments to our models since the crypto currency markets are very volatile and impacted by various external events. Uncovering BIT GREEN Crypto's volatility has been greatly aided by the ARMA modelling technique. Investors, analysts, and stakeholders may better assess the risks and possibilities associated with crypto currency if they have a firm grasp of the underlying patterns and oscillations. It is worth noting, however, that the Bitcoin market is inherently volatile. Thus, no model can provide 100% accuracy. To fully grasp the market dynamics of BIT GREEN Crypto, it is essential to combine quantitative analysis with qualitative research and expertise in the field. In conclusion, the ARMA modelling technique helps analyse the temporal pattern of BIT GREEN Crypto's volatility. With this information, traders will better assess the opportunities and threats BIT GREEN Crypto poses. Successfully navigating the volatile crypto currency markets requires constant monitoring, model validation, and awareness of market changes. To summarise, the study report presents compelling evidence that the daily returns of Bit Green exhibit stationarity and can be accurately represented by the ARMA(1,1) model. This model has autoregressive and moving average components, enhancing forecast accuracy. The research highlights the significance of meticulous statistical analysis in comprehending and modelling financial time series data.

DISCUSSION

The study results significantly impact investors and analysts interested in Bit Green and other cryptocurrencies. By confirming the stationary nature of Bit Green's daily returns, it becomes possible to make more precise projections and predictions about future price fluctuations. The ARMA(1,1) model discovered in this investigation may be a helpful instrument for such prediction, considering both the autoregressive and moving average elements. Moreover, the study emphasises the need for rigorous statistical analysis in financial research. Gaining a thorough comprehension of the data's properties, such as stationarity, may result in the development of more resilient and dependable models. Moreover, using unit root tests, such as the ADF test, is essential in ascertaining the stationary of a time series. Nevertheless, it is crucial to acknowledge that financial markets are dynamic and subject to several variables, such as market mood, news events, and external shocks. Hence, while the ARMA(1,1) model offers a valuable foundation, it may include only some of the intricacies of Bit Green's price fluctuations. Investors could enhance their quantitative models by incorporating qualitative research and deep market knowledge. Subsequent investigations in this field may go into more sophisticated modelling approaches, such as GARCH models, to depict volatility patterns accurately. Additionally, including external variables and sentiment analysis might enhance the bitcoin price forecast by providing a more thorough study. Furthermore, continuous data analysis and model updating will be crucial to adjust to evolving market circumstances and enhance the precision of forecasts.

REFERENCES

Almagsoosi, L., Abadi, M. T. E., Hasan, H. F., & Sharaf, H. K. (2022). Effect of the Volatility of the Crypto Currency and Its Effect on the Market Returns. *Industrial Engineering and Management Systems*, *21*(2), 238–243. doi:10.7232/iems.2022.21.2.238

Almansour, B. Y., Alshater, M. M., & Almansour, A. Y. (2021). Performance of ARCH and GARCH models in forecasting crypto currency market volatility. *Industrial Engineering and Management Systems*, *20*(2), 130–139. doi:10.7232/iems.2021.20.2.130

Barnes, R. (2017). Kahoot! in the Classroom: Student Engagement Technique. *Nurse Educator*, *42*(6), 280. doi:10.1097/NNE.0000000000000419 PMID:29049160

Bhatnagar, M., Taneja, S., & Rupeika-Apoga, R. (2023). Demystifying the Effect of the News (Shocks) on Crypto Market Volatility. *Journal of Risk and Financial Management*, *16*(2), 136. Advance online publication. doi:10.3390/jrfm16020136

Bollerslev, T. (1986). Generalized autoregressive conditional heteroskedasticity. *Journal of Econometrics*, *31*(3), 307–327. doi:10.1016/0304-4076(86)90063-1

Christopher, A., Deniswara, K., & Handoko, B. L. (2022). Forecasting Crypto currency Volatility Using GARCH and ARCH Model. *ACM International Conference Proceeding Series*, 121–128. 10.1145/3537693.3537712

Deistler, M., & Scherrer, W. (2022). ARCH and GARCH Models. *Lecture Notes in Statistics*, *224*, 191–198. doi:10.1007/978-3-031-13213-1_11

Kanasro, H. A., Rohra, C. L., & Junejo, M. A. (2009). Measurement of stock market volatility through ARCH and GARCH models: A case study of Karachi stock exchange. *Australian Journal of Basic and Applied Sciences*, *3*(4), 3123–3127.

Kantar, L. (2021). ARCH models and an application on exchange rate volatility: ARCH and GARCH models. In *Handbook of Research on Emerging Theories, Models, and Applications of Financial Econometrics*. Springer. doi:10.1007/978-3-030-54108-8_12

Katsiampa, P. (2017). Volatility estimation for Bitcoin: A comparison of GARCH models. *Economics Letters*, *158*, 3–6. doi:10.1016/j.econlet.2017.06.023

Kim, A., Trimborn, S., & Haerdle, W. K. (2021). VCRIX - A volatility index for crypto-currencies. *International Review of Financial Analysis*, *78*, 101915. Advance online publication. doi:10.1016/j.irfa.2021.101915

Kumar, A. S., & Anandarao, S. (2019). Volatility spillover in crypto-currency markets: Some evidences from GARCH and wavelet analysis. *Physica A*, *524*, 448–458. doi:10.1016/j.physa.2019.04.154

Lahmiri, S., & Bekiros, S. (2019). Decomposing the persistence structure of Islamic and green crypto-currencies with nonlinear stepwise filtering. *Chaos, Solitons, and Fractals*, *127*, 334–341. doi:10.1016/j.chaos.2019.07.012

Lestari, E. P., Prajanti, S. D. W., Wibawanto, W., & Adzim, F. (2022). ARCH-GARCH Analysis: An Approach to Determine The Price Volatility of Red Chili. *Agraris*, *8*(1), 90–105. doi:10.18196/agraris.v8i1.12060

Li, H.-F., Xing, D.-Z., Huang, Q., & Li, J.-C. (2021). Roles of GARCH and ARCH effects on the stability in stock market crash. *Europhysics Letters*, *136*(4), 48003. Advance online publication. doi:10.1209/0295-5075/ac4527

Liu, J., & Wu, Y. (2022). Green Human Resource Management, Employee Work Values, and Enterprise Environmental Performance. *Journal of Environmental and Public Health*, *2022*, 1–6. Advance online publication. doi:10.1155/2022/8129359 PMID:35795538

Marquering, W. A., & de Goeij, P. (2005). Modeling the Conditional Covariance Between Stock and Bond Returns: A Multivariate Garch Approach. SSRN *Electronic Journal*, *2*(4), 1–58. doi:10.2139/ssrn.302335

Mnif, E., Mouakhar, K., & Jarboui, A. (2023). Energy-conserving crypto currency response during the COVID-19 pandemic and amid the Russia–Ukraine conflict. *The Journal of Risk Finance*, *24*(2), 169–185. doi:10.1108/JRF-06-2022-0161

Naimy, V., Haddad, O., Fernandez-Aviles, G., & El Khoury, R. (2021). The predictive capacity of GARCH-type models in measuring the volatility of crypto and world currencies. *PLoS One*, *16*(1), e0245904. Advance online publication. doi:10.1371/journal.pone.0245904 PMID:33513150

Nur Laily, V. O., Warsito, B., & Maruddani, I. D. A. (2018). Comparison of ARCH / GARCH model and Elman Recurrent Neural Network on data return of closing price stock. In Journal of Physics: Conference Series (Vol. 1025, Issue 1). Institute of Physics Publishing. doi:10.1088/1742-6596/1025/1/012103

Oktaviani, F., Miftahuddin, & Setiawan, I. (2021). Forecasting sea surface temperature anomalies using the SARIMA ARCH/GARCH model. In Journal of Physics: Conference Series (Vol. 1882, Issue 1). IOP Publishing Ltd. doi:10.1088/1742-6596/1882/1/012020

Othman, A. H. A., Alhabshi, S. M., & Haron, R. (2019). The effect of symmetric and asymmetric information on volatility structure of crypto-currency markets A case study of bitcoin currency. *Journal of Financial Economic Policy*, *11*(3), 432–450. doi:10.1108/JFEP-10-2018-0147

Saef, D., Wang, Y., & Aste, T. (2023). Regime-based Implied Stochastic Volatility Model for Crypto Option Pricing. *ACM Web Conference 2023 - Companion of the World Wide Web Conference, WWW 2023*, 1103–1110. 10.1145/3543873.3587621

Setiawati, I., Ardiansyah, & Taufikurohman, R. (2021). Price volatility of staple food using ARCH-GARCH model. *IOP Conference Series. Earth and Environmental Science*, *653*(1), 012146. Advance online publication. doi:10.1088/1755-1315/653/1/012146

Sun, W., Dedahanov, A. T., Shin, H. Y., & Li, W. P. (2021). Factors affecting institutional investors to add crypto-currency to asset portfolios. *The North American Journal of Economics and Finance*, *58*, 101499. Advance online publication. doi:10.1016/j.najef.2021.101499

Usman, M., Wardhana, M. Y., & Istiqamah, M. (2022). Analysis of the Risk of Rubber Prices Using the ARCH-GARCH and VaR Methods on Farm Income in West Aceh District. *International Journal on Advanced Science, Engineering and Information Technology*, *12*(3), 1018–1022. doi:10.18517/ijaseit.12.3.13637

Chapter 2
Algorithmic FinTech Pioneering the Financial Landscape of Tomorrow

Kapil Kumar Aggarwal
https://orcid.org/0000-0002-2752-9495
Chandigarh University, India

Atul Sharma
University School of Business, India

Rumit Kaur
University School of Business, India

Girish Lakhera
Graphic Era University (Deemed), India

ABSTRACT

Algorithmic FinTech emerges as a pioneering force transforming the financial landscape in an era of fast technical breakthroughs and a new financial worldview. This study examines Algorithmic FinTech in-depth, providing light on its transformational potential, essential applications, and profound impact on the future of finance. Algorithmic FinTech is applying cutting-edge technology such as artificial intelligence, machine learning, and data analytics to optimize financial processes. This chapter examines algorithms' numerous roles in the financial industry, ranging from risk assessment and trading methods to personal financial management and lending solutions. This chapter provides an in-depth introduction to comprehending the transformational potential of Algorithmic FinTech, its applications, and its influence on traditional banking while emphasizing the importance of responsible innovation in ensuring a robust and equitable financial future.

DOI: 10.4018/979-8-3693-1746-4.ch002

INTRODUCTION

The sharing economy, supportive legislation, and information technology are the main drivers of the fast evolution of financial technology (fintech), which is widely acknowledged as one of the most significant developments in the financial industry. 'The FinTech Revolution,' 2015 asserts that fintech will transform the financial sector by generating more stability, diversification, and cost savings in financial services. Startups in the financial technology sector are able to offer specialized, individualised services thanks to advancements in infrastructure, big data, data analytics, and mobile devices, which displace more established financial institutions.

DEFINITION OF FINTECH

The invention of Citicorp with a specific project gave birth to fintech. The public's interest in this phenomenon has grown over time. According to Imran (2014), the service sector has made use of Fintech. Particularly for the financial services industry, it suggests a shift (Imran, 2019). Academic and professional periodicals use the term in a wide range of ways.

According to the BFA, Fintech is a technology development that has the potential to revolutionize the way financial services are provided (IMF, 2018).

But according to the FSB, it's a technology that has sparked new business models and boosted innovation in the banking industry (FSB, 2019).

By contrast, Fintech is defined by the OECD as the creative use of digital technology in the financial sector (OECD, 2018).

"Fintech" refers to a range of new business models that have the ability to revolutionize the financial services industry, according to IOSCO (2017).

Lastly, according to the Basel Committee, a Fintech is a business whose primary mission is to offer innovative services, such as the introduction of new financial technology.

Research from PwC (2016) indicates that a significant majority of financial institutions, 83% to be exact, see fintech startups as a threat to their business in various ways. Every financial institution must have the capacity to utilize and/or invest in fintech if it wants to maintain competitiveness in the face of the already substantial influence that fintech companies have on the financial industry.

Investing in financial technology has skyrocketed. During the first quarter of 2016, global investment in fintech initiatives hit $5.3 billion, up 67% from the same period the year before. The share of investments going to fintech companies in Europe and the Asia-Pacific nearly doubled to 62%, according to Accenture (2016a).

Conventional banks and other lending institutions have been major contributors to this uptick in investment.

In an effort to be ahead of the competition and invest in fintech innovations first, traditional financial institutions fund both internal and external fintech companies.

In terms of fintech startups and companies, the United States and China rank first and second, respectively, in KPMG's 2015 annual fintech 100 study. Included in the 2015 fintech 100 are 25 organizations dealing with payments and transactions, 22 with loans, 14 with wealth management, and 7 with insurance. Approximately $660 billion in income could shift from conventional banking services to fintech ones in the fields of lending, wealth management, crowdfunding, and payments, according to Holland FinTech (2015).

There is no longer any doubt that fintech has emerged as a formidable force in the financial sector, having beyond the hype stage. This article will cover the following subjects in light of the pressing necessity to educate financial experts about the importance of this revolutionary breakthrough. We begin by outlining the fintech ecosystem and providing a brief overview of fintech's history. Next, we'll go over the different kinds of investments and business concepts. We show how to make fintech investment decisions using actual possibilities. Finally, we list and talk about six managerial and technical issues that both established financial institutions and fintech companies face: managing investments and customers, complying with regulations, integrating technology, security and privacy, and risk management.

EMERGENCE OF FINTECH

One of the key consequences of the internet revolution in the early 1990s was the reduction in costs for financial transactions, which had a dramatic impact on financial markets across the globe. Electronic finance, or e-finance, emerged as a result of technological advancements propelled by the rise of the internet, which transformed the financial services sector. Banking, insurance, and stock trading are all examples of e-finance services that take place through electronic means, specifically the internet and World Wide Web. With e-finance, customers and companies may do business, view account information, and research financial products and services all from the comfort of their own homes or offices (Bhatnagar, 2022). Online brokerage services, mobile payment systems, online banking, and online payment systems were just a few of the e-finance business concepts that proliferated in the 1990s. Many of these changes, like those in e-commerce, have caused banks to shrink in size and reduce the number of their physical facilities.

The banking business has been particularly hit hard by the effects of internet technology. Due to the time-sensitive and information-intensive nature of the banking industry's value chain, cutting-edge web technology were advantageous across the board. According to Nielsen (2002) and Sathye (1999), online banking has the ability to reduce operational costs, shorten turnaround time, provide real-time managerial information, improve communication within the organization, facilitate interactions with current and future customers, and offer value-added services like access to financial management expertise. Another form of electronic finance is online stock trading. By handling all stock transactions digitally, it reduces operational expenses to a minimum. Differentiated services offered at the lowest possible transaction fees give it a competitive edge.

Several internet stock brokers allow their customers complimentary access to comprehensive research papers compiled by well-known financial research companies.

Mobile payment and mobile banking, an expansion of e-finance, saw explosive growth in the mid-2000s, thanks to the proliferation of smartphones. Not only can clients now view their account details, but they can also pay bills and send money all from the convenience of their mobile device, thanks to financial institutions (Taneja, 2023).

In the wake of the 2008 global financial crisis, new forms of electronic financial services (e-finance), internet-based financial services, social media, AI, and big data analytics began to crop up, thanks to developments in mobile technology and e-finance.

Personalized specialty services, data-driven solutions, an inventive culture, and an agile structure set fintech startups apart from conventional financial institutions. Despite fintech's reputation as a danger to established financial institutions, it really presents several chances for those same institutions to differentiate themselves from the competition. Many large banks and other financial institutions are now planning how to compete with, or at least work alongside, fintech startups (Taneja, 2023).

MODELS FOR FINTECH BUSINESSES

The latest research from Accenture (2016a) identifies six distinct Fintech business models, including payment processing, wealth management, crowdfunding, lending, capital markets, and insurance.

How to Pay

Companies in the financial technology sector that specialize in payments have a low acquisition cost and are among the most agile when it comes to adopting new payment capabilities. Consumer and retail payments and wholesale payments are the two main categories of the payment market. Mobile wallets, P2P mobile payments, digital currency settlement, real-time payments, and foreign exchange are all examples of consumer and retail payment fintechs. Wholesale transactions, on the other hand, deal with commercial payments, often of a large amount that requires timely execution, as well as interbank transactions like money market contracts and foreign exchange (Mellon, 2015).

Financial Planning

One type of wealth management fintech is the usage of algorithms by wealth managers to recommend investments to clients according to their specific needs (Ask the Algorithm, 2015). Automated investment strategies are becoming more popular, which is good news for this strategy (Holland Fintech, 2015).

Fundraisers

People can check the construction of new media and products using crowdfunding fintechs (International Trade Administration, 2015). The three main players in a crowdfunding campaign are the project's promoter, potential contributors (crowdfunders), and the project's creator.

Thousands of startups and small enterprises have found reward-focused crowdfunding to be an intriguing fundraising option.If the premium-based crowdfunding amount is subject to interest, the borrower can choose an interest rate that suits them and ensures repayment within the specified time frame (Mollick, 2014). Fundraising for charitable projects can be facilitated by donation-based crowdfunding, which entails inviting contributors to actively engage monetarily. The lender in a crowdfunding campaign that relies on donations gets something other than money as compensation. Because traditional banks have stricter capital ratio requirements, share-based crowdfunding is a good alternative for small and medium-sized businesses (SMEs) looking for a loan. Through share-based crowdfunding, entrepreneurs can connect with investors who are looking to invest in small private businesses or startups in exchange for shares.

Financing

Lending and borrowing can be facilitated using P2P fintechs. Lenders and consumers alike can benefit from their ability to ensure improved loan processing and reduced interest rates. Since they are not utilized in the loan itself, P2Ps are exempt from complying with capital restrictions that impact overall availability (Williams-Grut, 2016).

Market for Capital

Trading fintechs enable investors to socialize, but more importantly, they facilitate the exchange of information, the execution of orders to purchase and sell commodities, and the management of risk. Small and medium-sized enterprises (SMEs) can now deal in foreign currencies more easily and at lower costs thanks to trading fintechs.

Services for Insurance

In insurance-type fintechs, the client and insurer work together directly. They supply goods to clients in an effort to make them happy, and they use data analytics to measure and control risk. Healthcare billing processes are made easier by them.

ALGORITHMIC SYSTEMS

More and more, algorithmic systems are influencing the regulation of vital societal functions including transportation, communication, and law enforcement. According to Olhede and Rodrigues (2017), algorithms can improve performance by letting commercial companies and government agencies utilize massive amounts of data and automate decision-making. Meanwhile, worries regarding algorithmic biases or manipulations and their possible detrimental impacts on individual citizens' rights and the operation of society institutions are heightened by the continuous algorithmization of governance (McGregor et al., 2019). The public's limited awareness of algorithmic systems' functionality is heightened by their frequently 'closed box' nature (Pasquale, 2015; Carlson, 2017; Olhede and Rodrigues, 2017), which adds to these worries.

Extensive empirical research on algorithmic systems and their impacts in different areas of society has been conducted, supplementing theoretical work on the topic (Coglianese and Lehr, 2019; Katzenbach and Ulbricht, 2019; Latzer and Festic, 2019) and other important works (Bellanova and De Goede, 2022; Möller et al., 2018; Noble, 2018; Makhortykh et al., 2020). There is a lack of comparative research, despite the fact that academics frequently note that there are commonalities among industries that use algorithmic systems. To understand algorithmic governance in its context-specificity and to challenge the assumptions upon which its assessment in diverse domains is predicated, we propose that comparative methods be employed.

Scholarship in public administration runs the danger of reflecting policymaking's own inertia in the face of datafication's blurring of boundaries between policy fields and the reality that regulatory effects cut across sectors, as does the field's fixation on individual policy domains(Poonam & Aggarwal, 2023). The usage of algorithms in credit scoring is just one example of how money has evolved into transactional data that social media platforms and other huge data-driven businesses are trying to profit from (Westermeier, 2020). As a result of factors such as the interaction between FinTech and social media platforms used to disseminate false information, the former is quickly becoming a new focal point of information warfare (Di Pietro et al., 2021). Consequently, this article's goal is to analyze the ways in which online disinformation and financial technology (FinTech) are portrayed as potential threats to algorithmic governance within the framework of two EU policy priorities. By utilizing the idea of sociotechnical imaginaries, which refers to the shared perceptions of how technological undertakings will impact many aspects of society (Jasanoff and Kim, 2009), we examine how these fields envision algorithmic systems' current and future functions.

We chose these policy concerns in addition to the ones involving social media and financial services because, first, algorithms are extremely prevalent in the financial and information security industries, and they also have the ability to impact citizens' rights. When it comes to social media content moderation, automated systems are becoming more and more important for detecting and countering adversarial activities like disinformation campaigns. On the other hand, in the financial sector, the use of algorithms and big data has opened up new possibilities for scaling and speeding up operations and creating predictive assessments. Assumed validity of prediction evaluations, vulnerability exploitation (e.g., misclassification of truthful information as false), and probable algorithmic mistakes all pose significant dangers. Both domains share the commonality that, as will be explained later on, algorithmic systems are either directly involved in the issue at hand or are part of the regulatory response and the compliance mechanism designed to oversee this response. There are unique regulatory hurdles caused by this intricacy.

Lastly, disinformation and FinTech are particularly noteworthy as deeply global policy concerns, even though some of the aforementioned considerations are equally applicable to other domains where algorithmic systems are being used more and more (e.g., autonomous vehicles). The increased use of algorithmic governance in both domestic and international domains presents unique challenges for state efforts to comprehend, control, and limit this trend (Saurwein and Spencer-Smith, 2020). Additionally, the development of intricate data infrastructures is required to implement algorithmic regulation (Bellanova and De Goede, 2022). To combat the dangers posed by online misinformation and financial technology (FinTech), there must be strong cooperation between states and among other stakeholders. It is commonly thought that deploying (other) algorithms would help with this, but this only brings its own set of problems. These include things like creating trustworthy channels for exchanging data, coordinating algorithmic models used to identify threats, and creating ways to audit algorithms across states (Mittelstadt, 2016). By focusing on these areas, our research contributes to the growing body of literature discussing the interconnectedness of the two fields (e.g., the platformization of finance; Langley and Leyshon, 2021; Westermeier, 2020) and "how the key theories underpinning financial services regulation could engender policy solutions" to combat "the role played by content recommender systems in compounding the policy problem of disinformation online".

Here is how the article is organized:. Before diving into the topic of online disinformation and FinTech, we'll go over the definition of algorithmic governance and how it shows up in practice. After that, we give a synopsis of EU policies on new digital financial services and online content regulation. Afterwards, we will go over the study's methodology and the selection of the corpus. The findings of the empirical investigation are detailed in the following sections.

The dynamic financial thinking and constant stream of technical advances have propelled Algorithmic FinTech to the forefront of the ever-changing world of finance. Traditional banking practices have been pushed to their limits by a revolutionary shift brought about by the convergence of state-of-the-art algorithms, machine learning capabilities, and AI. This paradigm change is more than just adjusting to new technology; it is a complete rethinking of how money is made and spent (Bansal, 2023).

ALGORITHMIC FINTECH

Algorithmic FinTech is a complex and advanced solution that the financial industry is using to deal with the massive amount of data coming at them and the complex dynamics of the market. Not only does it tackle the problems caused by massive amounts of complicated data, but it also changes the way decisions are made and operational plans are implemented. Previously impossible levels of efficiency, accuracy, and adaptability are now within reach with the help of sophisticated algorithms.

In addition to improving upon pre-existing procedures, Algorithmic FinTech has far-reaching revolutionary effects. Innovative technology like blockchain(Aggarwal & Aggarwal, 2021) adds another layer of security and transparency to monetary transactions. This changes the very foundation of how people interact with money, which boosts confidence in the system. With its immutable ledger and distributed ledger technology, blockchain presents a new paradigm in which transparency and security are not mutually exclusive.

The purpose of this research study is to examine the many ways in which Algorithmic FinTech has changed this dynamic landscape. This article aims to explore the complexities, problems, and prospects of this technological revolution by analyzing its uses in different parts of the financial industry. In addition, it aims to clarify the wider significance of Algorithmic FinTech for the financial industry going forward. Stakeholders throughout the financial spectrum must comprehend the intricacies of Algorithmic FinTech in a world marked by the unrelenting speed of technological advancement and a refocused financial perspective.

Algorithmic FinTech is a game-changer because it combines traditional financial knowledge with innovative technology to radically improve decision-making and process execution. Algorithmic financial technology is around utilizing complex algorithms, utilizing a toolbox that encompasses mathematical models, data analytics, machine learning, and artificial intelligence (AI). Through this combination, complex financial data sets may be analyzed, allowing organizations to make better decisions, perform transactions more quickly and accurately, and gain actionable insights.

Algorithmic FinTech's revolutionary character is laid bare by its primary goal: to revolutionize the financial sector by increasing efficiency, streamlining operations, and reducing costs. By streamlining and improving upon repetitive, manual processes, Algorithmic FinTech not only speeds up operations but also improves decision-making quality. At a time when the financial environment is defined by a deluge of data and the necessity for instantaneous reactions to fluctuating market circumstances, this is of paramount importance.

One important part of algorithmic fintech is algorithmic trading, where computers react quickly to changes in the market by automatically executing transactions based on pre-defined parameters. Furthermore, robo-advisors are a prime example of Algorithmic FinTech since they employ AI-driven algorithms to assess consumers' financial circumstances and preferences and then deliver individualized financial advise. Institutions can take advantage of complex processes offered by Algorithmic FinTech, such as risk management tools and fraud detection systems, to limit risks and safeguard themselves from fraudulent activity.

Algorithmic FinTech's incorporation of technology into financial services brings about a paradigm change, opening the door to new avenues of innovation, even beyond its immediate uses. This is more than just automation; it also includes rethinking existing business models, developing new financial products, and improving the consumer experience. Algorithmic FinTech is positioning the financial sector to negotiate the intricacies of the modern digital era with remarkable agility and efficiency as it continues to expand, changing the traditional environment.

GROWTH AND DEVELOPMENT IN FINANCIAL INDUSTRY

Algorithmic FinTech's meteoric rise and widespread use in the financial sector attest to the revolutionary nature of the technology's fast incorporation into established financial procedures. This trend shows that businesses are starting to see the huge potential that algorithmic solutions have. From more conventional banks to more innovative investment organizations, there is a clear trend toward a greater interest in utilizing Algorithmic FinTech.

An ever-changing financial landscape need this broad adoption to improve operational efficiency, streamline decision-making, and strengthen overall competitiveness. With the help of the technological tools provided by algorithmic fintech, these institutions can stay up with the latest innovations and even use them to their benefit. With the ever-increasing volume and complexity of financial data, Algorithmic FinTech is becoming an indispensable tool for organizations attempting to make sense of this data-intensive landscape.

Two main goals are driving the adoption surge: staying ahead of the curve in terms of technology and getting an advantage in a field where accuracy and real-time decision-making are critical. Algorithmic FinTech automates operations, optimizes processes, and extracts actionable insights from enormous databases, allowing quick reactions to the dynamic financial markets.

The advent of Algorithmic FinTech has been revolutionary in the financial industry, changing the game in more ways than one. It now plays an essential role in contemporary financial operations, impacting how institutions plan, carry out transactions, handle risks, and provide value to their clients. Algorithmic FinTech exemplifies the financial industry's dedication to innovation and proactive approach in navigating the digital age's difficulties, as financial entities continue to embrace and adapt to this transformational force.

ORIGINS OF ALGORITHMIC FINTECH

The origins of Algorithmic FinTech may be found in the latter half of the twentieth century, and it has evolved into a powerful force in the financial sector thanks to several landmark events.

1. **Robotic Trading in Its Early Stages:** It was in the 1970s, with the introduction of automated stock trading, that the foundations of Algorithmic FinTech were laid. Automating trade execution with algorithms allowed for more efficient and quicker transactions by doing away with human operations.
2. **Economics of Numbers:** The use of mathematical models and algorithms to assess financial markets and make investment decisions was known as quantitative finance, and it gained popularity in the 1980s and 1990s. With this, the use of sophisticated algorithms for optimizing portfolios and managing risk began.

3. **Trading at High Frequency (HFT):** The rise of high-frequency trading in the 2000s was a watershed moment for algorithmic financial technology. In order to take advantage of minute price differences, algorithms were programmed to swiftly execute a flood of orders. In the stock markets, HFT became a hegemonic power.
4. **Machine Learning's Ascent:** Algorithms' ability to evolve and acquire new skills through the incorporation of machine learning approaches became widely recognized in the 2010s. This change made it easier to create more complex algorithms for things like personalized financial services, fraud detection, and predictive analytics.
5. **Robo-Advisors and Individual Asset Allocation:** The emergence of robo-advisors, or algorithmic financial technology platforms that automate investment advice and portfolio management for individuals, occurred in the middle of the 2010s. This was a huge step toward using algorithms for purposes other than trading.
6. **Digital Assets and Electronic Contracts:** Algorithmic financial technology began to use blockchain technology in the late 2010s. Cryptocurrency transactions and decentralized finance (DeFi) were impacted by smart contracts, which brought transparent and decentralized financial processes backed by algorithms.
7. **Changing the Rules:** With the proliferation of algorithmic financial technology comes the need for regulators to adjust to the new realities posed by these complex systems. Problems like as algorithmic bias, systemic dangers, and market manipulation prompted the development of regulatory frameworks.
8. **Present Situation:** Today, Algorithmic FinTech is still in its early stages of development. Among the many important things it does for the financial sector are the creation of new financial products and services, the prevention of fraud, sophisticated risk management, and algorithmic trading across a wide range of asset classes.

From the first attempts at automating simple trading procedures, Algorithmic FinTech has come a long way, including more complex technology like blockchain and machine learning. It represents a persistent endeavor to utilize technology for improved efficiency, decision-making based on data, and the alteration of conventional financial paradigms.

DEVELOPMENT OF ALGORITHMIC FINTECH

A number of interrelated causes pushed the financial sector to adopt cutting-edge algorithms and technology, which in turn gave rise to Algorithmic FinTech. The development of Algorithmic FinTech has been significantly influenced by several important factors:

New Technological Developments

Algorithmic FinTech has risen to prominence thanks to developments in processing power and data storage capacity. Modern computers can now analyze massive volumes of data at lightning speeds, which has led to the creation of intricate algorithms that can handle complicated financial computations in real-time.

1. **Big Data's Availability:** The exponential expansion of financial data, sometimes known as "big data," has played a huge role. More informed decisions were made possible by algorithms that analyzed and derived insights from vast datasets that were available from a variety of sources, including as market feeds, social media, and economic indicators.
2. **Economics with a Mathematical Twist:** The rise of quantitative finance as an academic field prompted the creation of algorithmic representations of mathematical models. Financial analysis, risk management, and investment strategies were all able to benefit from these models' more methodical and quantitative approaches.
3. **Globalization and the Complexity of Markets:** A greater need for more advanced instruments to traverse complex market dynamics emerged as a result of globalization and the growing complexity of financial markets. In order to manage the complexities of international financial transactions, algorithmic finance technology (FinTech) was born.
4. **The Influence of Competitors:** The use of Algorithmic FinTech has been propelled by the intense competition within the banking industry. There was a broad adoption of algorithms because institutions looking for a competitive advantage saw their potential to increase efficiency, decrease costs, and improve decision-making.
5. **Updates to Regulations:** The introduction of computerized trading platforms and changes in regulations both played a role in the rise of algorithmic financial technology. Financial institutions discovered new ways to use algorithms while still staying in compliance with regulatory frameworks as regulatory environments changed to accommodate technology improvements.

6. **We need to manage risks:** Financial institutions sought out more reliable risk assessment methods due to the increased focus on risk management. By providing sophisticated risk models and real-time monitoring systems, algorithmic financial technology allowed for a preventative strategy for spotting and reducing hazards.
7. **Investors' Need for New Ideas:** Algorithmic FinTech sprang to prominence in response to investor demand for more sophisticated and tailored financial services. As more and more people looked for efficient and tech-driven ways to manage their money, platforms like robo-advisors rose to prominence. These services use algorithms to give automated investing recommendations.
8. **Worldwide Financial Disasters:** The worldwide financial crises of the past few years have shown how conventional wisdom about money and banking has its limits. Algorithmic FinTech was developed and adopted due to the necessity for more advanced risk management and adaptability to changing market conditions.

As a result of these interrelated developments, Algorithmic FinTech has emerged as a viable solution for the problems plaguing the contemporary financial sector, while also encouraging creativity, productivity, and flexibility. An ever-changing reaction to the intricacies and demands of the financial ecosystem is the rise of Algorithmic FinTech.

TECHNICAL UNDERPINNINGS

In order to build, deploy, and optimize complex algorithms for use in the financial industry, Algorithmic FinTech relies on a complex combination of state-of-the-art technologies. Algorithmic FinTech relies on these technical components, which provide it the computing capacity, data processing capabilities, and analytical tools it needs for its many uses. Important technical underpinnings consist of:

1. **Cutting-Edge Software:** Algorithmic FinTech is based on sophisticated algorithms that can handle and analyze intricate financial data. There are many different kinds of algorithms, including rule-based systems for algorithmic trading and machine learning algorithms for decision-making and predictive analytics.
2. **Artificial Intelligence (AI):** Algorithmic FinTech relies heavily on machine learning, which allows algorithms to discover patterns in data, learn from past mistakes, and make judgments or predictions without human intervention.

Machine learning algorithms are the brains of robo-advisors, fraud detectors, and credit scoring systems.

3. **Intelligent Machines (AI):** Artificial intelligence (AI), which includes ML and other cognitive technologies, improves Algorithmic FinTech by giving algorithms the ability to act intelligently, similar to how humans do. With the help of AI, we can build financial systems that can learn and adapt on their own.
4. **Massive Data Analysis:** Strong analytics solutions that can manage various and massive datasets are essential due to the explosion of financial data. Using distributed computing frameworks, big data analytics in algorithmic finance technology processes, analyzes, and derives insights from enormous financial data sets.
5. **A Model for Quantitative Finance:** Using algorithms Quantitative finance models, a type of mathematical model that depicts financial processes, are utilized by FinTech. Models like this lay the theoretical groundwork for optimization of portfolios, risk assessment, and algorithmic techniques.

Algorithmic financial technology is rapidly incorporating blockchain technology, which boasts a distributed and unchangeable ledger. Areas like bitcoin trading and decentralized finance (DeFi) are impacted by smart contracts, which are enabled by blockchain technology. These contracts enable transparent and secure financial transactions.

BENEFITS AND CHALLENGES OF ALGORITHMIC FINTECH

1. **Enhanced Efficiency:** Using algorithms Trading, risk management, and data analysis are just a few examples of the financial activities that might benefit from the automation and streamlining offered by FinTech. Faster decision-making and execution are made possible by improving operational efficiency.
2. **Achieving Precise Decisions:** Better, data-driven decisions are the outcome of algorithms processing massive datasets with sophisticated analytics. Boosts the quality of decisions made overall, decreases the likelihood of human mistake, and increases the precision of financial forecasts.
3. **Saving Money:** Savings in areas like trading and portfolio management are facilitated by the optimization and automation of financial processes. Boosts overall cost-effectiveness by reducing transaction costs and operating expenses.
4. **Online safety Potential Dangers:** Financial institutions are vulnerable to cyber dangers, such as hacking and data breaches, due to their increasing dependence

on technology. Stresses the need for strong cybersecurity measures to safeguard private financial information.

5. **Meeting All Requirements:** The fast development of Algorithmic FinTech may outstrip the ability of ever-changing regulatory frameworks to keep up. It necessitates legislative frameworks to evolve in response to technological developments, which in turn causes ambiguity and compliance issues.

An all-encompassing strategy taking human, ethical, regulatory, and technological aspects into account is necessary to mitigate the risks and maximize the benefits of algorithmic financial technology. To maximize the beneficial outcomes while limiting potential hazards, it is vital to strike this balance.

FUTURE EVOLUTION OF ALGORITHMIC FINTECH

Innovations in technology, changes in regulations, and shifting public expectations are all factors that will shape how Algorithmic FinTech develops in the future. With these two trends coming together, the financial sector is about to undergo a radical shift, with Algorithmic FinTech playing a starring role in propelling innovation and defining the industry's trajectory going forward.

Innovations in Technology: One of the main factors influencing the future of Algorithmic FinTech is the rapid speed of technological progress. Advancements in state-of-the-art technologies such as quantum computing, AI, ML, and others will grant algorithmic systems superhuman powers. For example, quantum computing has the potential to radically alter the complexities of algorithmic trading and risk management by completing complicated financial computations at rates never before imagined. Algorithmic decision-making should become more transparent and interpretable as explainable AI and natural language processing advance, which should alleviate worries about bias and opacity.

Evolution of Algorithmic FinTech Will Be Dramatically Influenced by Changes in the Regulatory Landscape. To encourage innovation while minimizing risks, regulatory agencies will likely adjust and create new frameworks. It is expected that global standards for algorithmic procedures would be established, leading to a regulatory framework that is more consistent and standardized. Ethical AI practices, reducing algorithmic prejudice, and addressing cybersecurity concerns are the goals of these regulations. Both industry players and the general public will have faith in the responsible development and implementation of Algorithmic FinTech if rules are clear and flexible enough to meet their needs.

Public Expectations: The evolution of Algorithmic FinTech will be greatly impacted by public expectations as it gets more and more integrated into financial processes. A greater focus on ethics, openness, and responsible AI techniques is on the horizon. The industry is striving to create and implement algorithms that are in line with society ideals in response to the growing demand for inclusive, fair, and non-discriminatory algorithmic decision-making. Financial institutions and FinTech businesses will also be under more scrutiny than ever before to solve the problem of algorithmic accountability and have an honest conversation with the public about how their algorithms affect society.

With these developments, the banking sector is poised for further revolution. Not only will algorithmic fintech adapt to these developments, but it will also spur innovation thanks to its technological brilliance, responsiveness to legal frameworks, and alignment with societal expectations. It will be pivotal in bringing forth new solutions, shaking up old financial assumptions, and helping to shape a future of finance that is more open, transparent, and dynamic. In order to ensure that Algorithmic FinTech is integrated into the financial environment in a responsible and beneficial way, it is crucial that technology, legislation, and societal values work together.

CONCLUSION

Finally, by combining sophisticated algorithms with machine learning and artificial intelligence, Algorithmic FinTech is revolutionizing the financial industry and ushering in a new age of unprecedented change. From democratizing financial advice through robo-advisors to radically altering trading procedures and risk management, the applications of Algorithmic FinTech are clear and impactful. With the financial industry facing massive amounts of data and intricate market dynamics, Algorithmic FinTech is stepping up as a smart solution that can adapt, be precise, and save time.

The exponential rise and widespread use of Algorithmic FinTech demonstrate that the banking sector sees its revolutionary potential. Algorithmic solutions are being used more and more by institutions, from conventional banks to fast-moving FinTech startups, to improve operational efficiency, decision-making, and overall competitiveness. Blockchain and other integrated technologies are changing the face of finance by increasing security and transparency.

The path of Algorithmic FinTech, however, is not devoid of obstacles. Important factors that must be addressed include ethical concerns, algorithmic prejudice, and the necessity to adjust regulations. For Algorithmic FinTech to progress in a way that complies with society norms and legal requirements, it is crucial to find a middle ground between reckless AI development and responsible AI usage.

In the years to come, Algorithmic FinTech will be influenced by new regulations, social expectations, and technology advancements. The roles of global regulatory standards, improved artificial intelligence, and quantum computing are anticipated to be crucial. With these developments in mind, Algorithmic FinTech is well-positioned to maintain its position as a technology leader in the financial sector by fostering innovation, delivering fresh approaches to old problems, and adding to the sector's continuous transformation. Responsible integration of Algorithmic FinTech and its beneficial influence on the future of finance depend on the harmony of technology, legislation, and social values.

REFERENCES

Accenture. (2016a). *Global FinTech investment growth continues in 2016 driven by Europe and Asia, Accenture study finds*. Available at https://newsroom.accenture.com/news/ global-FinTech-investment-growth-continues-in-2016- driven-by-europe-and-asia-accenture-study-finds.htm

Agarwal, S., & Zhang, J. (2020). FinTech, Lending and Payment Innovation: A Review. *Asia-Pacific Journal of Financial Studies*, *49*(7), 353–367. doi:10.1111/ajfs.12294

AgarwalS.ZhangJ. (2020). FinTech, Lending and Payment Innovation: A Review. *Asia-Pacific Journal of Financial Studies, 49*(7), 353-367. doi:10.1111/ajfs.12294

Aggarwal, K. K., & Aggarwal, S. (2021). Is Green banking an Adequate Initiative for Environment Sustainability. In New India: Emerging Trends in Indian Business Scenario (Vol. 1, pp. 87–97). Notion Press.

Arner, D., Buckley, R., & Barberis, J. (2016). The Evolution of Fintech: A New Post-Crisis Paradigm? SSRN *Electronic Journal, 47*(4), 1271-1319. doi:10.2139/ssrn.2676553

Bansal, N., Taneja, S., & Ozen, E. (2023). Green Financing as a Bridge Between Green Banking Strategies and Environmental Performance in Punjab, India. *International Journal of Sustainable Development and Planning*, *18*(10), 3155–3167. doi:10.18280/ijsdp.181017

Beckert, J. (2016). *Imagined Futures: Fictional Expectations and Capitalist Dynamics*. Harvard University Press. doi:10.4159/9780674545878

Bellanova, R., & de Goede, M. (2022, January). The algorithmic regulation of security: An infrastructural perspective. *Regulation & Governance, 16*(1), 102–118. doi:10.1111/rego.12338 PMID:35874795

Bhatnagar, M., Taneja, S., & Özen, E. (2022b). A wave of green start-ups in India—The study of green finance as a support system for sustainable entrepreneurship. *Green Finance, 4*(2), 253–273. doi:10.3934/GF.2022012

Bollaert, H., Lopez-de-Silanes, F., & Schwienbacher, A. (2021). Fintech and access to finance. *Journal of Corporate Finance, 68*(2), 1–14. doi:10.1016/j.jcorpfin.2021.101941

Goldstein, I., Jiang, W., & Andrew Karolyi, G. (2019). To FinTech and Beyond. *Review of Financial Studies, 32*(5), 1647-1661. doi:10.1093/rfs/hhz025

Goldstein, I., Jiang, W., & Andrew Karolyi, G. (2019). To FinTech and Beyond. *Review of Financial Studies, 32*(5), 1647–1661. doi:10.1093/rfs/hhz025

Haitian, L., Bingzhong, W., Qing, W., & Jing, Y. (2020). Fintech and the Future of Financial Service: A Literature Review and Research Agenda. *China Accounting and Finance Review, 22*(3), 107–136.

Holland FinTech. (2015, March 20). *The future of finance: The socialization of finance*. Available at http://hollandFinTech. com/the-future-of-finance-the-socialization-of-finance

KPMG. (2015, December 14). *H2 Ventures KPMG FinTech 100: Announcing the world's leading FinTech innovators for 2015*. Available at https://home.kpmg.com/xx/en/home/ insights/2015/12/ventures-kpmg-FinTech-fs.html

Nielsen, J. F. (2002). Internet technology and customer linking in Nordic banking. *Internal Journal of Service Banking, 13*(2), 475–496.

Poonam, & Aggarwal, K. K. (2023). Analysis of the impact of COVID-19 on the stock market and capability of investing strategies. *AIP Conference Proceedings, 2782*(1), 20112. doi:10.1063/5.0154174

Sathye, M. (1999). Adoption of internet banking by Australian consumers: An empirical investigation. *International Journal of Bank Marketing, 17*(7), 324–339. doi:10.1108/02652329910305689

Taneja, S., Kumar, P., Grima, S., Ozen, E., & Sood, K. (2023). *Sustainable investments in Green Finance*. IGI Global. doi:10.4018/979-8-3693-1388-6

Taneja, S., & Özen, E. (2023). To analyse the relationship between bank's green financing and environmental performance. *International Journal of Electronic Finance*, *12*(2), 163–175. doi:10.1504/IJEF.2023.129919

Taneja, S., & Ozen, E. (2023). Impact of the European Green Deal (EDG) on the agricultural carbon (CO2) emission in Turkey. *International Journal of Sustainable Development and Planning*, *18*(3), 715–727. doi:10.18280/ijsdp.180307

Chapter 3
Disruptive Technologies in Computational Finance

Mohammad Kashif
https://orcid.org/0000-0002-4940-8264
Graphic Era University (Deemed), India

Puneet Kumar
IIMT University, India

Sachin Ghai
Graphic Era University (Deemed), India

Satish Kumar
IIMT University, India

ABSTRACT

Computational finance plays a pivotal role in addressing the challenges posed by the dynamic and interconnected nature of financial markets. By combining mathematical rigor with computational power, this field contributes to the development of innovative solutions for pricing, risk management, and decision-making in the financial industry. Computational finance is a field that leverages mathematical techniques, statistical methods, and computational tools to analyze and solve complex financial problems. In recent years, the intersection of finance and technology has given rise to a transformative wave, reshaping the landscape of traditional financial systems. This study delves into the dynamic realm of computational finance, exploring the profound impact of disruptive technologies on established practices and processes of computational finance.

DOI: 10.4018/979-8-3693-1746-4.ch003

1. INTRODUCTION

In recent years, the intersection of finance and technology has given rise to a transformative wave, reshaping the landscape of traditional financial systems. This chapter delves into the dynamic realm of computational finance, exploring the profound impact of disruptive technologies on established practices, processes, and paradigms within the financial industry (Hickey & Conway, 2021). As we navigate through an era characterized by rapid technological advancement, it becomes evident that these innovations are not mere catalysts but rather formidable forces that are fundamentally altering the way financial transactions are executed, risks are managed, and decisions are made.

1.1 Computational Finance

Computational Finance is an interdisciplinary field that leverages mathematical techniques, statistical methods, and computational tools to analyze and solve complex financial problems. It resides at the intersection of finance, mathematics, and computer science, aiming to develop models, algorithms, and numerical solutions to address challenges in the financial industry (in 't Hout et al., 2018; Mathis & Almarzoqi, 2022). At its core, Computational Finance seeks to enhance decision-making processes, risk management, and the understanding of financial markets through the application of advanced computational methods. This field emerged in response to the increasing complexity of financial instruments, the growing volume of financial data, and the need for more sophisticated modeling techniques to capture the dynamics of financial markets (Serov & Vasiliev, 2023; Trapletti & Hornik, 2017).

1.2 The Key Components of Computational Finance Include

Mathematical Models: Computational Finance relies on mathematical models to describe and understand financial phenomena. These models may range from simple ones, such as the Black-Scholes model for option pricing, to more complex models that account for factors like market frictions, transaction costs, and behavioral aspects.

Numerical Methods: Given the mathematical complexity of financial models, numerical methods play a crucial role in solving equations and simulating financial scenarios. Techniques such as finite difference methods, Monte Carlo simulations, and optimization algorithms are commonly employed to obtain numerical solutions.

Statistical Analysis: Computational Finance heavily incorporates statistical methods for data analysis, risk assessment, and model validation. Techniques like time series analysis, regression analysis, and econometrics help in extracting meaningful insights from financial data.

Algorithmic Trading: One practical application of Computational Finance is in the development of algorithmic trading strategies. Automated trading systems use computational algorithms to make real-time trading decisions, leveraging quantitative models and high-frequency data.

Risk Management: Computational Finance provides tools for assessing and managing financial risk. This includes the development of risk models, stress testing, and scenario analysis to evaluate the impact of various factors on the financial performance of portfolios and institutions.

Machine Learning: With the advent of big data, machine learning techniques have gained prominence in Computational Finance (Chiu, 2016). Algorithms such as neural networks, support vector machines, and ensemble methods are employed for tasks like predictive modeling, credit scoring, and fraud detection.

1.3 The Evolution of Computational Finance

The evolution of computational finance has been marked by a continuous quest for more efficient, accurate, and scalable methods of handling complex financial tasks. From the early adoption of computer-based models for pricing derivatives to the present era of algorithmic trading and decentralized finance, the financial industry has undergone a series of paradigm shifts (Locatelli et al., 2021). This evolution, however, has been significantly accelerated by the infusion of disruptive technologies that are challenging conventional norms and fostering a new era of financial innovation.

As we embark on this exploration of disruptive technologies in computational finance, it is essential to recognize that these advancements not only present unprecedented opportunities for innovation and efficiency but also pose challenges that demand careful consideration. The subsequent sections of this chapter will delve deeper into each of these disruptive technologies, offering insights into their applications, implications, and the transformative journey they embark upon within the intricate tapestry of computational finance. Disruptive technologies have reshaped various industries, and the field of computational finance is no exception. This chapter explores the impact of disruptive technologies on computational finance, examining how innovations in areas such as artificial intelligence, blockchain, and big data analytics have transformed traditional financial processes (Hout et al., 2018).

2. ARTIFICIAL INTELLIGENCE AND MACHINE LEARNING IN COMPUTATIONAL FINANCE

At the forefront of this revolution are artificial intelligence (AI) and machine learning (ML), which have become integral components of financial decision-making processes (Catania, 2021). These technologies enable sophisticated data analysis, pattern recognition, and predictive modeling, empowering financial institutions to make informed decisions in real-time. From optimizing investment portfolios to enhancing risk management strategies, AI and ML are ushering in a new era of computational finance characterized by adaptability and intelligence (Thacker, 2020).

This section delves into the applications of AI and ML algorithms in predictive modeling, algorithmic trading, credit scoring, and portfolio management. The integration of artificial intelligence (AI) and machine learning (ML) in computational finance has ushered in a new era, fundamentally transforming the way financial tasks are executed, risks are managed, and decisions are made. These technologies empower financial institutions to leverage vast amounts of data, discern complex patterns, and make informed predictions in real-time (Woodhead et al., 2018). Here's an in-depth exploration of how AI and ML are revolutionizing different aspects of computational finance:

2.1. Predictive Modeling and Forecasting

AI and ML algorithms excel at predictive modeling, allowing financial institutions to forecast market trends, asset prices, and economic indicators. By analyzing historical data and identifying patterns, these technologies help in making more accurate predictions about future financial movements. This capability is particularly valuable for traders, investment managers, and financial analysts seeking to optimize investment strategies.

2.2. Algorithmic Trading

Algorithmic trading, or algorithmic execution, involves the use of pre-programmed algorithms to execute trades based on predefined criteria. AI and ML play a crucial role in this domain by enabling algorithms to adapt and evolve in response to changing market conditions. These technologies enhance trading strategies, optimize execution, and contribute to more efficient market dynamics.

2.3. Credit Scoring and Risk Management

In the realm of lending and credit, AI and ML are employed for credit scoring and risk assessment. These technologies analyze a multitude of factors, including historical credit data, transaction patterns, and macroeconomic indicators, to assess the creditworthiness of individuals and businesses (Dedehayir et al., 2017). The result is a more nuanced and accurate risk evaluation, reducing the likelihood of defaults.

2.4. Portfolio Management

AI and ML are transforming portfolio management by providing sophisticated tools for asset allocation and risk diversification. These technologies analyze historical performance, market trends, and risk factors to optimize investment portfolios. Portfolio managers can leverage AI to identify opportunities, manage risks, and enhance overall portfolio performance (Schwartz et al., 2013).

2.5. Fraud Detection and Security

The ability of AI and ML to recognize patterns extends to the identification of fraudulent activities. In computational finance, these technologies are deployed to detect anomalies, unusual transaction patterns, and potential security threats. By continuously learning and adapting to new fraud patterns, AI and ML contribute to robust security measures within the financial ecosystem.

2.6. Natural Language Processing (NLP) for Sentiment Analysis

Natural Language Processing, a subset of AI, enables computers to understand, interpret, and generate human-like text. In finance, NLP is utilized for sentiment analysis of news articles, social media, and financial reports. This analysis helps in gauging market sentiment, which can be a valuable input for decision-making processes.

2.7. Customer Service and Chatbots

AI-powered chatbots are increasingly being used in customer service within the financial industry. These chatbots can provide personalized assistance, answer queries, and execute simple transactions. They enhance customer engagement and streamline routine tasks, allowing human resources to focus on more complex issues.

3. ROBOTIC PROCESS AUTOMATION (RPA) IN FINANCIAL OPERATIONS

Robotic Process Automation (RPA) is a technology that uses software robots, also known as "bots," to automate repetitive and rule-based tasks within business processes (Doguc, 2021). RPA is designed to perform tasks in the same way that a human employee would, interacting with digital systems to execute specific processes. These tasks can include data entry, data extraction, form filling, calculations, and other routine, rule-based activities.

RPA is commonly used in various industries, including finance, healthcare, human resources, customer service, and more. It is part of a broader trend towards digital transformation and the adoption of technologies that enhance operational efficiency (Januszewski & Kujawski, 2021). It's important to note that RPA is distinct from more advanced forms of automation, such as artificial intelligence (AI) and machine learning (ML), which involve technologies capable of learning and adapting to new scenarios. RPA, in contrast, follows pre-defined rules and instructions (Lorde & Joseph, 2019).

Robotic Process Automation (RPA) streamlines financial operations by automating repetitive tasks, reducing errors, and enhancing operational efficiency (Thekkethil et al., 2021; Vedder et al., 2016). This section explores how RPA is employed in areas such as transaction processing, compliance reporting, and data reconciliation, transforming the operational landscape of computational finance. In the context of financial operations, RPA has emerged as a transformative tool, streamlining workflows, reducing operational costs, and enhancing overall efficiency (Postolea & Bodea, 2022). Here's a comprehensive exploration of how RPA is applied in financial operations:

3.1. Automation of Repetitive Tasks

Financial operations often involve a multitude of repetitive and rule-based tasks, such as data entry, invoice processing, reconciliation, and report generation. RPA is designed to handle these routine tasks with speed and accuracy, freeing up human resources to focus on more complex and value-added activities (Postolea & Bodea, 2022).

3.2. Data Entry and Processing

RPA bots are capable of automating data entry tasks by extracting information from various sources, validating data accuracy, and entering it into relevant systems. This not only reduces the risk of human error but also accelerates data processing times, contributing to faster and more accurate financial transactions.

3.3. Invoice Processing and Accounts Payable

RPA is extensively used in automating invoice processing and accounts payable functions. Bots can extract data from invoices, validate against purchase orders and receipts, and update accounting systems. This leads to faster invoice processing cycles, improved accuracy, and a reduction in late payments or discrepancies.

3.4. Reconciliation and Data Validation

Financial reconciliation, whether it's bank reconciliation, ledger reconciliation, or transaction matching, can be a time-consuming task. RPA bots excel at comparing large volumes of data, identifying discrepancies, and reconciling accounts. This ensures data accuracy and compliance with financial regulations (Januszewski & Kujawski, 2021).

3.5. Report Generation and Financial Analysis

RPA can be employed to automate the generation of financial reports by pulling data from various sources, performing calculations, and formatting reports according to predefined templates. This enhances the speed and accuracy of financial reporting, allowing stakeholders to access up-to-date information for analysis and decision-making (Bhatnagar et al., 2022a, 2022b,2023a, 2023b; Dangwal et al., 2022a, 2022b; Kumar et al., 2023a, 2023b; Özen et al., 2022, Singh et al., 2021; Taneja et al., 2022a, 2022b; 2023a, 2023b, 2023c, 2023d, 2023e 2023f; Gupta et al. 2023; Dahiya 2023; Bansal 2023; Reepu 2023;).

3.6. Compliance and Regulatory Reporting

Financial institutions are subject to strict regulatory requirements. RPA plays a crucial role in automating compliance checks and generating reports for regulatory submissions. Bots can validate transactions, ensure adherence to compliance standards, and generate audit trails to facilitate regulatory compliance.

3.7. Customer Onboarding and KYC Processes

In the financial sector, customer onboarding and Know Your Customer (KYC) processes involve collecting and verifying customer information. RPA can automate these processes by extracting, validating, and updating customer data across multiple systems, ensuring compliance with regulatory requirements and minimizing the time required for onboarding.

4. CYBERSECURITY IN COMPUTATIONAL FINANCE

As computational finance becomes more technology-dependent, ensuring robust cybersecurity measures is crucial (Ch et al., 2020). This section explores the role of cybersecurity technologies in safeguarding financial systems, protecting sensitive data, and mitigating the risks associated with cyber threats. The increasing reliance on digital technologies and interconnected systems in the financial industry has elevated the significance of cybersecurity in computational finance. Cybersecurity encompasses a set of practices, technologies, and measures designed to safeguard financial systems, data, and transactions from unauthorized access, attacks, and disruptions (Malhotra, 2015). In the context of computational finance, which involves the use of advanced technologies for financial modeling, algorithmic trading, and data analytics, robust cybersecurity measures are essential to protect sensitive information and ensure the integrity and availability of financial services. Here's a comprehensive exploration of the role of cybersecurity in computational finance:

4.1. Data Protection and Privacy

Data is a cornerstone of computational finance, and the protection of financial data is paramount. Cybersecurity measures in this context involve encryption, access controls, and secure storage to prevent unauthorized access or data breaches. Additionally, compliance with data protection regulations, such as GDPR (General Data Protection Regulation), ensures the privacy of customer information (Liao et al., 2022).

4.2. Secure Transaction Processing

In computational finance, where transactions occur at high speeds and volumes, ensuring the security of these transactions is crucial. Cybersecurity measures, including secure communication channels, transaction monitoring, and authentication mechanisms, help mitigate the risk of unauthorized access, fraudulent transactions, and man-in-the-middle attacks.

4.3. Protection Against Cyber Threats

Financial institutions are prime targets for cyber threats such as malware, ransomware, and phishing attacks. Cybersecurity practices involve implementing robust antivirus software, firewalls, and intrusion detection systems to identify and prevent these threats. Regular security audits and vulnerability assessments are conducted to identify and address potential weaknesses in the system.

4.4. Identity and Access Management

Controlling and monitoring user access is a critical aspect of cybersecurity in computational finance. Identity and Access Management (IAM) systems are implemented to ensure that only authorized personnel have access to sensitive financial data and systems. Multi-factor authentication adds an additional layer of security by requiring multiple forms of verification for user access.

4.5. Network Security

Computational finance relies heavily on networked systems for communication and data transfer. Network security measures, such as secure network protocols, virtual private networks (VPNs), and intrusion prevention systems, are implemented to protect against unauthorized access and data interception during transit.

4.6. Incident Response and Cybersecurity Training

Given the evolving nature of cyber threats, having a robust incident response plan is crucial. Financial institutions in computational finance conduct regular cybersecurity training for employees to enhance awareness and preparedness. Incident response plans outline the steps to be taken in the event of a security incident, facilitating a swift and effective response to mitigate potential damages.

4.7. Regulatory Compliance

Governments and regulatory bodies have introduced cybersecurity regulations specific to the financial sector. Adherence to these regulations, such as the NIST Cybersecurity Framework or sector-specific guidelines, ensures that financial institutions maintain a baseline level of cybersecurity hygiene.

4.8. Continuous Monitoring and Threat Intelligence

Real-time monitoring of system activities and leveraging threat intelligence sources help financial institutions stay ahead of emerging cyber threats. Continuous monitoring allows for the prompt identification of suspicious activities, enabling proactive responses to potential security incidents.

5. CONCLUSION

Disruptive technologies continue to reshape the landscape of computational finance, offering new opportunities and challenges. This chapter provides insights into the transformative impact of artificial intelligence, big data analytics, robotic process automation, and cybersecurity on various aspects of financial operations (Kim et al., 2020). As the financial industry adapts to these technological advancements, it is essential for practitioners, researchers, and policymakers to stay abreast of the latest developments to navigate the evolving landscape of computational finance.

While AI and ML offer tremendous potential in computational finance, it's crucial to acknowledge the challenges. These include issues related to data privacy, algorithmic bias, and the interpretability of complex models. Additionally, the reliance on historical data assumes that future market conditions will resemble the past, which may not always be the case (Ziritt Trejo et al., 2018). The integration of AI and ML in computational finance has democratized access to sophisticated analytical tools, enabling financial institutions to make data-driven decisions with greater speed and accuracy. As these technologies continue to evolve, their impact on financial markets and institutions is likely to deepen, necessitating a balance between innovation and the prudent management of associated risks.

Computational finance plays a pivotal role in addressing the challenges posed by the dynamic and interconnected nature of financial markets. By combining mathematical rigor with computational power, this field contributes to the development of innovative solutions for pricing, risk management, and decision-making in the financial industry. While cybersecurity measures in computational finance are robust, challenges persist. These include the sophistication of cyber threats, the need for international collaboration on cybersecurity standards, and the evolving landscape of technology. Future trends in cybersecurity for computational finance may involve the integration of advanced technologies like artificial intelligence and machine learning to enhance threat detection and response capabilities. As computational finance continues to evolve, so does the need for robust cybersecurity measures. Financial institutions must adopt a proactive and comprehensive approach to these technologies to protect sensitive data, maintain the trust of stakeholders, and ensure the resilience of computational finance systems in the face of evolving cyber threats.

REFERENCES

Bansal, N., Taneja, S., & Ozen, E. (2023). Green Financing as a Bridge Between Green Banking Strategies and Environmental Performance in Punjab, India. *International Journal of Sustainable Development and Planning*, *18*(10), 3155–3167. doi:10.18280/ijsdp.181017

Bhatnagar, M., Özen, E., Taneja, S., Grima, S., & Rupeika-Apoga, R. (2022a). The Dynamic Connectedness between Risk and Return in the Fintech Market of India: Evidence Using the GARCH-M Approach. *Risks*, *10*(11), 209. doi:10.3390/risks10110209

Bhatnagar, M., Taneja, S., Kumar, P., & Özen, E. (2023a). Does Financial Education Act as a Catalyst for SME Competitiveness. *International Journal of Education Economics and Development*, *1*(1), 1. doi:10.1504/IJEED.2023.10053629

Bhatnagar, M., Taneja, S., & Özen, E. (2022b). A wave of green start-ups in India—The study of green finance as a support system for sustainable entrepreneurship. *Green Finance*, *4*(2), 253–273. doi:10.3934/GF.2022012

Bhatnagar, M., Taneja, S., & Rupeika-Apoga, R. (2023b). Demystifying the Effect of the News (Shocks) on Crypto Market Volatility. *Journal of Risk and Financial Management*, *16*(2), 136. doi:10.3390/jrfm16020136

Catania, L. J. (2021). The evolution of artificial intelligence (AI). Foundations of Artificial Intelligence in Healthcare and Bioscience. doi:10.1016/B978-0-12-824477-7.00002-X

Ch, R., Gadekallu, T. R., Abidi, M. H., & Al-Ahmari, A. (2020). Computational system to classify Cyber Crime offenses using machine learning. *Sustainability (Basel)*, *12*(10), 4087. Advance online publication. doi:10.3390u12104087

Chiu, H. (2016). Fintech and Disruptive Business Models in Financial Products, Intermediation and Markets- Policy Implications for Financial Regulators. *Journal of Technology Law and Policy*, *21*(1).

Dahiya, K., Taneja, S., & Özen, E. (2023). To Analyse the Impact of Multi-Media Technology on the Rural Entrepreneurship Development. In Contemporary Studies of Risks in Emerging Technology, Part A (pp. 221-240). Emerald Publishing Limited. doi:10.1108/978-1-80455-562-020231015

Dangwal, A., Kaur, S., Taneja, S., & Taneja, S. (2022a). A Bibliometric Analysis of Green Tourism Based on the Scopus Platform. In J. Kaur, P. Jindal, & A. Singh (Eds.), *Developing Relationships, Personalization, and Data Herald in Marketing 5.0* (Vol. 1, pp. 1–327). IGI Global. doi:10.4018/978-1-6684-4496-2.ch015

Dangwal, A., Taneja, S., Özen, E., Todorovic, I., & Grima, S. (2022b). Abridgement of Renewables: It's Potential and Contribution to India's GDP. *International Journal of Sustainable Development and Planning*, *17*(8), 2357–2363. doi:10.18280/ijsdp.170802

Dedehayir, O., Ortt, J. R., & Seppänen, M. (2017). Disruptive change and the reconfiguration of innovation ecosystems. *Journal of Technology Management & Innovation*, *12*(3), 9–21. Advance online publication. doi:10.4067/S0718-27242017000300002

Doguc, O. (2021). Applications of Robotic Process Automation in Finance and Accounting. *Beykent Üniversitesi Fen ve Mühendislik Bilimleri Dergisi*, *14*(1), 51–59. Advance online publication. doi:10.20854/bujse.906795

Gupta, M., Arora, R., & Taneja, S. (2023). Bibliometric Analysis on Employee Engagement and Human Resource Management. In *Enhancing Customer Engagement Through Location-Based Marketing* (pp. 185–205). IGI Global. doi:10.4018/978-1-6684-8177-6.ch013

Hickey, A. J., & Conway, J. (2021). Historical perspective - Disruptive technologies and strategies. Inhaled Medicines: Optimizing Development through Integration of In Silico, In Vitro and In Vivo Approaches. doi:10.1016/B978-0-12-814974-4.00003-1

Hout, K., Itkin, A., von Sydow, L., & Toivanen, J. (2018). Special issue—Computational and algorithmic finance. *Journal of Computational Science*, *24*, 180–181. doi:10.1016/j.jocs.2017.12.009

Januszewski, A., & Kujawski, J. (2021). Best practices in robotic process automation in global business services. *27th Annual Americas Conference on Information Systems, AMCIS 2021.*

Kim, J., Shah, P., Gaskell, J. C., Prasann, A., & Luthra, A. (2020). Scaling Up Disruptive Agricultural Technologies in Africa. Scaling Up Disruptive Agricultural Technologies in Africa. doi:10.1596/978-1-4648-1522-5

Kumar, P., Taneja, S., Özen, E., & Singh, S. (2023b). Artificial Intelligence and Machine Learning in Insurance: A Bibliometric Analysis. In Smart Analytics, Artificial Intelligence and Sustainable Performance Management in a Global Digitalised Economy (pp. 191-202). Emerald Publishing Limited. doi:10.1108/S1569-37592023000110A010

Kumar, P., Verma, P., Bhatnagar, M., Taneja, S., Seychel, S., Todorović, I., & Grim, S. (2023). The financial performance and solvency status of the Indian public sector banks: A CAMELS rating and Z index approach. *International Journal of Sustainable Development and Planning*, *18*(2), 367–376. doi:10.18280/ijsdp.180204

Liao, B., Huang, Z., Cao, X., & Li, J. (2022). Adopting Nonlinear Activated Beetle Antennae Search Algorithm for Fraud Detection of Public Trading Companies: A Computational Finance Approach. *Mathematics*, *10*(13), 2160. Advance online publication. doi:10.3390/math10132160

Locatelli, R., Schena, C., & Tanda, A. (2021). *A Historical Perspective on Disruptive Technologies*. doi:10.1007/978-3-030-81835-7_2

Lorde, T., & Joseph, T. S. D. (2019). Airbnb, technological change and disruption in Barbadian tourism: A theoretical framework. *Third World Quarterly*, *40*(12), 2190–2209. Advance online publication. doi:10.1080/01436597.2019.1633913

Malhotra, Y. (2015). Cybersecurity & Cyber-Finance Risk Management: Strategies, Tactics, Operations, &, Intelligence: Enterprise Risk Management to Model Risk Management: Understanding Vulnerabilities, Threats, & Risk Mitigation (Presentation Slides). SSRN *Electronic Journal*. doi:10.2139/ssrn.2693886

Mathis, F. J., & Almarzoqi, R. M. (2022). Global innovation, finance, and international commerce. In *Global Innovation*. Finance, and International Commerce. doi:10.4324/9781003024675

Özen, E., & Sanjay, T. (2022a). Empirical Analysis of the Effect of Foreign Trade in Computer and Communication Services on Economic Growth in India. *Journal of Economics and Business Issues*, *2*(2), 24–34. https://doi.org/https://jebi-academic.org/index.php/jebi/article/view/41

Postolea, I. D., & Bodea, C. N. (2022). Building RPA solutions for customer-oriented processes automation. *Issues in Information Systems*, *23*(2). Advance online publication. doi:10.48009/2_iis_2022_108

Reepu, R., Taneja, S., Ozen, E., & Singh, A. (2023). A Globetrotter to the Future of Marketing: Metaverse. In *Cultural Marketing and Metaverse for Consumer Engagement* (pp. 1–11). IGI Global. doi:10.4018/978-1-6684-8312-1.ch001

Schwartz, R. A., Byrne, J. A., & Schnee, G. (2013). The quality of our financial markets: Taking stock of where we stand. In *The Quality of Our Financial Markets*. Taking Stock of Where We Stand. doi:10.1007/978-1-4614-5592-9

Serov, E. R., & Vasiliev, S. A. (2023). Application of quantum technologies in banking. *Economics and Management*, *29*(3), 248–255. Advance online publication. doi:10.35854/1998-1627-2023-3-248-255

Singh, V., Taneja, S., Singh, V., Singh, A., & Paul, H. L. (2021). Online advertising strategies in Indian and Australian e-commerce companies:: A comparative study. *Big Data Analytics for Improved Accuracy, Efficiency, and Decision Making in Digital Marketing*, 124–138. doi:10.4018/978-1-7998-7231-3.ch009

Taneja, S., Bhatnagar, M., Kumar, P., & Grima, S. (2023c). A panel analysis of the effectiveness of the asset management in Indian agricultural companies. *International Journal of Sustainable Development and Planning*, *18*(3), 653–660. doi:10.18280/ijsdp.180301

Taneja, S., Bhatnagar, M., Kumar, P., & Rupeika-apoga, R. (2023b). India ' s Total Natural Resource Rents (NRR) and GDP : An Augmented Autoregressive Distributed Lag (ARDL) Bound Test. *Journal of Risk and Financial Management*, *16*(2), 91. doi:10.3390/jrfm16020091

Taneja, S., Gupta, M., Bhushan, P., Bhatnagar, M., & Singh, A. (2023f). Cultural Marketing in the Digital Era. In *Cultural Marketing and Metaverse for Consumer Engagement* (pp. 109–122). IGI Global. doi:10.4018/978-1-6684-8312-1.ch008

Taneja, S., Jaggi, P., Jewandah, S., & Ozen, E. (2022b). Role of Social Inclusion in Sustainable Urban Developments: An Analyse by PRISMA Technique. *International Journal of Design & Nature and Ecodynamics*, *17*(6), 937–942. doi:10.18280/ijdne.170615

Taneja, S., Kaur, S., & Özen, E. (2022a). Using green finance to promote global growth in a sustainable way. *International Journal of Green Economics*, *16*(3), 246–257. doi:10.1504/IJGE.2022.128930

Taneja, S., Kumar, P., Grima, S., Ozen, E., & Sood, K. (2023). *Sustainable investments in Green Finance*. IGI Global. doi:10.4018/979-8-3693-1388-6

Taneja, S., & Özen, E. (2023a). To analyse the relationship between bank's green financing and environmental performance. *International Journal of Electronic Finance*, *12*(2), 163–175. doi:10.1504/IJEF.2023.129919

Taneja, S., & Ozen, E. (2023d). Impact of the European Green Deal (EDG) on the agricultural carbon (CO2) emission in Turkey. *International Journal of Sustainable Development and Planning*, *18*(3), 715–727. doi:10.18280/ijsdp.180307

Taneja, S., & Sharma, V. (2023e). Role of Beaconing Marketing in Improving Customer Buying Experience. In *Enhancing Customer Engagement Through Location-Based Marketing* (pp. 176–184). IGI Global. doi:10.4018/978-1-6684-8177-6.ch012

Thacker, J. (2020). The Age of AI: Artificial Intelligence and the Future of Humanity. *Perspectives on Science and Christian Faith*, *72*(4), 252–254. Advance online publication. doi:10.56315/PSCF12-20Thacker

Thekkethil, M. S., Shukla, V. K., Beena, F., & Chopra, A. (2021). Robotic Process Automation in Banking and Finance Sector for Loan Processing and Fraud Detection. *2021 9th International Conference on Reliability, Infocom Technologies and Optimization (Trends and Future Directions), ICRITO 2021*. 10.1109/ICRITO51393.2021.9596076

Trapletti, A., & Hornik, K. (2017). tseries: Time Series Analysis and Computational Finance. *R Package Version 0.10-42*.

Vedder, R., Welters, M., Mints, A., & Ramkhelawan, A. (2016). *Robotic process automation in the Finance function of the future*. Ernst & Young.

Woodhead, R., Stephenson, P., & Morrey, D. (2018). Digital construction: From point solutions to IoT ecosystem. *Automation in Construction*, *93*, 35–46. Advance online publication. doi:10.1016/j.autcon.2018.05.004

Ziritt Trejo, G., Taboada Hernandez, R., Moreno, Z., & Isabel Castellano, M. (2018). Public Management and Sustainable Development: Expression of Social Responsibility. Innovation Management and Education Excellence Through Vision 2020, Vols I -Xi.

Chapter 4
Challenges and Opportunities of Machine Learning in the Financial Sector

Manjit Kour
https://orcid.org/0000-0003-1043-3187
Chandigarh University, India

ABSTRACT

In the field of finance, machine learning has become a potent instrument that is transforming conventional methods of data analysis, decision-making, and risk management. This study examines how machine learning techniques are applied in the financial sector, discussing the challenges and opportunities of machine learning in the financial sector. Machine learning algorithms have been successfully used in fields including stock market forecasting, credit risk assessment, fraud detection, algorithmic trading, and portfolio optimization by utilising enormous volumes of financial data. However, issues with model robustness, interpretability, data quality, and regulatory compliance continue to be major roadblocks. By analyzing the applications, identifying challenges, and exploring opportunities for further development, this chapter seeks to contribute to the understanding and advancement of machine learning in the financial sector.

DOI: 10.4018/979-8-3693-1746-4.ch004

INTRODUCTION

In the branch of artificial intelligence known as "machine learning," algorithms and statistical models are used to help computers learn from data without having to be explicitly programmed (Batta, 2020). Due to its capacity for processing and analysing massive amounts of data, finding patterns, and making predictions, machine learning has seen an exponential increase in its application across a wide range of fields. The banking industry is one such area where machine learning has had a substantial impact. The financial industry produces a huge amount of data that may be used to improve decision-making, lower risk, and improve customer experience (Kour, 2023). By automating activities, increasing accuracy, and opening up new business prospects, machine learning has the potential to revolutionise the financial sector.

The ability of machine learning to analyse and interpret massive volumes of data, find patterns, and make predictions has made it a crucial tool in the financial industry. In the financial industry, machine learning is utilised for a number of purposes, including fraud detection, risk management, trading and investment, personalised customer care, and credit score and loan approval. Machine learning has enormous potential for the financial industry, and more companies will certainly start using it in the future. Machine learning techniques have become increasingly popular in the financial sector, offering the potential to enhance efficiency, reduce costs, and make more accurate predictions (Lee & Shin, 2020). However, the implementation of these techniques is not without challenges. In this paper, we will discuss the challenges and opportunities of machine learning in the financial sector.

METHODOLOGY

The purpose of this work is exploration. To investigate the potential of big data analytics in the banking industry, secondary data is used. Secondary data is gathered from a variety of publicly available sources, including publications, journals, etc. The research paper is organized in three main sections. The first section discusses use of machine learning in the financial sector, the second section deliberates on the challenges and opportunities of machine learning in financial sector and the third section explores the future of machine learning in the financial sector.

Machine Learning Techniques in the Financial Sector

In the financial industry, the use of machine learning techniques to automate numerous processes and anticipate a variety of outcomes is on the rise. Three groups of strategies can be distinguished: reinforcement learning, unsupervised learning, and supervised learning. Each method has particular benefits and uses in the financial industry.

Supervised Learning

A type of machine learning called supervised learning involves training the algorithm using labelled data. In supervised learning, the algorithm picks the best instances from the training dataset to learn how to translate input variables to output variables (Ouadah et al., 2022). In the financial industry, this method is frequently applied to tasks like stock price forecasting, fraud detection, and credit scoring. For instance, while determining credit scores, an algorithm is trained using data on loan applicants' credit histories, income, and work status as well as their repayment patterns. The model can then be applied to determine a new loan applicant's creditworthiness. Statistical regression, decision trees, random forests, and support vector machines (SVMs) are examples of supervised learning techniques frequently employed in the finance industry (Rakshit et al., 2022).

Figure 1. Machine learning techniques in the financial sector

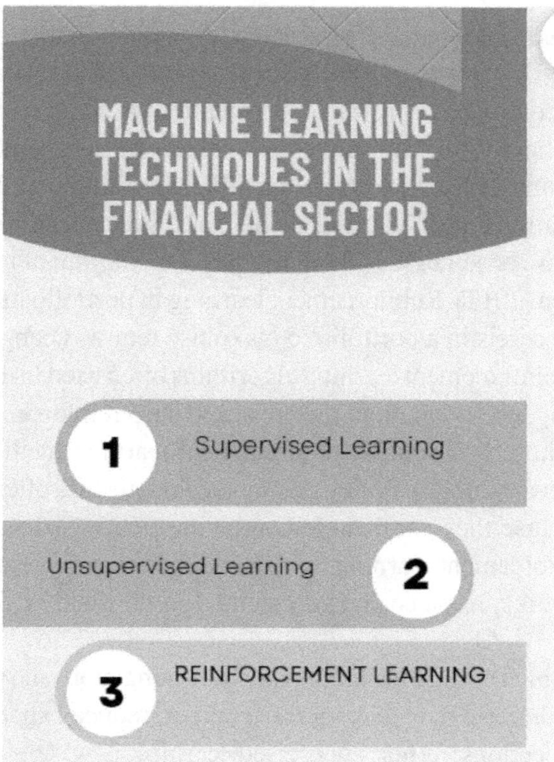

Unsupervised Learning

Unsupervised learning techniques require the system to be trained on unlabelled data. Without being provided specific samples to learn from, the algorithm learns to detect patterns and structure in the data through unsupervised learning (Batta, 2020). In the banking sector, this method is frequently utilised for activities including fraud detection, client segmentation, and anomaly identification (Rakshit et al., 2022). Unsupervised learning techniques, for instance, can be used to find patterns in financial transaction data that can point to fraudulent behaviour. Financial institutions can customise their services to distinct customer categories by using unsupervised learning algorithms to categorise consumers based on their transactional behaviour (Allegue et al., 2023). In the banking sector, unsupervised learning methods including clustering, PCA, and association rule mining are extensively used. Clustering is widely used in customer segmentation, whereas PCA is frequently used in anomaly detection (Farrugia., 2020). Association rule mining is commonly used in market basket research to identify the products that are frequently purchased together (Li et al., 2018).

Reinforcement Learning

Reinforcement learning is a sort of artificial intelligence that educates an agent to base decisions on information received from the outside world (Arulkumaran et al., 2017). Since it receives rewards or penalties based on its actions, the agent gradually learns how to maximise the advantages. In the financial industry, this method is frequently utilised for operations like algorithmic trading and portfolio management. Reinforcement learning agents, for instance, can be trained to decide whether to purchase or sell based on market data with the aim of maximising profits (Théate & Damien, 2017). Reinforcement learning in portfolio management can be used to distribute assets in a portfolio to maximise returns (Jiang & Liang, 2017).

Examples of reinforcement learning algorithms often used in the financial sector include Q-learning, policy gradient methods, and deep reinforcement learning. The Q-learning algorithm is a popular reinforcement learning method in algorithmic trading (Karthik et al., 20123). Policy gradient techniques are often used in portfolio management because they can handle continuous action spaces (Jiang & Liang, 2017). Deep reinforcement learning, which combines reinforcement learning with deep neural networks, has also shown potential in the field of finance (Théate & Damien, 2021).

In short, machine learning techniques are becoming more and more important in the financial sector since they may increase output, reduce expenses, and generate more precise projections. While supervised learning is widely used in tasks like credit scoring, fraud detection, and stock price prediction, unsupervised learning is frequently utilised in occupations like fraud detection, customer segmentation, and anomaly detection. Reinforcement learning is often used in algorithmic trading and portfolio management.

Challenges and Opportunities of Machine Learning in the Financial Sector

In this section we will discuss the challenges and opportunities of machine learning in the financial sector.

Figure 2. Challenges and opportunities of machine learning in the financial sector

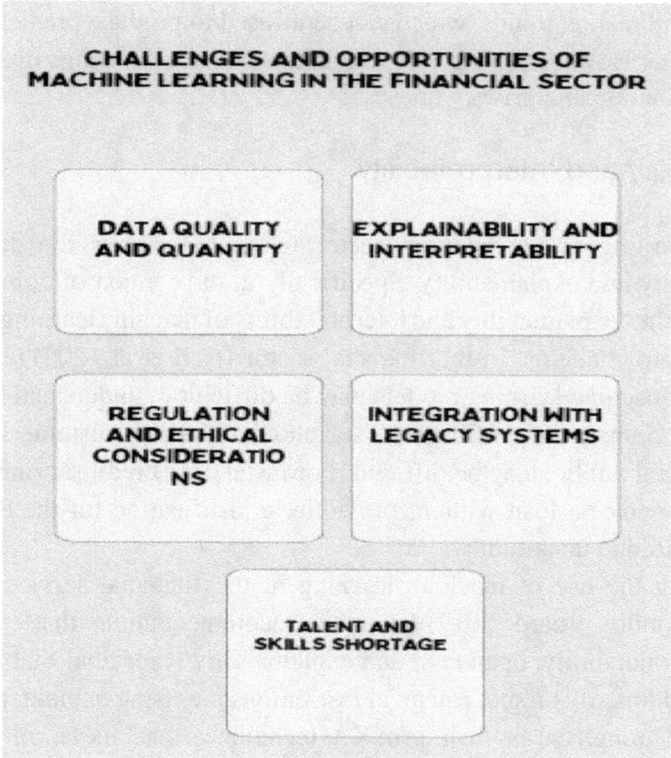

Data Quality and Quantity

One of the main challenges for machine learning in the banking industry is the quality and quantity of data. The incomplete, chaotic, and complex character of financial data can make machine learning algorithms less accurate (Bao et al., 2022). Machine learning algorithms require a large amount of data to be trained and to make accurate predictions. Financial information, however, is usually hard to come by, especially for young or small businesses. Additionally, there can be bias in financial data, which could make machine learning models less accurate. Using a credit score model, for instance, that was developed using false data may result in unethical lending practises.

Financial organisations are using alternate data sources to address the problems with data quantity and quality. Satellite imaging, online reviews, and social media are some more data sources. These sources can offer more information about consumer behaviour and market trends, which can be utilised to produce predictions that are more accurate. However, using different data sources also brings up moral issues like discrimination and privacy abuses.

Explainability and Interpretability

Machine learning in the banking sector needs to address the difficulties of interpretability and explainability. Specifically in the context of compliance with regulations, the "explainability and interpretability of machine learning algorithms" is a significant challenge in the financial sector (Hall et al., 2021). Due to their complexity, machine learning models may be difficult to understand how they get their results. Gaining the confidence of stakeholders, such as customers, authorities, and the general public, may be difficult. For instance, a credit scoring system that approves or denies a loan without providing a justification for the decision may cause mistrust and uncertainty.

Regarding the use of machine learning in the financial services sector, the Financial Stability Board (2017) has made recommendations that emphasise the need for accountability, openness, and explainability (Financial Stabilioty Board, 2021). To address this issue, financial institutions are using explainable AI (XAI) techniques. Through the application of XAI techniques, machine learning models are meant to be more transparent and understandable. Combining model-agnostic XAI methods like LIME (Local Interpretable Model-Agnostic Explanations) and SHAP (Shapley Additive Explanations) with model-specific methods like decision trees and rule-based systems. These techniques can help financial institutions justify the decision-making procedures underlying their machine learning models, increasing responsibility and trust.

Regulation and Ethical Considerations

Machine learning applications in the financial sector are subject to regulations and ethical constraints. Financial institutions are required to abide by laws including the Fair Credit Reporting Act (FCRA) and the General Data Protection Regulation (GDPR). In addition, ethical considerations including justice, accountability, and transparency must be made. A credit score system that prejudices certain groups of people, for instance, may violate anti-discrimination laws.

Significant regulatory issues face the banking sector, and machine learning has only made compliance more challenging. As machine learning is applied increasingly frequently in the financial sector, there is an increasing demand for legal frameworks to ensure the fair and ethical use of algorithms (Zhu et al., 2022). Additionally, biased information or biased judgements may have an impact on algorithms, posing moral dilemmas. If an algorithm builds a model using biased data, it may produce biased results that unfairly discriminate against specific groups.

Financial organisations are creating responsible AI frameworks to address these issues. Guidelines for the moral and open application of machine learning are included in responsible AI frameworks, as are controls for governance and accountability (Zhu et al., 2022). These frameworks can assist financial organisations in adhering to rules and moral standards while also preserving the confidence of its stakeholders and clients.

The General Data Protection Regulation (GDPR) of the European Union and the Consumer Financial Protection Bureau (CFPB) of the United States are two regulatory bodies that have developed guidelines for the ethical application of machine learning in the financial sector. Financial organisations are currently setting up their own ethical frameworks to ensure the ethical deployment of machine learning algorithms. For instance, JPMorgan has developed an AI Ethics Framework with the aim of making sure that its AI systems are transparent, comprehensible, and accountable.

Integration with Legacy Systems

Another challenge facing the banking sector is how to integrate machine learning with traditional systems. Sometimes, financial firms have complex IT systems that are difficult to change or upgrade. These outdated systems might not be compatible with contemporary machine learning techniques, which could limit their usefulness.

To get over this problem, financial organisations are using APIs (application programming interfaces) to link machine learning with old systems (Benmoussa, 2019). Thanks to APIs, which allow connection between different software systems, machine learning may be more simply incorporated into current IT systems. To fix compatibility problems, financial institutions also use cloud-based machine learning tools like Microsoft Azure and Amazon Web Services (AWS).

Legacy systems from numerous financial institutions were developed utilising outdated infrastructure and technology. Because they might not be able to manage the enormous volumes of data required for these models, it can be challenging to integrate machine learning into these systems. It may also be difficult to make sure that the machine learning algorithms work with the current systems.

Talent and Skills Shortage

A highly qualified workforce with understanding in fields like data science, computer science, statistics, and financial domain knowledge is needed to implement machine learning in the financial sector. There is a talent and skills deficit in the industry as a result of the demand for certain abilities developing far faster than the supply (PwC, 2020). According to a World Economic Forum study from 2018, there is a shortage of 1.5 million data scientists worldwide, and by 2021, this number is projected to climb to 3.5 million (Morales et al., 2022).

The lack of educational programmes that give the necessary skills and knowledge required for machine learning in the financial sector is one of the major obstacles to addressing the talent and skills gap. Only 10% of colleges worldwide, and less than 1% of those specifically, offer degrees in fintech, according to an EY research from 2019 (Marevac et al., 2023). Additionally, the curriculum of currently offered courses could not be in line with market demands, resulting in a discrepancy between graduates' skills and what employers want. Financial institutions are implementing a variety of initiatives to solve the talent and skills deficit, including working with universities to create educational programmes, providing training and development opportunities for current employees, and engaging with technology companies. Utilising freelance talent and the gig economy, which can offer specialised talents on a project-by-project basis, is another strategy. A further development in this direction is the usage of low-code or no-code platforms, which make it possible for non-experts to create and use machine learning models.

There is a talent and skill gap due to the finance sector's growing need for machine learning experts. It can be difficult to find candidates with the requisite technical and analytical skills because they are frequently in great demand across sectors. Further boosting the need for qualified professionals is the financial sector's requirement for people who are familiar with its rules and business procedures.

Financial institutions are working with universities and investing in training programmes to make sure that their staff members have the abilities to use machine learning. In order to supply the necessary expertise, several universities are also collaborating with outside suppliers and technology companies.

In conclusion, a significant obstacle to the adoption of machine learning in the financial sector is the lack of people and abilities. Financial institutions must devise plans for luring and keeping skilled workers, collaborating with educational institutions, and utilising emerging technology to democratise machine learning in order to meet this problem.

Future of Machine Learning in the Financial Sector

The financial sector is crucial to the global economy because of its capacity to handle massive amounts of data and make difficult decisions. Due to the recent rapid rise of machine learning techniques, the financial sector now presents new opportunities. Machine learning algorithms have the potential to enhance several aspects of finance, including risk management, fraud detection, trading strategies, customer service, and investment decision-making. This research segment examines the key potential that machine learning will bring to the financial sector in the future.

Risk Management and Fraud Detection

Machine learning algorithms can identify patterns in the examination of enormous volumes of financial data that may indicate potential risks or fraudulent activity. By training models on historical data, financial institutions can develop predictive models that assess creditworthiness, identify anomalies, and forecast market patterns (Li et al., 2020). By employing machine learning to dramatically improve the accuracy and speed of risk assessment, financial firms may be able to make better decisions and minimise potential losses.

Trading Strategies and Algorithmic Trading

Machine learning has allowed for the development of sophisticated algorithms that can assess vast amounts of market data, which has drastically altered trading practises (Buczynski et al., 2020). These algorithms have the capacity to foretell market moves, identify patterns and trends in real-time, and execute trades without human intervention. Machine learning algorithms can also optimise trading strategies and minimise human biases. They can also adapt to changing market conditions. As a result, financial organisations can increase the effectiveness and performance of their trade.

Customer Service and Personalization

Machine learning algorithms can examine consumer data, including transaction history, preferences, and behaviour patterns to provide customised financial services. By applying natural language processing (NLP) techniques, chatbots and virtual assistants may interact with customers, answer to their inquiries, and offer tailored recommendations. By increasing contact, reducing processes, and offering individualised financial advice, these AI-powered tools can improve client happiness.

Investment Decision-Making

Machine learning algorithms can assist in investment decision-making processes by assessing enormous volumes of financial and economic data. These algorithms can find relevant factors and relationships, elucidate mysterious patterns, and provide asset value prediction models (Kour & Sharma, 2023). By applying machine learning, investors can improve portfolios, make data-driven decisions, and improve investment performance.

Fraud Prevention and Cybersecurity

The banking sector is vulnerable to numerous cybersecurity risks, including identity theft, phishing attacks, and data breaches [23]. Machine learning algorithms can examine network traffic, user behaviour, and historical data to find and stop fraudulent activities. These algorithms are able to adjust to shifting threats, learn from previous errors, and identify odd patterns that can indicate security problems. Machine learning is crucial for increasing the security measures and safeguarding sensitive data in financial organisations.

CONCLUSION

With unprecedented opportunities for productivity, accuracy, and profit, machine learning has the potential to change the banking sector. Machine learning has several financial applications, including trading, investing, risk management, and fraud detection. Financial organisations are now able to extract knowledge from massive volumes of data using machine learning techniques including supervised learning, unsupervised learning, and reinforcement learning. Nevertheless, there are a number of challenges in using machine learning in the finance industry. The lack of people and skills, as well as problems with data quality and quantity, explainability and interpretability, legal and ethical challenges, integration with legacy systems, and regulatory and ethical considerations, are some of the main problems the industry is currently facing. To get over these barriers, cooperation is required between financial institutions, regulatory bodies, and tech firms. The financial industry must solve these challenges while ensuring the moral and ethical use of algorithms in order to properly exploit machine learning. Financial institutions must seek to establish solid governance frameworks and invest money on the personnel and resources they require in order to foster innovation and growth.

Machine learning algorithms can help in investment decision-making by studying vast volumes of financial and economic data. These algorithms are capable of uncovering hidden patterns, identifying relevant relationships and components, and creating asset value prediction models. Making data-driven judgements, optimising portfolios, and boosting investing success are all possible for investors who use machine learning.

REFERENCES

Allegue, S., Abdellatif, T., & El Abed, H. (2023). SBM: A Smart Budget Manager in banking using machine learning, NLP, and NLU. *Concurrency and Computation*, *35*(11), e6673. doi:10.1002/cpe.6673

Arulkumaran, K., Deisenroth, M. P., Brundage, M., & Bharath, A. A. (2017). Deep reinforcement learning: A brief survey. *IEEE Signal Processing Magazine*, *34*(6), 26–38. doi:10.1109/MSP.2017.2743240

Bao, Y., Hilary, G., & Ke, B. (2022). Artificial intelligence and fraud detection. Innovative Technology at the Interface of Finance and Operations, 1, 223-247.

Benmoussa, M. (2019). Api "Application Programming Interface" Banking: A Promising Future For Financial Institutions (International Experience). *Revue Des Sciences Commerciales*, *18*(2), 31–34.

Buczynski, W., Cuzzolin, F., & Sahakian, B. (2021). A review of machine learning experiments in equity investment decision-making: Why most published research findings do not live up to their promise in real life. *International Journal of Data Science and Analytics*, *11*(3), 221–242. doi:10.100741060-021-00245-5 PMID:33842690

Farrugia, M. (2020). *Imputation and anomaly detection for consumer load profiles* [Master's thesis]. University of Malta.

Financial Stability Board. (2017). *Artificial Intelligence and Machine Learning in Financial Services: Market Developments and Financial Stability Implications.* Retrieved from https://www.fsb.org/wp-content/uploads/P300117.pdf

Hall, P., Cox, B., Dickerson, S., Kannan, A. R., Kulkarni, R., & Schmidt, N. (2021). A United States fair lending perspective on machine learning. *Frontiers in Artificial Intelligence*, *4*, 695301. doi:10.3389/frai.2021.695301 PMID:34164616

Jiang, Z., & Liang, J. (2017). *Cryptocurrency portfolio management with deep reinforcement learning. In 2017 Intelligent Systems Conference (IntelliSys) (pp. 905-913)*. IEEE.

Karthik, K., Ranjithkumar, V., Kiran, S., & Kumar, S. P. (2023). A Survey of Price Prediction using Deep Learning Classifier for Multiple Stock Datasets. In *2023 Second International Conference on Electronics and Renewable Systems (ICEARS)* (pp. 1268-1275). IEEE.

Kour, M. (2023). Blockchain Technology Changing Landscape of Banking Industry. In *2023 2nd International Conference on Applied Artificial Intelligence and Computing (ICAAIC)* (pp. 1212-1216). IEEE. 10.1109/ICAAIC56838.2023.10140854

Kour, M., & Sharma, N. (2023). Security Issues in e-Banking. In *2023 2nd International Conference on Applied Artificial Intelligence and Computing (ICAAIC)* (pp. 1291-1294). IEEE. 10.1109/ICAAIC56838.2023.10140397

Lee, I., & Shin, Y. J. (2020). Machine learning for enterprises: Applications, algorithm selection, and challenges. *Business Horizons*, *63*(2), 157–170. doi:10.1016/j.bushor.2019.10.005

Li, Y., Jiang, W., Yang, L., & Wu, T. (2018). On neural networks and learning systems for business computing. *Neurocomputing*, *275*, 1150–1159. doi:10.1016/j.neucom.2017.09.054

Li, Y., Ni, P., & Chang, V. (2020). Application of deep reinforcement learning in stock trading strategies and stock forecasting. *Computing*, *102*(6), 1305–1322. doi:10.100700607-019-00773-w

Mahesh, B. (2020). Machine learning algorithms—A review. *International Journal of Scientific Research*, *9*, 381–386.

Marevac, E., Patković, S., & Žunić, E. (2023). Decision-making AI for customer worthiness and viability. In *2023 22nd International Symposium INFOTEH-JAHORINA (INFOTEH)* (pp. 1-6). IEEE. 10.1109/INFOTEH57020.2023.10094207

Morales, L., Gray, G., & Rajmil, D. (2022). Emerging Risks in the FinTech Industry–Insights from Data Science and Financial Econometrics Analysis. *Economics, Management & Financial Markets, 17*(2).

Ouadah, A., Zemmouchi-Ghomari, L., & Salhi, N. (2022). Selecting an appropriate supervised machine learning algorithm for predictive maintenance. *International Journal of Advanced Manufacturing Technology, 119*(7-8), 4277–4301. doi:10.100700170-021-08551-9

Rakshit, S., Clement, N., & Vajjhala, N. R. (2022). Exploratory review of applications of machine learning in finance sector. In *Advances in Data Science and Management. Proceedings of ICDSM, 2021*, 119–125.

Théate, T., & Ernst, D. (2021). An application of deep reinforcement learning to algorithmic trading. *Expert Systems with Applications, 173*, 114632. doi:10.1016/j.eswa.2021.114632

World Economic Forum Boston Consulting Group (BCG). (2018). *Towards a reskilling revolution: A future of jobs for all.* World Economic Forum.

Zhu, L., Xu, X., Lu, Q., Governatori, G., & Whittle, J. (2022). AI and ethics—Operationalizing responsible AI. In *Humanity Driven AI* (pp. 15–33). Productivity, Well-being, Sustainability and Partnership. doi:10.1007/978-3-030-72188-6_2

Chapter 5
Sustainability-Driven Finance: Reshaping the Financial World

Sanjay Taneja
https://orcid.org/0000-0002-3632-4053
Graphic Era University (Deemed), India

Reepu
Chandigarh University, India

ABSTRACT

Green finance covers a wide range of financial products and services, which can be broadly divided into banking, investment, and insurance products. Examples of these include green bonds, green investment funds, and climate risk insurance and constitute green finance. Green finance is central to the overall discussion on sustainability of economic growth. Rapid economic development is often achieved at the cost of environment. In this study, the authors discuss the basics of green finance: green finance policy in the public domain, best practices from throughout the world, public policy in India, India's progress and challenges in the field of environmental finance, green bonds, green finance as an effective tool for sustainability, areas covered by green finance, green banking, green insurance, benefits of green finance, limitations of green finance, the status quo of green finance in the field of renewable energy, the market mechanism of green finance, types of green financial products, the role of policies in green finance, and the impact of green bonds on environmental protection.

DOI: 10.4018/979-8-3693-1746-4.ch005

INTRODUCTION

Financing initiatives that are environmentally friendly or take climate change into account is referred to as "green finance." Solar, wind, and biogas power; clean transportation that minimizes greenhouse gas emissions; energy-efficient initiatives like green construction; and waste management including recycling, effective disposal, and conversion to electricity are all part of a sustainable approach to building. Green Debt Securities projects must disclose information on how they will deal with environmental issues such as climate change adaptation, resource conservation, waste and water management, land use, and biodiversity. Carbon market mechanisms (like a carbon tax) and new financial institutions (like green banks and funds) are all being created to help fund these sorts of projects. Green finance is the sum of all of these elements put together in one package.

Sustainable economic growth and green funding are linked. Rapid economic expansion is not often accompanied with environmental degradation. Health and economic consequences of environmental deterioration, loss of natural resources, and pervasive pollution are becoming more and more apparent. In an effort to protect and improve the environment, countries throughout the world are rapidly adopting environmentally friendly technologies. The development of an acceptable incentive structure would be required, however, to increase the amount of money provided to initiatives that promote environmental sustainability. It's possible that established enterprises may divert land and man power to more sustainable ventures. (Berensmann, K., & Lindenberg, N. 2016), As a consequence, long-term resources are allocated in a way that fosters long-term growth. Governments, companies, and central banks all play a role in economic growth via the implementation of specific green finance policies.

Environment and natural resource conservation are becoming increasingly important as more and more environmental problems arise. This is due in large part to the rise in pollution, ozone layer depletion, global warming, and other environmental difficulties. The goal of green finance is to strike a balance between the needs of the environment and the interests of the financial system. Though there isn't a clear definition for Green finance, any financial assistance given to projects with the primary goal of promoting sustainability, such as the construction of green buildings, efficient management of energy, waste management, preservation of biodiversity, renewable energy projects, and other related projects, can be referred to as Green financing. Investments from the public sector will fall short of what is needed to complete these projects. Government and business sector efforts should be encouraged to fulfill the expanding need. However, to deal with the issues of fundraising and the use of that money, a regulatory framework and appropriate policy measures are needed as well. (Mohd, S., & V K, K. 2018) As a result, funding for renewable energy, energy efficiency management, and green investment products is not prioritized due to a lack of awareness, subsidies given to fossil fuels in various countries, the bias toward low returns, fear of breaching trust, and mismanagement of funds invested, and other such reasons At the moment, there is little effort being made to connect the concepts of finance and the environment. As part of the long-term aims of the 2015 Paris accord, the financial component was included, along with limiting global average temperature increase and enhancing capacity to adapt to climate change consequences. We need international agreements, policy initiatives, and regulations to bring these two parts together so they may be integrated. Green Financing has been examined in this article as an effective instrument for sustainability and the different possibilities and problems that occur when merging the methods of finance and the environment in India.

GREEN FINANCE POLICY IN THE PUBLIC DOMAIN

Best Practices From Throughout The World

Since the G20's first summit in 2008, the circular carbon economy (CCE) has come up for debate, although climate change has been on the table for a long time. In order to increase the funding and public knowledge of environmentally friendly projects all over the globe, a number of well-known initiatives have been launched. Companies in both the financial and non-financial sectors may benefit from programmes like this that encourage them to include environmental considerations into their financial planning. Financial institutions' commitment to sustainable development may be shown in initiatives like UNEP's Statement of Commitment on Sustainable Development, Principles for Responsible Investment, and Equator Principles. In India, a number of groups have agreed to support these efforts. Environmental and social risks can only be mitigated if a credible source of information on how the entities manage them and a track record of the entities' ability to identify opportunities with both an acceptable rate of return and environmental benefits are in place. (UNEP) As part of the Sustainable Stock Exchange, stock exchanges in signatory countries are urged to create stock price indices that track the stock performance of a select group of companies operating in the signatory countries that are leaders in incorporating ESG principles into their financing strategies.

Environmentally conscious investors may use these indices to their advantage. Members of this initiative include the Bombay Stock Exchange (BSE) and the National Stock Exchange (NSE) of India, which each develop their own ESG indexes. There are four broad types of legal frameworks in use across the world: Financial and non-financial businesses are required to report on their exposure to ESG risks as part of their sustainability disclosures, which is the first step. (Dikau, S., & Volz, U. 2018,) These kinds of disclosures have grown increasingly widespread since the G20 called on firms to voluntarily adopt the principles of the Task Force on Climate-related Financial Disclosures (TCFD). In order to adopt TCFD by June 2020, 60 percent of the 100 largest publicly listed companies worldwide have committed. A system for disclosing ESG-related risks by publicly traded companies has been introduced in many countries. China is one of these Hong Kong (2012) (2012) England and Wales (2012) a country called India (2012) a chronology of events: Philippines, Vietnam, Singapore (2016). (Chowdhary, T. U., Datta, R., & Mohajan, H. K. 2013) Annual CSR reporting by commercial banks started in 2008, and the obligation was extended to non-banking financial institutions (NBFIs) in 2013, with an extra review of social hazards included to the credit evaluation in 2017. Bangladesh's banks were required to use a common risk reporting format as early as 2013. Physical and transitional risks must be reported by asset owners and managers in accordance with France's Energy Transition for Green Growth Law.

Public Policy In India

India has made green finance a top goal since 2007. Corporate Social Responsibility, Sustainable Development, and Nonfinancial Reporting - The Role of Banks" in which it highlights the importance of global warming and climate change for sustainable development, the Reserve Bank of India released a notice in December 2007. In 2008, the NAPCC was established to lay out a comprehensive strategy for mitigating the harmful consequences of climate change in the United States. CCFU, the Ministry of Finance's climate change finance unit, was set up in 2011 to serve as a coordinating body for India's several green funding organisations. The implementation of sustainable disclosure guidelines was the most major strategic move since 2012. Since 2012, the Securities and Exchange Board of India has mandated that companies provide annual reports on corporate social responsibility (SEBI). (Soundarrajan, P., & Vivek, N. 2016) SEBI's guidelines for green bond issuance in May 2017 said that disclosure requirements must be satisfied. A compulsory CSR report was imposed in 2013 by the Ministry of Corporate Affairs under the Companies Act, 2013. (Corporate Social Responsibility) 9 At least once a year, the Committee on Corporate Governance advised that the board of directors meet to discuss strategy, budgeting, board assessment, risk management, environmental and social responsibility (ESR), as well as succession planning.

In India, there are several tax and financial benefits. Following India's 2015 Paris Agreement goals to reduce greenhouse gas emission intensity by 33 to 35 percent below 2005 levels and to attain 40 percent of installed electric generating capacity from non-fossil sources by 2030, these incentives are being implemented. Almost all Indian governments give a 30 percent subsidy for the installation of solar panels on rooftops11. Up to 70% of the installation expenses are subsidized by certain of the special-category states12. If the yearly generation exceeds 1100 kWh1500 kWh, beneficiaries may additionally benefit from a generation-based incentive, which pays '2 per unit of generation. The government may set a price for excess power, which can then be sold on the open market. Additionally, the Indian government launched the Faster Adoption and Manufacturing of Hybrid and Electric Vehicles (FAME) programme in 2015 and 2019 with the goal of increasing credit availability, lowering upfront costs for all vehicles, and developing infrastructure (such as charging stations) to promote the production and sale of environmentally friendly automobiles in the future (Geddes A., Schmidt T. S. and Steffen, B. 2018). There will be a 20 basis point reduction in upfront fees for electric automobiles under the State Bank of India's "green auto loans" scheme, as well as an extended payback period for customers for the production of high-efficiency renewable energy modules; the government has also developed a Production-Linked Incentive (PLI) Scheme.

It has also adopted active policy measures to assist and stimulate green finance operations. The small renewable energy sector is now part of the bank's Priority Sector Lending (PSL) strategy, which began in 2015. Family members may borrow up to'10 lakh to invest in renewable energy, while businesses can borrow up to'30 crore (rising to'15 crore from September 4, 2020). It was announced by the Indian government in September that the country expects to create 450 (GW) of renewable energy by the year 2030.

INDIA'S PROGRESS AND CHALLENGES IN THE FIELD OF ENVIRONMENTAL FINANCE

Increased General Awareness

Green finance and sustainable development aren't often discussed in the mainstream media; therefore it's difficult to gauge public opinion. If you're curious about how people search the internet from various areas at different times, Google Trends is an excellent resource. Based on the volume of Google searches, we may get a sense of how much interest there is in a certain issue or subject area. As a percentage of all searches done in an area during the selected period, the number of Google searches on each subject is normalized in Google Trends. (Keerthi, B.S. 2013) Because Google's general search activity has changed over time, this normalization eliminates any bias. Overall search traffic is substantially bigger now than it was in 2004, for example, due to the global increase of internet access. This means that the total number of searches for a certain topic may not be a useful indicator of how much interest the public has shown in that subject over time. Green finance and its role in sustainable economic growth are becoming more popular, according to Google Trends.

Green Bonds

In this case, the bond's issuer undertakes to use the bond proceeds to support environmentally friendly goods, reforestation, and climate-related initiatives, among other things. To properly allocate money to environmentally friendly projects while also taking into account the risk and reward associated with the bonds, a balanced strategy is required. In addition to strengthening the reputation of the issuing firm or financial institution, green bonds allow investors who only want to invest in environmentally friendly goods to do so. At the same time, it assists those investors who wish to engage in socially responsible initiatives, and so fulfills their desire to incorporate investment and social responsibility into a single transaction. The European Investment Bank and the World Bank initially issued green bonds in 2007. Private businesses, banks, and other financial organizations began issuing green bonds in the following years. For the listing and issuance of these debt instruments in India, the Securities and Exchange Board of India (SEBI) published rules. For SEBI standards, the revenues of such bonds should be invested in green projects including renewable energy and climate change action as well as efforts to preserve biodiversity and reduce pollution levels.

Green bonds may be issued by any sovereign entity, intergovernmental coalition, or company and the earnings from the bonds can be used for environmentally beneficial activities. Bloomberg has provided extensive data on green bonds issued by Indian firms and governments. In India, we started by looking at all bonds issued since January 21, 2015, regardless of whether they were green bonds or not. Bonds with "India" indicated as the risk country have been selected regardless of where the issuer is based. Over 5000 Indian bonds have been issued since 2015,(Berensmann, K. & Lindenberg, N. 2019)and our data includes the initial issuance amount in US dollars, the coupon rate and debt to total assets ratio, as well as whether the bond revenues were to be utilized for green initiatives or not. The Bloomberg terminal was used to get summary information, but not detailed information, for international comparisons.

Green bonds have been issued by the Indian government since 2015. There are now $16.3 billion in green bonds outstanding in India. Approximately $8 billion in green bonds were issued in the Indian financial market at the beginning of 2018, accounting for approximately 0.7% of all bonds issued in India. Some of the world's most powerful and emerging economies have experienced a large increase in green bond investments over the last few years.

"Most green bonds issued since 2015 have maturities of five years or more, but less than 10 years. Yes, Bank Ltd. (2015), the Indian Renewable Energy Development Agency Ltd. (2017, 2019), the Rural Electrification Corporation Limited or REC Limited (2017), the Power Finance Corporation Ltd. (2017), and the Indian Railway Finance Corporation Limited (2017) have all issued long-term green bonds (2017). Renew Power Pvt. Ltd. issued short-term green bonds earlier this year, expiring in less than five years. India's green bonds have been issued in US dollars at a rate of 76% since 2015. It isn't only the World Bank that issues green bonds for Indian projects; it has done so on occasion. India's Green Bond Impact report (2019) estimates that as of June 30, 2019, the amount of Green Bond proceeds earmarked to help finance such projects in India is expected to be US$640 million. (Jain, S. 2020), summary: India's eco-finance sector has only begun to take shape. A total of 7.9% of all outstanding bank credit in the power sector was accounted for by non-conventional energy as of March 2020, whereas green bonds accounted for only 0.7% of all bonds issued in India since 2018. In the next section, we'll discuss some of the most pressing concerns facing the Indian green bond market."

Table 1. Since January 1, 2018, green bonds have been sold (corporate and government: all maturities)

Country	Amount Issued ($Mn)	Number of Bonds Issued	The Amount Issued as a Percent of All Bond Issuance (Percent)	Number of Bonds Issued as a Percent of All Bond Issuance (Percent)
Euro Area	1,96,854	594	1.7	0.4
China	63,023	183	0.3	0.2
USA	35,421	71	0.2	0.2
Japan	11,815	88	0.1	1.1
South Korea	11,781	44	1.0	0.4
Central and Southern America	8,869	53	0.5	1.0
India	**7,992**	**22**	**0.7**	**0.3**
South-east Asia	7,208	86	0.6	1.4
Australia and New Zealand	5,878	15	1.1	0.8
UK	5,311	17	0.4	0.5
Hong Kong	4,781	19	0.5	1.0
Singapore	496	9	0.05	1.2

Source: Compiled by author

Meaning of Green Finance

It's difficult to agree on what defines green funding. "Green Finance" refers to financing initiatives and businesses that do not affect the environment. Environment-friendly projects and investments in renewable energy, clean energy, and pollution control and water sanitation are funded with consideration for both the positive and negative impacts on the environment. This includes the development of green products for end-users like cloth-cotton bags, etc. When we talk about "green finance," we mean financial planning that is both publically and privately funded, with an eye toward long-term sustainability.

GREEN FINANCE AS AN EFFECTIVE TOOL FOR SUSTAINABILITY

Sustainable development, the environment, and the financial system can all coexist in harmony when green financing is used to support initiatives aimed at reaching that end. As a result, it protects natural resources, stimulates the use of renewable energy resources, and so tries to decrease human exploitation of the environment. For the sake of attaining sustainable development objectives, it serves as an effective method.

Areas Covered by Green Finance

Green Banking

It focuses on promoting environmentally friendly behaviors via banking activity. Green banking is beneficial to both the environment and the financial industry since it aids in environmental conservation. Technology advances, shifting stakeholder expectations, and operational innovations are all part of its functioning. (Dikau, S., & U. Volz. 2018) SBI, Punjab National, Bank of Baroda, Canara, ICICI and DFC Bank, Kotak Mahindra, and IDBI are among the Indian banks that provide green banking services to their clients. Other green banking institutions in India include the State Bank of India, Punjab National Bank, Bank of Baroda, Canara, and IDBI.

In the following table, you will find a collection of green banking practices.

Table 2. Green banking practices

S.No	Areas Covered	Explanation
1	Online Banking	Using the internet to provide clients with financial services. Encourages the use of electronic payment methods rather than paper checks or cash.
2	Green mortgage	For the acquisition of green buildings or the renovation of existing buildings to green buildings, financing is given.
3	The green home equity loan	Purchase and installation of home energy-saving equipment made possible thanks to the loan.
4	Home office conversion loans	Loans to set up a home office and begin working from home.
5	Green car loan	discounts on financing for non-zero emission automobiles
6	Green credit cards	Environmentally-friendly initiatives are funded by deducting a portion of each payment from the cardholder's account.
7	Energy-efficient loans	Loans for energy management that is more efficient
8	Loans towards the development of alternative fuel vehicles and infrastructure.	Incentives and loans provided to the conversion of existing vehicles to cleaner and more efficient fuels

Source: Compiled by author

GREEN INSURANCE

As a member of the green financial sector, the insurance business has a critical role to play in achieving long-term sustainability objectives. As a backbone for green financing, the insurance industry provides information on risk management and significantly lowers the risk associated with its various strategies and its business of underwriting, Dipika (2015). Although it has not been directly involved in environmental degradation or framing regulations about these issues.

For private electric cars insured by the Insurance Regulatory and Development Authority of India (IRDAI), the third-party premium rates would be cut by 15% from FY 2019-20.

BENEFITS OF GREEN FINANCE

Green finance will have a positive impact on both the environment and the economy. It aids in creating a balance between the financial and natural worlds. There are a variety of advantages to be had,

Table 3. Green insurance types

S.No	Type of Green Insurance	Explanation
1	Green car insurance	Insurance premiums will be based on the number of miles driven, which will encourage people to drive less and help the environment at the same time.
2	Green business insurance	Incentive programs for company owners to renovate or rehabilitate damaged structures using environmentally friendly materials
3	Eco-friendly home insurance	Insures renewable energy power systems with technology and maintenance assistance, as well as insurance coverage
4	Green travel insurance	By contributing a portion of the premium to programs aimed at reducing carbon dioxide emissions, this insurance compensates for the environmental impact of traveling.
5	Green life insurance	Insurance companies will give a portion of the premiums they collect to environmental causes.
6	Carbon insurance	Protects the plantation woodlands from weather-related dangers by providing insurance coverage.

Source: Compiled by author

1) **Efficient energy management:** Under green finance, various incentives and money are made available for the installation and use of renewable energy resources. As a result, energy efficiency may be improved.
2) **Environmental protection:** Green finance is all about supporting sustainable development initiatives, and environmental preservation is an essential element of that funding. So the notion will help reduce pollution, mitigate climate change, mitigate the loss of the ozone layer, and protect biodiversity, which is essential for the existence of living beings.
3) **Enhances reputation:** As the number of stakeholders who want to have a positive impact on society via their investments grows, they will give preference to firms who are doing their part to protect the environment. (Wang, K., Tsai, S.-B., Du, X., & Bi, D. 2019) Even the government offers financial assistance to environmentally beneficial initiatives. As a result, firms will be able to create and strengthen their reputation via green finance in the long term.
4) **Helps in attracting FDI:** Concerns about environmental preservation are on the rise across the world. Therefore, international investors that invest in local enterprises are going to take into account the social costs and benefits while evaluating the initiatives. As a result, releasing green investment instruments would help our nation attract FDI.

LIMITATIONS OF GREEN FINANCE

1) **Ambiguity regarding definition:** The term "green finance" has no universally agreed-upon meaning. Investing in green projects will be challenging for investors since there is a lack of clarity on what constitutes a "green" project, which leads to misunderstanding and so acts as a barrier.
2) **No proper regulatory framework:** When it comes to the appraisal of green projects and the implementation of green investment policies, no formal laws, rules, or regulations exist, As a result of this regulatory void, green investment has had difficulty expanding and developing.
3) **Lack of awareness:** Many stakeholders are unaware of green finance, even though some groups of individuals are becoming more receptive to environmentally responsible investments. Insufficient knowledge and awareness of green investment goods will result in less capital accumulation than necessary. As a result, there will be an imbalance between the supply and demand for financial resources.
4) **Give rise to unhealthy competition:** There is a rising demand for green investment goods, and market players will take advantage of this need to increase their market share by utilizing the term "green projects." Prioritizing short-term economic gain above long-term sustainability creates unhealthy competition.

RECOMMENDATIONS

- To begin, governments, banks, and financial institutions should work together to educate the general people on the importance of environmental protection as well as the vast range of green investment options available. Innovative goods that both attract investors and contribute to environmental progress may be created by combining technology and money.
- To properly analyze green finance projects and safeguard the interests of investors, a robust regulatory framework must be established. All monies received for a certain project must be utilized for the intended purpose, according to the regulations.
- To penalize market players who unfairly take advantage of the increased demand for green initiatives, strict legislation must be implemented to govern the abuse of money. (Volz, U. 2018) Additionally, the legislation should be concerned with the use of monies generated. In the event of a policy infringement, appropriate measures must be implemented.

- Research in the area of green finance should be encouraged to bring forth novel green investment products and efficient green projects as well as the right legislative measures required for complete development and growth in the financial industry.

THE STATUS QUO OF GREEN FINANCE IN THE FIELD OF RENEWABLE ENERGY

Energy sources including natural gas, crude oil, wind and solar power are the primary focus of green finance research today rather than an overall picture of the energy industry. (Reddy, A. S. 2018) we can help reduce the risk and cost of financing, enhance the financial system, and support the expansion of renewable energy via green finance. Solar energy's expansion has been slowed for years due to a lack of adequate financing. Renewable energy processors and consumer demand should be taken into consideration by the financial system in order to promote broad use of renewable energy. The cost of renewable energy technologies electricity is directly influenced by the cost of financing. The future structure of renewable energy sources may be influenced by the power market's competitiveness. (Sachs, J.D., Woo, N., Yoshino, N.,& Hesary, T. Hesary 2019)If financing for renewable energy projects can be made more affordable via competition, they should accomplish their stated goals. There are many ways to look at wind energy funding for the banks; the need for efficient use of funds over time; financial instruments must be aligned with scientific and technological progress and renewable energy financing requirements; and political objectives must be aligned with energy security legislation and the energy fund in order to better promote development However, no research has been done on the interconnected expansion of the energy and financial sectors, and no in-depth examination of the internal mechanism addressing the link, mutual penetration, and reciprocal influence between the two businesses is known yet.

THE MARKET MECHANISM OF GREEN FINANCE

"Environmental funds, weather derivatives, nature-linked securities, and ecological options are just a few of the green financial products available. Ecosystem-based financial products and methods are also part of the green finance sector, which aims to protect firms against unanticipated natural disasters"

Emissions Trading Market Mechanism

The first stage in constructing an emissions trading market is to identify the total amount of emissions trading in the region, as well as the initial number of tradable permits that will be available for trading. Emissions trading market creation also includes the transaction subject, the transaction protocol, and how the market will be governed and controlled among other aspects. The Slovak government and Japan's Sumitomo Corporation inked an agreement in 2002 for the trading of emissions totaling 200000 tones, which is generally recognized as a milestone in the worldwide emissions trading market. Air pollution, water pollution, and biodiversity challenges have all been addressed via the application of financial market mechanisms by environmental regulatory authorities.

Table 4. Types of green financial products

Biodiversity Funds and Environmental Funds	Biodiversity conservation funds and environmental funds provide financial assistance directly to conservation initiatives or indirectly to businesses engaged in the protection of biodiversity. RBI (2019), Sustainability in forests and fisheries may be achieved via the establishment of environmental funds and funds dedicated to biodiversity.
Debt-for environment Swaps	In exchange for contributions to an environmental fund, the more developed country may avoid incurring debt. Over 30 countries have previously benefited from debt-for-environment swaps programmes in the US, Sweden, and Germany; one of the most notable debt-for-environment swap agreements between the US and Polish governments had a total value of approximately $370 million.
Securitizations in Forestry	Companies that set up securities transfer all of their profits to a new legal entity, which then obtains funds from investors by issuing securities in the capital market and lends the revenues to the companies of forestry extraction, for example in mitigation banking of wetland and endangered species in the United States and the system tradable native vegetation obligations in Brazil.
Derivatives on the weather	Climate change-related financial losses may now be offset by these new financial solutions. Companies entering weather derivative contracts may be required to pay compensation if the degree of climate change exceeds a certain benchmark. Since 2002, the transactions in weather derivatives have reached billions of dollars, according to data from CME, which dates back to the energy sector's mid-1990s.
Nature-linked Securities	Nature-linked Natural catastrophes and climate change may be transferred to investors in the global financial market using securities. A special purpose vehicle (SPV) is often set up by the sponsors of natural catastrophe securities before they issue debt securities. As a result of this agreement, SPV commits to compensate sponsors in the case of natural catastrophes in exchange for the sponsors' monthly payment of an insurance premium to SPV.
Green investment funds	For example, "many investment firms and trust funds refuse to invest in pollution-producing industries. Fund managers were encouraged to implement environmentally friendly investing methods under the Equator principles of green finance"

Source: Compiled by author

THE ROLE OF POLICIES IN GREEN FINANCE

Due to the large initial investment and the lengthy payback time, environmental protection sector expansion needs a specialized financing strategy. Green finance policies may help alleviate some of the government's funding shortfalls when paired with reform and new financial instruments. Reform and innovation of existing financial tools are part of a two-pronged approach to achieving the goals of green finance development: first, an examination of fiscal policy and the most feasible means of raising funds; and second, a review of the efficiency and direction of the use of fiscal funds.

THE IMPACT OF GREEN BONDS ON ENVIRONMENTAL PROTECTION

The use of financial tools is essential to the practical application of green financing. The worldwide market for green bonds has grown at an incredible rate. The terms "green bonds" and "bonds" are used interchangeably here. Bonds that are classified as "green" have many of the same features and functions as regular ones. Issuers have a low capital cost to issue bonds since the interest is pre-tax and investors' desire for yield is low, therefore lowering the cost of capital. For big-scale infrastructure projects that need enormous amounts of cash and long-term investment returns, bonds are ideal since they can generate a substantial amount of funds and have relatively long periods. There is a wide range of funding sources, including the government, financial institutions, and corporations, as well to suit the needs of a wide range of investors, bonds outperform bank deposits when it comes to profitability, liquidity, and stability. (Shen, C., Zhao, K., & Ge, J. 2020), Investors benefit from greater liquidity management due to bonds' lower entry/exit fees as well as the ability to change their investment portfolios more easily. Green bonds have stricter environmental standards than traditional bonds. The monies received must be used for renewable energy and green initiatives that are long-term and sustainable. Environmental and climate change risks may be hedged by investing in green bonds. The government may introduce green bond-related preferential policies such as lower investment thresholds and more favorable tax treatment in the future. (Nassiry, D. 2018), some national and local government subsidies may be used to fund green bond projects shortly. The transparency standards for green bonds are also more stringent, allowing investors to invest with less risk while still fulfilling their social obligation and benefiting from it. The first worldwide Climate Awareness Bond was issued by the European Investment Bank (EIB) in June 2007. (Geddes A., Schmidt T. S. and Steffen, B. 2018) It was used to finance renewable energy and energy efficiency initiatives. From 2007 to 2012, the worldwide green bond market went through the earliest stages of development before entering a period of significant growth in 2013. Scale expansion and the variety of issuers are two of the most important aspects of the green bonds market. From Europe to all across the globe, particularly in developing nations, distribution is becoming more widespread.

REFERENCES

Bansal, N., Bhatnagar, M., & Taneja, S. (2023). Balancing Priorities Through Green Optim000ism: A Study Elucidating Initiatives, Approaches, and Strategies for Sustainable Supply Chain Management. In *Handbook of Research on Designing Sustainable Supply Chains to Achieve a Circular Economy* (pp. 60–81). IGI Global. doi:10.4018/978-1-6684-7664-2.ch004

Berensmann, K., & Lindenberg, N. (2019). *Green finance: actors, challenges and policy recommendations.* Briefing Paper 23. German Development Institute/ Deutsches Institut für Entwicklungspolitik (DIE).

Bhatnagar, M., Özen, E., Taneja, S., Grima, S., & Rupeika-Apoga, R. (2022a). The Dynamic Connectedness between Risk and Return in the Fintech Market of India: Evidence Using the GARCH-M Approach. *Risks*, *10*(11), 209. doi:10.3390/ risks10110209

Bhatnagar, M., Taneja, S., Kumar, P., & Özen, E. (2023a). Does Financial Education Act as a Catalyst for SME Competitiveness. *International Journal of Education Economics and Development*, *1*(1), 1. doi:10.1504/IJEED.2023.10053629

Bhatnagar, M., Taneja, S., & Özen, E. (2022b). A wave of green start-ups in India— The study of green finance as a support system for sustainable entrepreneurship. *Green Finance*, *4*(2), 253–273. doi:10.3934/GF.2022012

Bhatnagar, M., Taneja, S., & Rupeika-Apoga, R. (2023b). Demystifying the Effect of the News (Shocks) on Crypto Market Volatility. *Journal of Risk and Financial Management*, *16*(2), 136. doi:10.3390/jrfm16020136

Chowdhary, T. U., Datta, R., & Mohajan, H. K. (2013). Green Finance is Essential for Economic Development and Sustainability. *International Journal of Research in Commerce, Economics and Management*, *3*(10), 104–108. https://mpra.ub.uni-muenchen.de/id/eprint/51169

Dahiya, K., Taneja, S., & Özen, E. (2023). To Analyse the Impact of Multi-Media Technology on the Rural Entrepreneurship Development. In Contemporary Studies of Risks in Emerging Technology, Part A (pp. 221-240). Emerald Publishing Limited. doi:10.1108/978-1-80455-562-020231015

Dangwal, A., Kaur, S., Taneja, S., & Taneja, S. (2022a). A Bibliometric Analysis of Green Tourism Based on the Scopus Platform. In J. Kaur, P. Jindal, & A. Singh (Eds.), *Developing Relationships, Personalization, and Data Herald in Marketing 5.0* (Vol. 1, pp. 1–327). IGI Global. doi:10.4018/978-1-6684-4496-2.ch015

Dangwal, A., Taneja, S., Özen, E., Todorovic, I., & Grima, S. (2022b). Abridgement of Renewables: It's Potential and Contribution to India's GDP. *International Journal of Sustainable Development and Planning*, *17*(8), 2357–2363. doi:10.18280/ijsdp.170802

Dikau, S., & Volz, U. (2018). *Central Banking, Climate Change and Green Finance.* ADBI Working Paper 867. Tokyo: Asian Development Bank Institute.

Dipika. (2015). Green Banking in India: A Study of Various Strategies Adopted by Banks for Sustainable Development. *International Journal of Engineering Research & Technology.*

Falcone, P. M., & Sica, E. (2019). Assessing the Opportunities and Challenges of Green Finance in Italy: An Analysis of the Biomass Production Sector. *Sustainability (Basel)*, *11*(2), 517. doi:10.3390u11020517

Geddes, A., Schmidt, T. S., & Steffen, B. (2018). The multiple roles of state investment banks in low-carbon energy finance: An analysis of Australia, the UK and Germany. *Energy Policy*, *115*, 158–170. doi:10.1016/j.enpol.2018.01.009

Group of Twenty. (2016). *G20 Green Finance Synthesis Report 2016*. https://unepinquiry.org/wpcontent/uploads/2016/09/Synthesis_Report_Full_EN.pdf

Gupta, M., Arora, R., & Taneja, S. (2023). Bibliometric Analysis on Employee Engagement and Human Resource Management. In *Enhancing Customer Engagement Through Location-Based Marketing* (pp. 185–205). IGI Global. doi:10.4018/978-1-6684-8177-6.ch013

Jain, S. (2020). *Financing India's green transition. ORF Issue Brief No. 338.* Observer Research Foundation.

Jayasubramanian, P., & Shanthi, M. (2014). Green Finance. *Indian Journal of Applied Research, 4(* 8). doi:10.15373/2249555X/August2014/161

Keerthi, B. S. (2013). A Study on Emerging Green Finance in India: Its challenges and Opportunities. *International Journal of Management and Social Sciences Research*, *2*(2), 49–53.

Kumar, P., Taneja, S., Özen, E., & Singh, S. (2023b). Artificial Intelligence and Machine Learning in Insurance: A Bibliometric Analysis. In Smart Analytics, Artificial Intelligence and Sustainable Performance Management in a Global Digitalised Economy (pp. 191-202). Emerald Publishing Limited. doi:10.1108/S1569-37592023000110A010

Kumar, P., Verma, P., Bhatnagar, M., Taneja, S., Seychel, S., Todorović, I., & Grim, S. (2023). The financial performance and solvency status of the indian public sector banks: A CAMELS rating and Z index approach. *International Journal of Sustainable Development and Planning*, *18*(2), 367–376. doi:10.18280/ijsdp.180204

Mohd, S., & V K, K. (2018). Green Finance: A Step towards Sustainable Development. *MUDRA Journal of Finance and Accounting*, *5*(1), 59–74. doi:10.17492/mudra.v5i01.13036

Nassiry, D. (2018). *Green Bond Experiences in Nordic Countries.* ADBI Working Paper No. 816.

Olga, B., & Smorodinov, O. (2017). Challenges to green finance in G20 countries. *Mirovaya ekonomika i mezhdunarodnye otnosheniya*, *61*(10), 16-24.

Özen, E., & Sanjay, T. (2022a). Empirical Analysis of the Effect of Foreign Trade in Computer and Communication Services on Economic Growth in India. *Journal of Economics and Business Issues*, *2*(2), 24–34. https://doi.org/https://jebi-academic.org/index.php/jebi/article/view/41

Reddy, A. S. (2018). Green Finance- Financial Support for Sustainable Development. *International Journal of Pure and Applied Mathematics*, *118*(20), 645–650.

Reepu, R., Taneja, S., Ozen, E., & Singh, A. (2023). A Globetrotter to the Future of Marketing: Metaverse. In *Cultural Marketing and Metaverse for Consumer Engagement* (pp. 1–11). IGI Global. doi:10.4018/978-1-6684-8312-1.ch001

Sachs, J. D., Woo, N., Yoshino, N., & Hesary, T. (2019). *Hesary; Why is Green Finance Important?* ADBI working paper 917. https://www.adb.org/publications/why-green-finance-important

Shen, C., Zhao, K., & Ge, J. (2020). An Overview of Green Building Performance Database. *Journal of Engineering*, *2020*, 1–9. doi:10.1155/2020/3780595

Singh, V., Taneja, S., Singh, V., Singh, A., & Paul, H. L. (2021). Online advertising strategies in Indian and Australian e-commerce companies: A comparative study. *Big Data Analytics for Improved Accuracy, Efficiency, and Decision Making in Digital Marketing*, 124–138. doi:10.4018/978-1-7998-7231-3.ch009

Soundarrajan, P., & Vivek, N. (2016). Green finance for sustainable green economic growth in India. *Zemedelská Ekonomika*, *62*(1), 35–44. doi:10.17221/174/2014-AGRICECON

Taneja, S., Bhatnagar, M., Kumar, P., & Grima, S. (2023). A panel analysis of the effectiveness of the asset management in Indian agricultural companies. *International Journal of Sustainable Development and Planning*, *18*(3), 653–660. doi:10.18280/ijsdp.180301

Taneja, S., Bhatnagar, M., Kumar, P., & Rupeika-apoga, R. (2023). India ' s Total Natural Resource Rents (NRR) and GDP : An Augmented Autoregressive Distributed Lag (ARDL) Bound Test. *Journal of Risk and Financial Management*, *16*(2), 91. doi:10.3390/jrfm16020091

Taneja, S., Gupta, M., Bhushan, P., Bhatnagar, M., & Singh, A. (2023). Cultural Marketing in the Digital Era. In *Cultural Marketing and Metaverse for Consumer Engagement* (pp. 109–122). IGI Global. doi:10.4018/978-1-6684-8312-1.ch008

Taneja, S., Jaggi, P., Jewandah, S., & Ozen, E. (2022). Role of Social Inclusion in Sustainable Urban Developments: An Analyse by PRISMA Technique. *International Journal of Design & Nature and Ecodynamics*, *17*(6), 937–942. doi:10.18280/ijdne.170615

Taneja, S., Kaur, S., & Özen, E. (2022). Using green finance to promote global growth in a sustainable way. *International Journal of Green Economics*, *16*(3), 246–257. doi:10.1504/IJGE.2022.128930

Taneja, S., & Özen, E. (2023a). To analyse the relationship between bank's green financing and environmental performance. *International Journal of Electronic Finance*, *12*(2), 163–175. doi:10.1504/IJEF.2023.129919

Taneja, S., & Ozen, E. (2023b). Impact of the European Green Deal (EDG) on the agricultural carbon (CO2) emission in Turkey. *International Journal of Sustainable Development and Planning*, *18*(3), 715–727. doi:10.18280/ijsdp.180307

Taneja, S., & Sharma, V. (2023e). Role of Beaconing Marketing in Improving Customer Buying Experience. In *Enhancing Customer Engagement Through Location-Based Marketing* (pp. 176–184). IGI Global. doi:10.4018/978-1-6684-8177-6.ch012

Volz, U. (2018). *Fostering green finance for sustainable development in Asia.* ADBI Working Paper Series (814).

Wang, K., Tsai, S.-B., Du, X., & Bi, D. (2019). Internet Finance, Green Finance, and Sustainability. *Sustainability (Basel), 11*(14), 3856. doi:10.3390u11143856

Chapter 6
Masters of the Market: Unleashing Algorithmic Wizardry in Finance

Jaspreet Kaur
Chandigarh University, India

Ercan Ozen
USAK University, Turkey

ABSTRACT

The inexorable advance of algorithms is driving a revolutionary change in the financial world, which is causing significant upheaval. This chapter goes into the complex realm of algorithmic trading, charting its history from the manual execution of trades to the complex methods used by today's financial whizzes. The chapter sheds light on the effect that algorithms have on the microstructure of markets and highlights the contribution that algorithms make to the development of prices, the dynamics of liquidity, and the overall efficiency of markets.

BACKGROUND AND CONTEXT: SIGNIFICANCE OF ALGORITHMIC TRADING IN FINANCE

Using computer algorithms for automating the procedure of trading financial products in the stock exchange, the forex market, or other kinds of markets is known as algorithmic trading, sometimes referred to as algo trading or black-box trading. It involves executing transactions automatically with the use of preset criteria and procedures. The emergence of algorithmic trading, which is now a common occurrence in contemporary financial markets, is directly related to changes in

DOI: 10.4018/979-8-3693-1746-4.ch006

market structure, technological breakthroughs, and the complexity of financial products (Auer et al., 2023).

Development of Trading Algorithms: Over time, algorithmic trading has seen substantial change. Trading was mostly done manually in the early days of financial markets, with traders executing orders on the trading floor. Algorithmic trading became more popular with the introduction of computers and computerised trading platforms. The 1987 stock market crisis and the events that followed brought attention to the necessity of automated systems capable of reacting quickly to market conditions. The creation and acceptance of algorithmic trading tactics resulted from this.

Developments in connectivity, processing power, and data availability have all contributed to the rise of algorithmic trading. A branch of algorithmic trading known as high-frequency trading (HFT) was created by traders who wanted to profit from incredibly brief price swings.

Technology and Facilities: A lot of cutting-edge technology, such as potent computers, fast data feeds, and complex algorithms, are necessary for algorithmic trading. With the help of this technology, traders may quickly execute orders, find trading opportunities, and analyse enormous volumes of data. Co-location services have grown in popularity as a way for trading companies to cut down on latency and have a performance advantage over exchange servers (Barzykin et al. 2023).

Algorithmic Trading's Importance in Finance

- **Productivity and Velocity:** Trades can be executed more quickly and effectively by automating trading procedures, which is made possible by algorithmic trading. This is important because swift decision-making gives you a competitive advantage in markets where pricing can fluctuate quickly. As a subset of algorithmic trading, high-frequency trading entails the execution of several orders at incredibly fast speeds. This helps to reduce bid-ask spreads and increase market liquidity.
- **Market Transparency:** Because algorithmic trading makes it easier to enter and exit positions, it has boosted market liquidity. Algorithms help create a more liquid and tradeable market by quickly executing deals in response to changing market conditions (Bumin & Ozcalici, 2023).
- **Risk Control:** Complex risk management measures can be implemented thanks to algorithmic trading. In order to reduce possible losses, algorithms can automatically monitor and manage risk factors, modify positions, and put stop-loss orders in place.

- **Making Markets:** Market makers frequently use trading algorithms to constantly quote buy and sell prices. This helps guarantee that there are always buyers and sellers accessible, especially in less liquid markets, and it also adds to market liquidity.
- **Lessening of Human Bias:** When making trading judgements, automation lessens the influence of human emotions and prejudices. Trading may become more methodical and disciplined as a result of algorithms' execution of deals in accordance with predetermined rules and objective standards (Eichengreen, 2023).
- **Arbitrage Possibilities**: The process of finding and taking advantage of arbitrage opportunities resulting from price differences between several markets or financial instruments is known as algorithmic trading. Prices in different trading venues line more closely as a result, improving market efficiency.
- **Trade in Quantitative Forms:** Quantitative trading, which uses statistical analysis and mathematical models to create trading strategies, is closely related to algorithmic trading. The optimisation of trading techniques and the methodical assessment of market conditions are made possible by quantitative approaches (Chakrabarty & Pascual, 2023).
- **Market Monitoring and Adherence:** Algorithmic techniques for market monitoring are frequently used by regulators and exchanges to identify and stop market manipulation, fraud, and other illegal actions. Data from algorithmic trading is also essential for regulatory compliance and inquiry.

In summary, algorithmic trading, which provides efficiency, liquidity, and sophisticated risk management skills, has emerged as a key component of contemporary financial markets. Its importance will probably only increase in the future as financial markets and technology develop. It also brings up issues with justice, market stability, and the requirement for suitable regulatory frameworks to handle potential hazards (Bumin & Ozcalici, 2023).

An Historical Perspective on the Development of Algorithmic Trading

When financial markets first started using computerised trading platforms in the 1970s and 1980s, algorithmic trading was only getting its start. These decades are considered to be the cradle of algorithmic trading. During this time period, exchanges made the switch from floor-based trading to electronic systems, which enabled order matching to occur at a much quicker and more efficient rate as depicted in Figure 1.

Figure 1. Development of algorithmic trading

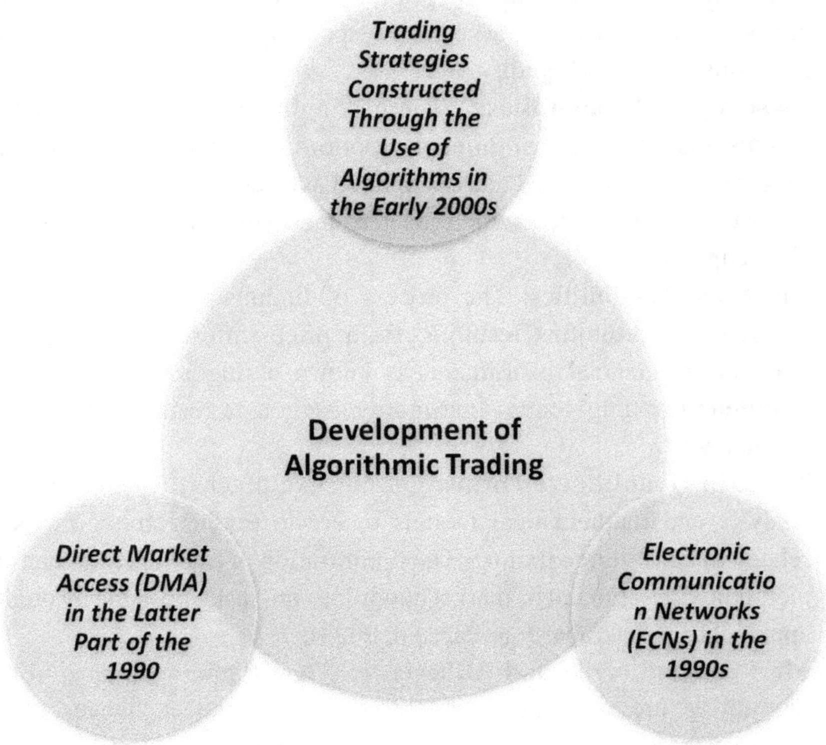

The Development of Electronic Communication Networks (ECNs) in the 1990s: Electronic Communication Networks (ECNs), which provide a platform for traders to electronically execute orders, began to emerge in the 1990s after decades of slow development. Because ECNs made it feasible for buyers and sellers to speak directly with one another, the necessity for the customary intermediaries was significantly reduced (Dhoni, 2023).

The Introduction of Direct Market Access (DMA) in the Latter Part of the 1990s: Direct Market Access (DMA), which enables institutional investors to trade directly on exchanges without the need for the manual intervention of brokers, rose to prominence in the late 1990s and quickly spread throughout the financial industry in the early 2000s. DMA acquired general acceptance during this time period. It is common practise to attribute DMA with being the driving force behind the automation of order execution.

Trading Strategies Constructed Through the Use of Algorithms in the Early 2000s: At the turn of the 21st century, algorithmic trading strategies started to gain traction as a viable option for investors. These included ways that were less complicated, such as the Volume-Weighted Average Price (VWAP) and the Time-Weighted Average Price (TWAP). Traders started employing algorithms so that they could place massive orders without visibly affecting the price of the market's asset (Dhoni, 2023).

Achievements in the Field of Technology

1. Recent Developments in Computer Processing Power: Because of advancements in computing power, algorithmic trading systems have become capable of handling increasingly sophisticated calculations and processing large volumes of market data. Because of this, complex algorithms that are able to analyse several factors simultaneously and in real time were able to be developed (Eichengreen, 2023).
2. High-Frequency Trading (HFT) - During the Middle of the 2000s: High-Frequency Trading (HFT), a subset of algorithmic trading that is distinguished by high-speed execution and a huge number of orders in extremely short timescales, began to gain popularity around the middle of the 2000s. Co-location services are extremely important to HFT because they help to lower latency.
3. Enhancements to the Market's Data and Connectivity: The development of algorithmic trading was significantly aided by developments in market data feeds as well as network enhancements. It has become vital to have data transmitted at a high speed and with a low latency in order to execute trades accurately (Dhoni, 2023).
4. Services related to co-location: Co-location services, in which trading companies position their servers in close proximity to exchange servers, have gained broad adoption in recent years. This helped to reduce latency, which in turn provided algorithmic traders with a competitive advantage in terms of the speed with which they could execute their deals.

Moving Away From Manual Trading and Towards Automated Trading

Historically speaking, trading was a procedure that was carried out manually on the trading floors of stock exchanges. This era of trading is referred to as the "Age of Manual Trading." Traders would communicate with one another both vocally and via the use of hand gestures when they were placing orders (Chakrabarty & Pascual, 2023).

The Initial Steps Towards the Implementation of Electronic Trading: With the widespread deployment of electronic trading platforms in the 1980s, the transition away from manual trading and towards automated trading got under way in a serious way at that time. The use of electronic technology sped up the process of carrying out orders, which also contributed to an improvement in overall production (Fertani, 2023).

Trading Strategies Constructed on the Basis of Algorithms: The development and subsequent widespread adoption of algorithmic trading strategies in the 2000s was the driving force behind the quickening pace of the shift. Traders and institutions started using algorithms as a way to automate trading decisions on the basis of predetermined guidelines and standards. This trend began in the 1990s (Eichengreen, 2023).

Integrating Human and Machine Learning: Over the past few years, the field of algorithmic trading has started to implement a number of different machine learning strategies. These include neural networks, reinforcement learning, and natural language processing, and they give computers the ability to learn from market data and modify themselves accordingly (Bhatnagar et al., 2023; Kumar et al., 2023; Reepu et al., 2023; Taneja et al., 2023).

Obstacles to Regulation and Possible Solutions: The proliferation of algorithmic trading spurred regulatory bodies to address the possible dangers and difficulties posed by the practise. The integrity of the market, the prevention of manipulation, and the promotion of trading practises that are fair and transparent all led to the development of regulatory frameworks (Chakrabarty & Pascual, 2023).

The Constantly Changing Evolution: The practise of algorithmic trading is constantly advancing, and recent developments in artificial intelligence, big data analytics, and blockchain technology are all being incorporated into it. The ongoing pursuit of algorithms that are not just faster but also more efficient and adaptive is also pushing additional innovation in the financial markets.

In a nutshell, the development of algorithmic trading mirrors the transition away from human, floor-based trading and towards highly automated, technology-driven systems. The landscape of algorithmic trading has been defined by technological breakthroughs, which, when combined with changes in market structure, have made algorithmic trading an essential component of today's modern financial markets (Garcia et al., 2023).

Building Blocks of Different Algorithmic Strategies

Analysis of the Market: Comprehensive research of financial markets is typically where algorithmic trading methods get their start. This includes looking at past price data, trends in the market, and any other pertinent indicators that may be available.

Traders make use of this knowledge to determine the potential opportunities and hazards in a given situation.

Administration of Risk: An essential component of algorithmic strategies is the implementation of an efficient risk management system. This requires the establishment of preset risk factors, such as stop-loss levels, position sizes, and portfolio diversification, among other things. The purpose of developing algorithms is to automatically manage and modify risk based on the conditions of the market (Chakrabarty & Pascual, 2023).

Algorithms for the Execution of Code: It is absolutely necessary to have order execution algorithms in place in order to both reduce the market's influence and get the best possible fill pricing. These algorithms intend to carry out trades in an effective manner by taking into consideration aspects like as the liquidity of the market, the depth of the order book, and the transaction costs.

Impact Analysis of the Market: Models that assess the possible effect that a significant trade could have on the market could be incorporated into algorithms. When prices are affected by trade, it is important to understand how those changes will occur so that mitigation solutions can be developed accordingly.

Testing in reverse and making adjustments: Prior to being put into action, algorithmic trading techniques are put through exhaustive back testing, which evaluates how well the strategies performed under a variety of different market scenarios using data from the past. The parameters are fine-tuned using optimisation techniques, which also help to improve the effectiveness of the strategy (Gomez & Lambertz, 2023).

The Application of Quantitative Analysis to Finance: Quantitative analysis is the process of analysing financial markets via the application of mathematical models and statistical methods in order to arrive at educated conclusions regarding investments. The following are important components:

Analysis of Time Sequences: The study of past price data with the goal of recognising patterns, trends, and possible predicting signals. Understanding the dynamics of the market and constructing effective forecasting models requires the use of time series analysis.

The practise of statistical arbitrage: Utilising statistical models in order to locate price differences between connected financial products and then capitalising on such differences. Trading in pairs is a prominent tactic utilised in the statistical arbitrage field (Hambly et al., 2023).

Optimisation of the Portfolio: Constructing investment portfolios by the application of mathematical optimisation techniques in order to get maximum returns for a specified degree of risk. The Modern Portfolio Theory (also known as MPT) and the Capital Asset Pricing Model (also known as CAPM) are two theories that are considered to be foundational in this field.

Simulations with the Monte Carlo method: The evaluation of a portfolio's risk and potential return by modelling thousands of different possible outcomes through simulation. The uncertainty that is involved with making financial decisions can be quantified with the use of Monte Carlo simulations (Gomez & Lambertz, 2023).

Modelling the Volatility of Events: In order to effectively manage risks, it is necessary to model and forecast volatility. Quantitative tools such as GARCH models, which stand for generalised autoregressive conditional heteroskedasticity, and implied volatility analysis are frequently utilised in this context.

The Importance of Statistical Models and Their Functions

An Examination of Regression: Used in order to comprehend the connection between variables that are dependent and those that are independent. In the field of finance, regression analysis is a technique that can be utilised to estimate the impact of many factors, such as interest rates, economic indicators, or the performance of companies, on asset prices.

Models Based on Time Series: The Autoregressive Integrated Moving Average (ARIMA) and the Generalised Autoregressive Conditional Harrell (GARCH) models are utilised in order to analyse and forecast time-series data, particularly in regards to stock prices and volatility (Hambly et al., 2023).

Trading With the Help of Machine Learning Algorithms

In order for algorithms to be able to make accurate predictions, they must first be trained using data that has been labelled. Support Vector Machines (SVM), Random Forests, and Neural Networks are a few examples of the types of software that can be used to anticipate prices and perform categorization tasks (Huang et al., 2023).

Learning Without Supervision: The K-means clustering method is one example of a clustering algorithm that may recognise patterns and groupings in data. Market segmentation and the detection of anomalies are two applications of these methodologies.

Learning through Reinforcement: Learning occurs when algorithms engage in activity with their surroundings and are provided with feedback in the form of incentives or punishments. Trading techniques can be optimised over time with the help of reinforcement learning thanks to its use.

Processing of natural language (Natural Language Processing): Textual data, such as news stories or the sentiment expressed on social media, is analysed and interpreted using NLP algorithms. This information can be utilised to assess the mood of the market and to make judgements on trading (Irani, 2023).

The Effect That Large Amounts of Data Have on Decision-Making Algorithms

The term "big data" refers to an umbrella term that includes a variety of data formats, such as structured, unstructured, and semi-structured data. Trading algorithms can take use of this diversity to obtain a more in-depth picture of how the market is currently functioning. The speed of the data High-frequency data streams can provide access to information that is current and accurate regarding the state of the market. The most recent information that is accessible can be used by algorithmic strategies to make decisions in a split second, and these strategies are also able to react swiftly to changing situations.

The Authenticity of the Data and the Quality of the Data is of the utmost importance to validate the data and ensure that they are of a superior standard. Big data technologies make it possible to clean, validate, and combine data from a broad variety of sources; as a result, the accuracy of algorithmic decision-making is considerably improved. Analytics that Predict the Future The application of big data analytics makes it possible to develop predictive models that are founded on extraordinarily large datasets. Because these models are able to recognise patterns and trends, algorithmic procedures can produce more accurate projections with their help (Irani, 2023).

Decision-Making That Is Informed by Data Because algorithmic trading now uses significant quantities of data, the focus has shifted to decision-making that is driven by the data itself. The capacity of algorithms to self-modify and learn from vast datasets throughout the course of their development enables them to grow more robust and effective over time. Big data technologies offer scalability, which makes it possible for algorithmic trading systems to effectively manage massive volumes of data. This is extremely important considering that the financial markets produce enormous amounts of data on a regular basis (Huang et al., 2023).

In general, algorithmic strategies are only as strong as their foundations, which are a comprehensive study of the market, sound risk management, and efficient algorithmic execution. In the fast-paced and intricate sector of finance, algorithmic decision-making has become increasingly sophisticated thanks to the contributions of quantitative analysis, statistical models, machine learning algorithms, and large amounts of data. Big data also plays an important part in this development.

High-Frequency Trading, Sometimes Known as HFT, Is Characterised by the Following Features

In this sense, the term "High-Frequency Trading" (HFT) refers to the practise of executing a large number of orders at lightning-fast speeds by utilising sophisticated computer algorithms and high-speed data networks. HFT techniques involve making hundreds of millions of trades in fractions of a second, leveraging technology to detect and exploit market inefficiencies and price disparities. HFT strategies can be used to identify and exploit market inefficiencies and price discrepancies as depicted in figure 2 below:

Figure 2. Features of high-frequency trading

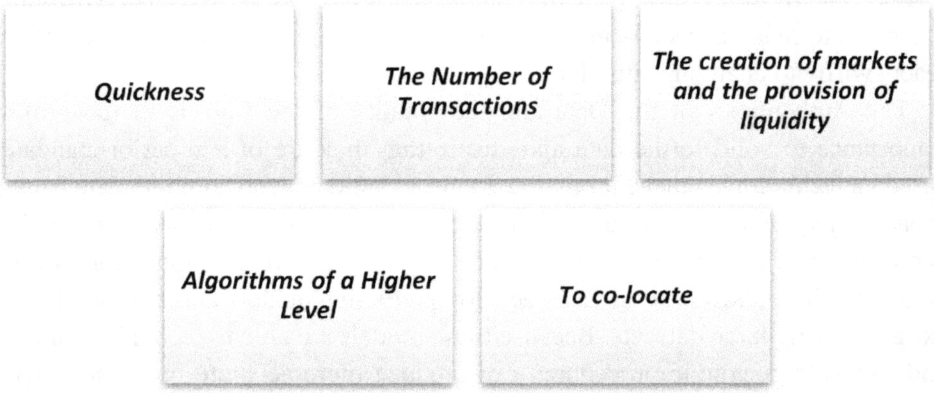

- **Quickness:** High-frequency trading (HFT) functions at extremely rapid rates, with trade executions timed in microseconds or even nanoseconds. The objective is to make a profit off of relatively little pricing differences that might only be available for a very brief period of time (Iandoli, 2023).
- **The Number of Transactions**: Executing a high number of deals in a short period of time is a key component of high-frequency trading (HFT). One of its defining characteristics is the massive volume of deals that take place, which differentiates it from more traditional trading tactics.
- **Algorithms of a Higher Level**: High-frequency trading is dependent on complex algorithms that do data analysis on the market in real time and execute orders according to predetermined criteria. In order to respond appropriately to shifting market conditions, these algorithms frequently use machine learning techniques (Huang et al., 2023).
- **To co-locate:** Co-locating their servers in close proximity to exchange servers is a common practise among HFT firms. This results in a decrease in latency, which enables orders to be executed more quickly and minimises the amount of time it takes for trade orders to reach the exchange

- **The creation of markets and the provision of liquidity**: Market-making, which is when companies consistently quote buy and sell prices, is one of the most common HFT tactics. HFT helps the market function more efficiently by providing liquidity, which also contributes to a reduction in the size of the bid-ask spread.

Regarding the HFT's Technology Infrastructure

Networks with a High Bandwidth: HFT companies put a significant amount of money into developing high-speed data networks in order to cut down on latency. This includes the utilisation of dedicated connections that have low latency and the utilisation of fiber-optic cables for the rapid transmission of data.

Services Relating to Co-location: Co-location refers to the practise of installing servers in the same data centres as the exchanges themselves. Due to this proximity, the amount of physical distance that data needs to travel is reduced, which in turn minimises latency and provides a competitive edge in terms of execution speed (Huang et al., 2023).

Trading Systems with a Low Impact of Latency: HFT systems are intended to have as little delay as possible and have their hardware and software settings optimised. This comprises networking switches that are quick, high-performance computing systems, and data processing that has been optimised.

Access to Direct Markets (also Known as DMA): HFT companies can avoid going through middlemen by using DMA to establish direct connections to exchanges. This makes it possible to execute orders more quickly and cuts down the amount of time it takes for trade orders to get to the market.

Order Types for Advanced Customers: HFT systems use a variety of sophisticated order types to execute trades with pinpoint accuracy. These order types include market orders, limit orders, and iceberg orders. Orders are routed via many trading venues using sophisticated algorithms to achieve the best possible execution (Iandoli, 2023).

High-Frequency Trading Makes Use of the Following Strategies

Market-making is an activity that HFT companies participate in by constantly quoting buy and sell prices. Both the bid-ask spread and the volume of trades that are carried out contribute to the generation of profits as mentioned in Figure 3.

Arbitrage: HFT algorithms seek for and capitalise on price disparities that exist across a number of different marketplaces or trading venues. This includes statistical arbitrage, which is the practise of trading instruments with associated prices in order to capture relative price fluctuations.

Figure 3. Strategies used by high-frequency trading

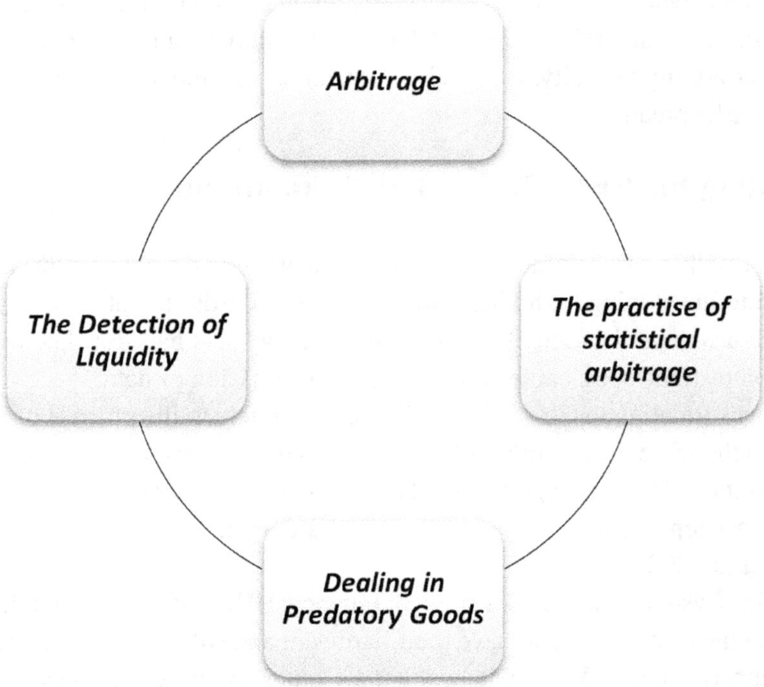

The practise of statistical arbitrage: HFT makes use of statistical models to analyse historical data in order to discover patterns and trends. Statistical probability of future price fluctuations is used to guide the execution of trades (Liu et al., 2023).

The Detection of Liquidity: Trading tactics can be adapted in response to shifts in market liquidity that can be detected and analysed by HFT algorithms. This requires a quick response to imbalances in the order book as well as rapid shifts in the activity level of trade.

Dealing in Predatory Goods: Identifying large institutional orders and "front-running" them by quickly completing trades in advance of these orders is one strategy that can be used in high-frequency trading (HFT). This has sparked conversations about the integrity of the market and its fairness (Iandoli, 2023).

The Advantages and Disadvantages of High-Frequency Trading Are as Follows

Advantages:

- Liquidity on the Market: High-frequency trading (HFT) adds to the liquidity of the market since it takes an active part in trading and provides constant buy and sell quotes.
- Bid-Ask Spreads Are Closer Together: Market-making actions in high-frequency trading (HFT) lead to bid-ask spreads becoming narrower, which is to the benefit of all market participants.
- Effectiveness: The incorporation of fresh information into pricing and the facilitation of rapid price discovery are two ways that high-frequency trading (HFT) increases market efficiency.
- The Discovery of Prices: By rapidly reacting to newly available information, high-frequency trading (HFT) can help to make price discovery more accurate and timelier (Liu et al., 2023).

The Obstacles:

- Integrity of the Market: Concerns have been raised regarding the possibility that high-frequency trading (HFT) practises could undermine the integrity of the market, particularly when predatory methods are utilised.
- Risks to the System: The rapidity and interconnection of high-frequency trading (HFT) systems can lead to systemic hazards, which includes the possibility of sudden swings in market prices and flash crashes.
- Access Denied to Some: Co-location and high-speed networks have the potential to create an uneven playing field, which provides considerable advantages to businesses that have larger financial resources (Iandoli, 2023).
- Challenges in Regulatory Affairs: In order to maintain fair and transparent markets while keeping up with the rapid speed of technology improvements in HFT, regulators face a number of obstacles.

High-Frequency Trading and the Implications of Regulatory Considerations

Surveillance of the Market: Surveillance systems are put into place by regulators in order to monitor high-frequency trading operations, identify instances of potentially manipulative market behaviour, and assure compliance with regulations.

Ratios of Orders to Trade: Limits on the order-to-trade ratio are imposed by some authorities in order to prevent high order volumes, which could contribute to the instability of the market.

Breakers of the Circuit: Circuit breakers are procedures that, in the event of substantial price changes, momentarily suspend trading. They were developed with the purpose of halting severe and erratic market swings (Makhlouf, 2023).

Conditions Demanding Openness to Information: HFT firms may be required to provide more information about their trading activity if regulators decide to enforce enhanced openness and make it a requirement.

Obligations Regarding the Market: HFT companies in certain countries are subject to market-making duties to guarantee that they make a contribution to market liquidity.

In conclusion, high-frequency trading (HFT) does help to the liquidity and efficiency of the market; yet, it also poses issues in relation to the integrity of the market, threats to the system, and legal considerations. In the context of high-frequency trading, one of the most important challenges for regulators is to find a way to strike a balance between encouraging innovation and preserving a market that is both fair and transparent (Liu et al., 2023).

Microstructure of the Market and Its Liquidity

1. A Comprehension of the Market's Microscopic Structure: The study of the specific organisational and operational characteristics of financial markets is referred to as market microstructure. It entails analysing how orders are placed, matched, and executed, in addition to the dynamics of bid-ask spreads and the process of discovering prices.
2. The Impact of Algorithms on the Formation of Prices: The mechanism by which prices are established in financial markets is significantly influenced by algorithmic trading in a substantial way. Trades can now be executed at speeds and frequencies that were previously unreachable thanks to algorithms, notably high-frequency trading (HFT) algorithms. This has the potential to impact the supply and demand dynamics that are responsible for price changes (Omidvar et al., 2023).
3. Contribution to the Efficacy of the Market as a Whole: Trading based on algorithms is beneficial to the overall efficiency of the market in a number of ways, including the following:

Increased Liquidity: The constant provision of buy and sell quotes is one of the contributions that algorithmic trading methods, and notably market-making algorithms, make to the increased liquidity of the market (Liu et al., 2023).

Bid-Ask Spreads That Are Closer Together: The bid-ask spreads that result from the use of market-making algorithms are often reduced, which results in lower transaction costs for market participants.

Quicker Incorporation of New Information into Prices Algorithms are able to rapidly incorporate new information into prices, which enables quicker and more accurate price discovery.

Trading Process Efficiency Is Improved Because Algorithms Can Execute Large Volumes Of Trades At High Speeds, Trading Process Efficiency Is Improved.

4. The Dynamics of the Order Book: The order book is a real-time list that is constantly updated with any new buy or sell orders for a specific security. Because it continually interacts with the order book, algorithmic trading plays a significant part in the dynamics of that document. In response to changes in market conditions, algorithms can place, amend, or cancel orders, which has an effect on the depth and structure of the order book.

Orders to Buy and to Sell: When an algorithm forecasts that prices will go up, it will place buy orders, and when it forecasts that prices will go down, it will place sell orders. The order book's dynamics are improved thanks to the constant interaction that takes place.

The depth of the order book: The depth of the order book, which is the total quantity of buy and sell orders at a variety of price levels, is impacted by algorithmic trading. High-frequency algorithms have the ability to quickly increase or remove liquidity, which can have an effect on the depth of the order book (Omidvar et al., 2023).

Influence on the Market: Market effect can be caused when massive deals are executed by algorithms, which can influence the following movement of prices. The goal of many algorithms is to reduce their market influence by employing a variety of different tactics and approaches.

5. Obstacles and Things to Take into Account: Even though algorithmic trading makes markets more efficient; it also presents a number of obstacles and things to think about, including the following:

Potential for Manipulation of the Markets Some algorithmic trading tactics might be vulnerable to being manipulated or used in unethical ways, which would necessitate close regulatory oversight (Pallathadka et al., 2023).

Liquidity can become fragmented as a result of the expansion of different trading venues and the use of dark pools, which creates difficulties for market participants and regulators.

The speed and interconnection of algorithms raise the possibility of sudden and dramatic market swings, which can ultimately result in flash crashes.

In nutshell, having an awareness of the microstructure of the market is absolutely necessary in order to comprehend the complexities of the process of price formation and the dynamics of liquidity. While algorithmic trading does contribute to the general efficiency of the market, it also poses issues that demand constant monitoring, regulation, and risk management in order to preserve a financial environment that is both fair and transparent.

Considerations of an Ethical Nature in Algorithmic Finance

1. Bias and Fairness in the Use of Algorithms: The term "algorithmic bias" refers to discrimination that occurs in the outcomes that are created by algorithms in a methodical and unjust manner. It frequently arises as a consequence of the use of biased training data or the development of algorithms that unintentionally favour some groups over others (Omidvar et al., 2023).

Concerns: Unfair treatment, the perpetuation of existing inequities, and a contribution to social injustice may result from the presence of bias in the decision-making process that is carried out by algorithms.

2. Accountability and Openness to the Public: Openness and honesty: Clarity of communication regarding the inner workings of algorithms, including the data they draw upon and the processes that guide their decisions.

Taking Responsibility: Imposing human or organisational responsibility for the outcomes of decisions made by computer programmes or other automated systems.

Worries about: Mistrust can develop when there is a lack of transparency, and if accountability is lacking, there may be no consequences for the negative effects of algorithmic decisions (Pallathadka et al., 2023).

3. The Ethical and Social Consequences of Algorithmic Trading: Inequality in terms of Wealth: The distribution of wealth may become more unequal as a result of algorithmic trading since those who have access to more sophisticated algorithms and high-speed trading infrastructure may have a disproportionate advantage.

Dynamics of the Market: Trading with a high frequency can have an effect on the dynamics of the market, which could result in an increase in market volatility and instability.

Considerations of an Ethical Nature: The social consequences of algorithmic trading include concerns about fairness and accessibility, in addition to the wider economic impact of this form of trade.

Strategies for Risk Avoidance in Light of Ethical Considerations

The importance of diversity and inclusion:

Encourage diversity in the teams responsible for the design and implementation of algorithms in order to reduce the likelihood of biased perspectives being used.

Guidelines for Ethical Conduct: Establishing and adhering to explicit ethical criteria in the process of developing and deploying algorithms will ensure a commitment to fairness and social responsibility and will help ensure the integrity of the process (Pallathadka et al., 2023).

Always Keeping an Eye on It: Implement ongoing monitoring of algorithmic processes in order to detect and address any biases that may develop over the course of time.

Participation of Stakeholders: Engage with different stakeholders, like as regulators, advocacy groups, and the general public, in order to collect a variety of opinions and respond to issues.

Ability to be Explained: Create algorithms with explainability in mind, so that consumers and other parties affected by algorithmic decisions may comprehend the reasoning that underpins those decisions.

Training in Ethical Conduct: It is important to provide persons involved in the creation of algorithms and decision-making processes with ethics training in order to improve their awareness and ability to make ethical decisions (Reppen et al., 2023).

Assessments of the Impact: Before deploying algorithmic systems, it is important to conduct impact assessments to analyse the potential social, economic, and ethical ramifications of using such systems.

Overall, addressing ethical considerations in algorithmic finance requires reducing computational bias, increasing transparency and accountability, as well as comprehending the societal ramifications of algorithmic trading and resolving those implications. In order to guarantee that algorithms contribute to a just and equitable monetary ecosystem, it is necessary to take preventative steps and conduct regular evaluations.

The Current Regulatory Climate Regarding Algorithmic Trading

1. The Development of New Regulations as a Reaction to the Rise of Algorithmic Trading:

The Initial Phases: In the beginning, there was a focus on developing regulatory frameworks for traditional manual trading. The proliferation of algorithmic trading forced regulatory bodies to modify and improve the aforementioned frameworks in order to address the specific issues that are brought by automated and high-frequency trading (Reppen et al., 2023).

Responses from Regulatory Agencies: Global regulators have put in place a number of safeguards to protect investors, preserve the integrity of the market, and mitigate the dangers that are connected with algorithmic trading. The establishment of risk controls, circuit breakers, and greater market surveillance capabilities are some of the initiatives that fall under this category.

2. Worldwide Regulatory Patterns and Their Variations:

United States of America: The Securities and Exchange Commission (SEC) and the Commodity Futures Trading Commission (CFTC) are two of the most important regulatory agencies in the United States when it comes to algorithmic trading. Market surveillance, risk controls, and transparency are the primary focuses of regulatory agencies (Tulchinsky & Mason, 2023).

The European Union (EU): The European Union's MiFID II (Markets in Financial Instruments Directive) and MiFIR (Markets in Financial Instruments Regulation) address algorithmic trading by mandating pre-trade risk controls, monitoring, and reporting duties. These regulations were enacted in response to the financial crisis of 2008.

Asia and the Pacific: Different regulatory approaches are taken throughout the Asia-Pacific region. Several nations, including Japan and Singapore, have put in place regulatory frameworks to monitor algorithmic trading, with a particular emphasis on risk management and market surveillance.

3. The Difficulties in Maintaining Compliance Faced by Algorithmic Traders:

Prerequisites for Risk Management: Algorithmic traders face a big problem when it comes to meeting the expectations of regulatory bodies on risk management. These requirements include the implementation of circuit breakers, order quantity limits, and price collars.

Maintenance of Records and Submission of Reports: Due to the high-frequency nature of algorithmic trading, it might be difficult to comply with record-keeping and reporting obligations. Traders are obligated to provide regulatory authorities with reports that are both accurate and timely (Tulchinsky & Mason, 2023).

A Landscape of Regulation That Is Fragmented: Those algorithmic traders who operate in numerous jurisdictions are going to have a difficult time navigating the regulatory landscape because it is so fragmented. Because of the variety of needs and standards, having a thorough awareness of the local rules is required.

Abuse of the Market and Manipulation of It: The algorithmic trading process is under regulatory scrutiny to detect any potential market misuse or manipulation. In order to detect and avoid engaging in manipulative practises, traders are required to set up monitoring procedures (Weber et al., 2023).

Fairness and openness to the public: Continuous work is required in order to maintain both openness and fairness in the algorithmic trading procedures. The importance of publicly sharing information about algorithms and the market impact they have is emphasised by regulatory authorities.

Considerations Relevant Across Borders: The process of complying with many regulations is made more complicated by international trade. Traders using algorithms are required to navigate the various regulatory regulations that exist in the various jurisdictions in which they operate (Dhoni, 2023).

Compliance Obstacles and Their Potential Mitigation Strategies

Management of Risk in Its Totally Extent: For the purpose of ensuring compliance with the regulatory requirements, it is imperative to put in place stringent protocols for risk management, which should include pre-trade risk controls and real-time monitoring.

Regulatory Technology, abbreviated as "RegTech": Utilise solutions that are offered by RegTech companies in order to automate and simplify compliance procedures such as record-keeping, reporting, and surveillance.

Collaboration Across Functional Boundaries: Encourage communication between the compliance, legal, and IT teams in order to guarantee a thorough understanding of the regulatory requirements and effective implementation of those needs (Weber et al., 2023).

Training That Is Constant: It is important to provide continual training for algorithmic traders so that they can be kept up to date on changes in regulatory requirements and compliance best practises.

Engagement with Regulatory Bodies: Engage with the regulatory authorities to ask for clarification on the requirements for compliance and to contribute to the development of regulations that strike a balance between innovation and risk management.

Regulatory Intelligence on a Global Scale: Create a global regulatory intelligence framework so that you can keep up with the ever-changing regulatory trends and needs in many jurisdictions.

In nutshell, the regulatory landscape for algorithmic trading is constantly shifting as a result of regulators adjusting to the rapid improvement of technology as well as the increasing complexity of the market. In order to successfully manage the hurdles presented by the global regulatory environment, algorithmic traders need to maintain a state of vigilance, take a proactive approach to compliance, and utilise tactics (Irani, 2023).

CASE STUDIES SHOWING NOTABLE APPLICATIONS OF ALGORITHMIC TRADING STRATEGIES

1. Medallion Fund, a product of Renaissance Technologies: quantitative and systematic trading is a trading method, relying on well-developed mathematical models and machine learning. Success: The Medallion Fund, which is managed by Renaissance Technologies, has achieved huge returns over the course of several decades by utilising algorithms to analyse large volumes of data and find profitable trading opportunities. These successes can be attributed to the use of these algorithms (Weber et al., 2023).
2. According to Citadel LLC, the categories of strategy include market-making, high-frequency trading, and quantitative techniques. Citadel, a multinational financial firm, has shown great success in applying algorithmic trading strategies to the trading of a diverse range of asset classes. The use of algorithmic trading by the corporation has led to consistent financial gains for the enterprise, and the company's market-making algorithms contribute to an increase in the general level of market liquidity (Dhoni, 2023).
3. Investing in Two Sigma is trading with a quantitative and systematic approach, with an emphasis on making judgements based on data. This strategy was developed by Michael Covel. The use of algorithmic approaches is a major contributor to Two Sigma's capacity to successfully assess a wide variety of data and choose appropriate investments. This skill was achieved by Two Sigma. Because they use technology and data science into their strategies,

the organisation has enjoyed a great deal of success in managing quantitative hedge funds. This success may be attributed to the fact that they employ these two fields (Liu et al., 2023).

4. The business firm Virtu Financial: The three pillars of this strategy are market-making, high-frequency trading, and execution services. The success of Virtu Financial may be attributed in large part to the company's market-making algorithms. These algorithms play an essential part in the provision of liquidity across a wide range of financial markets. The business has a proven track record of achieving success in understanding the dynamics of market microstructures and successfully executing trades in an efficient manner (Reppen et al., 2023).

Notable Defeats and the Lessons That Were Learned From Them

1. The Knight Capital Group (2012): A software bug prompted Knight Capital to carry out a large number of erroneous trades in a short amount of time, which ultimately led to the company's catastrophic failure. The incident showed the significance of robust risk controls, comprehensive testing of algorithmic systems, and the need for quick response mechanisms to address technological concerns. Lessons Learned The incident highlighted the value of robust risk controls, thorough testing of algorithmic systems, and the need (Irani, 2023).
2. A Long-Term Capital Management Report from 1998: The hedge fund LTCM, which was run by people who had won Nobel prizes, went bankrupt as a result of large losses brought on by highly leveraged and complex algorithmic trading tactics. The incident brought to light the dangers connected with using an excessive amount of leverage, as well as the significance of having a solid grasp of the constraints imposed by sophisticated computational models; as a result, risk management procedures were improved.
3. The movie "Flash Crash" from 2010: The Flash Crash was characterised by a fast decrease in market value, which was partly explained by the presence of algorithmic trading and high-frequency trading (Weber et al., 2023).

What We Have Taken Away: The occurrence brought to light the importance of having circuit breakers, pre-trade risk controls, and increased coordination among market participants in order to reduce excessive volatility and to slow down the rate at which markets fluctuate.

4. Initial Public Offering (IPO) of Facebook in 2012: During Facebook's first public offering (IPO), technical difficulties led to delayed order executions, which in turn led to confusion among investors (Dhoni, 2023).

Lessons Learned: The incident brought to light the significance of performing exhaustive testing and being well-prepared for high-profile events. It also brought to light the necessity of utilising robust systems that are able to manage increasing trading volumes (Liu et al., 2023).

5. Initial Public Offering for BATS Global Markets (2012): During its initial public offering (IPO), BATS was plagued by technological issues, which ultimately led to the cancellation of the company's stock listing.

Lessons Learned: The incident served as a reminder of the significance of doing exhaustive testing; maintaining open lines of communication during the resolution of technical issues; and emphasising the requirement for resilient algorithmic systems (Irani, 2023).

Important Discoveries and Broader Life Lessons

Management of risks is of the Utmost Importance: It is impossible to exaggerate how vital it is to have effective risk management. It is imperative to conduct exhaustive testing in addition to implementing comprehensive risk controls in order to reduce the likelihood of failures occurring (Reppen et al., 2023).

Ability to Adapt and Flexibility: Because markets and technologies are always changing, algorithmic traders need to constantly modify and improve their trading tactics in order to maintain their competitive edge and avoid falling behind the pack.

Transparency and Communication: It is essential to have clear communication while dealing with technical challenges. The confidence of market players might be increased by increased transparency regarding algorithmic procedures and associated hazards (Dhoni, 2023).

Compliance with Regulatory standards: It is essential to ensure that financial markets are both stable and fair by complying with all of the regulatory standards. Traders that use algorithms are required to keep up with constantly changing rules and to comply with them (Liu et al., 2023).

In nutshell, successful applications of algorithmic trading methods demonstrate the potential for innovation and profitability. Notable failures, on the other hand, highlight the significance of risk management, flexibility, and regulatory compliance in the dynamic landscape of algorithmic finance (Weber et al., 2023).

The Difficulties and Dangers Involved With Algorithmic Trading

1. Difficulties of a Technical Nature: Infrastructure with a Low-Latency Time Delay: The achievement of and continued commitment to a low-latency infrastructure presents a persistent challenge. The efficiency of high-frequency trading techniques may be negatively affected if there is a delay in the data transmission or execution speed. Investing in high-performance technology, hosting data in close physical proximity, and improving network connectivity are some potential mitigation strategies for latency issues (Irani, 2023).

The Processing of Data and Its Quality: The task of ensuring the quality and integrity of the data is a very important one. Trading decisions might be negatively impacted by data that is either inaccurate or delayed. The implementation of dependable data validation procedures, the utilisation of information obtained from trustworthy sources, and the utilisation of efficient data cleaning strategies are all critical components of an effective mitigation strategy.

Dangers posed by Cyberspace: Algorithmic trading is susceptible to cybersecurity risks because algorithms are becoming increasingly complicated, and financial systems are becoming increasingly interconnected. Use of advanced cybersecurity techniques, such as encryption, multi-factor authentication, and regular security audits, are all examples of mitigation strategies that can assist guard against cyber-attacks (Dhoni, 2023).

Ability to scale up: Ensuring that algorithmic trading systems can scale to manage increasing trade volumes and data is a key issue, particularly for growing trading organisations. Specifically, the challenge lies in ensuring that algorithmic trading systems can handle increasing trade volumes. Utilising scalable design, cloud computing, and persistently improving both code and infrastructure's overall efficiency are examples of mitigation strategies (Liu et al., 2023).

Overfitting and Data Snooping: Overfitting happens when a trading algorithm is excessively adjusted to past data, leading to poor performance in real-world settings. This can be avoided by limiting the amount of historical data used in the tuning process. Risks related with overfitting can be reduced by implementing correct validation procedures, doing out-of-sample testing, and avoiding over-optimization, which are all examples of mitigation strategies (Reppen et al., 2023).

2. Risks to the overall economy and fluctuations in the market:

Crashing in a Flash: The use of high-frequency trading and algorithmic techniques carries with it the potential risk of contributing to abrupt and dramatic market changes that could ultimately result in flash crashes. The use of circuit breakers, pre-trade risk controls, and market surveillance techniques can all be helpful in mitigating the danger of flash crashes and preventing their occurrence.

Lack of Availability of Liquidity: There is a possibility that algorithmic trading, in particular during periods of acute market stress, could lead to a drying up of liquidity in the market as automated systems withdraw from it. The mitigation strategy consists of ensuring that the algorithms integrate risk management protocols that take into consideration the market stress and the liquidity conditions (Dhoni, 2023).

The concepts of correlation and contagion: Algorithms have the potential to unintentionally contribute to correlated trading activity, which can result in contagion effects. These effects occur when the actions of one algorithm influence the actions of other algorithms and exacerbate market fluctuations. Contagion risks can be reduced by diversifying trading techniques, introducing randomization into algorithms, and keeping an eye on correlations. These are all examples of mitigation strategies (Irani, 2023).

The fragmentation of the market: The emergence of various trading venues and dark pools poses a potential risk because it may lead to the fragmentation of liquidity and contribute to market inefficiencies. The market fragmentation issues are being attempted to be mitigated by the implementation of regulatory measures such as best execution criteria and standardised protocols for trading venues.

Risks Involved in Operations: The risk is that algorithmic trading activity could be disrupted if operational difficulties, such as hiccups in the system or problems with connectivity, occur. The implementation of redundant systems, the routine testing of those systems, and the development of detailed disaster recovery plans are all examples of mitigating factors that can reduce the likelihood of operational risks.

3. Risks Associated with Ethical and Regulatory Issues:

A Bias Inherent in Algorithms: The possibility exists that unintentional biases in algorithmic models could result in unfair outcomes, hence contributing to the perpetuation of existing societal inequities. The implementation of ethical rules, the incorporation of fairness indicators, and the performance of regular audits are all potential mitigation strategies that might assist discover and mitigate algorithmic bias (Reppen et al., 2023).

Controlled Administration: Changing regulatory landscapes and growing focus on algorithmic trading practises can present issues in terms of complying with the regulations. For mitigating effects, it is essential to maintain a proactive attitude to regulatory compliance, engage with relevant regulatory bodies, and be informed about any changes to applicable regulations.

In nutshell, a complete approach to risk management, technological resilience, and regulatory compliance is required due to the technical obstacles and systemic hazards involved with algorithmic trading. Taking action to address these difficulties is absolutely necessary in order to protect the integrity and stability of the financial markets (Irani, 2023).

CONCLUDING REMARKS

The financial markets have entered a new era, heralded in by the advent of algorithmic trading, which has brought about a transformation in the manner in which prices are established and assets are traded. The transition from manual trading to algorithmic tactics has been characterised by leaps in technology, complex market dynamics, and ethical considerations. The results of this investigation have shed light on the historical development, technological milestones, and the subtle interplay of algorithms in the process of sculpting financial landscapes. The development of algorithmic trading has been a winding path that has involved many different aspects. The introduction of computerised trading platforms and the growth of high-frequency trading are two examples of important technological breakthroughs that have contributed significantly. Quantitative analysis, statistical modelling, and the incorporation of machine learning algorithms have evolved to become the fundamental building blocks of algorithmic methods. Case studies, market microstructure analysis, ethical issues, regulatory environments, and other research have all contributed to a more sophisticated understanding of the benefits and challenges presented by algorithmic finance.

The convergence of technical innovation, regulatory adaptation, and ethical responsibility will determine the course of the financial industry in the future. The development of algorithmic trading methods will be significantly influenced by cutting-edge technology, especially artificial intelligence (AI) and machine learning (ML). Regulatory frameworks are expected to evolve, which will result in a greater emphasis being placed on risk management, ethical issues, and transparency. It is expected that algorithmic trading will continue to have an impact on market dynamics, overall efficiency, and liquidity, hence reshaping the fundamental structure of financial ecosystems.

In conclusion, the path that algorithmic trading has taken sheds light on the successes and failures that have been associated with financial innovation. The huge potential for profit and efficiency is demonstrated by successful applications, such as those developed by companies such as Renaissance Technologies and Citadel. Concurrently, cautionary tales such as the catastrophe that occurred with the Knight Capital Group serve as clear reminders of the risks that are linked with the rapid growth of technology.

As we navigate the future of finance, we need to find a way to strike a balance between being innovative and being responsible. The stakeholders in the financial business have a responsibility to maintain vigilance, responding to changes in technology while preserving ethical standards and fulfilling the requirements set forth by regulators. The continual development of algorithmic trading calls for a concerted effort on the part of industry participants, regulatory authorities, and technological experts, all of whom must work in tandem. The road that lies ahead calls for a dedication to transparency, accountability, and ongoing adaptation; these are essential aspects that will define the future of algorithmic finance and its place in the larger financial environment.

REFERENCES

Auer, R., Haslhofer, B., Kitzler, S., Saggese, P., & Victor, F. (2023). *The Technology of Decentralized Finance (DeFi)*. Bank for International Settlements, Monetary and Economic Department. doi:10.100742521-023-00088-8

Barzykin, A., Bergault, P., & Guéant, O. (2023). Algorithmic market making in dealer markets with hedging and market impact. *Mathematical Finance*, *33*(1), 41–79. doi:10.1111/mafi.12367

Bhatnagar, M., Pathak, N., & Taneja, S. (2023). Tech-Optimists and Financial Education - A Research on the Efficacy of Communication Mediums of Government Economic Policies. *International Journal of Sustainable Development and Planning*, *18*(7), 2245–2252. doi:10.18280/ijsdp.180729

Bumin, M., & Ozcalici, M. (2023). Predicting the direction of financial dollarization movement with genetic algorithm and machine learning algorithms: The case of Turkey. *Expert Systems with Applications*, *213*, 119301. doi:10.1016/j.eswa.2022.119301

Chakrabarty, B., & Pascual, R. (2023). Stock liquidity and algorithmic market making during the COVID-19 crisis. *Journal of Banking & Finance*, *147*, 106415. doi:10.1016/j.jbankfin.2022.106415

Dhoni, P. (2023). *Unleashing the Potential: Overcoming Hurdles and Embracing Generative AI in IT Workplaces: Advantages*. Guidelines, and Policies.

Eichengreen, B. (2023). Financial regulation in the age of the platform economy. *Journal of Banking Regulation*, *24*(1), 40–50.

Fertani, O. (2023). *A Digital Marketing Toolbox Architecture For The Electronic Dance Music Industry: The Use Of Digital Marketing Tools To Reshape The Edm Scenery In The 21st Century* (Doctoral dissertation).

Garcia, D., Hu, X., & Rohrer, M. (2023). The colour of finance words. *Journal of Financial Economics*, *147*(3), 525–549. doi:10.1016/j.jfineco.2022.11.006

Gomez, P., & Lambertz, M. (2023). *Leading by Weak Signals: Using Small Data to Master Complexity* (Vol. 5). Walter de Gruyter GmbH & Co KG. doi:10.1515/9783110797886

Hambly, B., Xu, R., & Yang, H. (2023). Recent advances in reinforcement learning in finance. *Mathematical Finance*, *33*(3), 437–503. doi:10.1111/mafi.12382

Huang, A. H., Wang, H., & Yang, Y. (2023). FinBERT: A large language model for extracting information from financial text. *Contemporary Accounting Research*, *40*(2), 806–841. doi:10.1111/1911-3846.12832

Iandoli, L. (2023). *When solutions are in search of problems: New venture creation in the booming market of digital speech recognition*. SAGE Publications.

IraniL. (2023). Algorithms of Suspicion: Authentication and Distrust on the Amazon Mechanical Turk Platform. Available at SSRN 4482508. doi:10.2139/ssrn.4482508

Kumar, P., Taneja, S. M., & Ozen, E. (2023). Digital transformation of the insurance industry - a case of the Indian insurance sector. In *The Impact of Climate Change and Sustainability Standards on the Insurance Market*. Wiley. https://www.scopus.com/inward/record.uri?eid=2-s2.0-85168611885&partnerID=40&md5=6c2fb77610b1390b55b6945d955c0955

Liu, P., Zhang, Y., Bao, F., Yao, X., & Zhang, C. (2023). Multi-type data fusion framework based on deep reinforcement learning for algorithmic trading. *Applied Intelligence*, *53*(2), 1683–1706. doi:10.100710489-022-03321-w

Makhlouf, A. (2023). *Workshop Report: Cryptos: Distinguishing Hype and Realities in Islamic Finance*. Academic Press.

Omidvar, O., Safavi, M., & Glaser, V. L. (2023). Algorithmic routines and dynamic inertia: How organizations avoid adapting to changes in the environment. *Journal of Management Studies*, *60*(2), 313–345. doi:10.1111/joms.12819

Pallathadka, H., Ramirez-Asis, E. H., Loli-Poma, T. P., Kaliyaperumal, K., Ventayen, R. J. M., & Naved, M. (2023). Applications of artificial intelligence in business management, e-commerce and finance. *Materials Today: Proceedings*, *80*, 2610–2613. doi:10.1016/j.matpr.2021.06.419

Reepu, R., Taneja, S., Ozen, E., & Singh, A. (2023). A globetrotter to the future of marketing: Metaverse. In *Cultural Marketing and Metaverse for Consumer Engagement*. IGI Global. doi:10.4018/978-1-6684-8312-1.ch001

Reppen, A. M., Soner, H. M., & Tissot-Daguette, V. (2023). Deep stochastic optimization in finance. *Digital Finance*, *5*(1), 91–111. doi:10.100742521-022-00074-6

Taneja, S., Grima, S., Kumar, P., & Ozen, E. (2023). Special Issue: 'Green Asset and Risk Management for Promoting Sustainable Entrepreneurship in the Building of the Green Economy.'. *International Journal of Technology Management & Sustainable Development*, *22*(2), 127–130. doi:10.1386/tmsd_00071_7

Tulchinsky, I., & Mason, C. E. (2023). *The Age of Prediction: Algorithms, AI, and the Shifting Shadows of Risk*. MIT Press. doi:10.7551/mitpress/13872.001.0001

Weber, P., Carl, K. V., & Hinz, O. (2023). Applications of Explainable Artificial Intelligence in Finance—a systematic review of finance, information systems, and computer science literature. *Management Review Quarterly*, 1-41.

Chapter 7
The Impact of Corruption on Economic Growth in Tunisia:
An Application of ARDL Approach

Hayet Kaddachi
Faculty of Economics and Management, University of Sfax, Tunisia

Naceur Benzina
https://orcid.org/0009-0004-4097-6718
Faculty of Economics and Management, University of Sfax, Tunisia

ABSTRACT

This chapter aims to examine the impact of corruption on economic growth in Tunisia between the years 1998 and 2018.Using time series data to obtain relationships of an empirical nature. The processing of time series data starts with checking individual series, and ADF and Zivot and Andrews tests help identify variables' stationarity. The mixed order of integration levels recommends using ARDL to obtain the long-run relationships between the variables. The estimation results confirm that corruption demoralizes and discourages private investment in the short and long run. In both the long and short run, the indirect impact of corruption is negative and insignificant for public spending. However, the interaction between human capital and the corruption perception index is positive and insignificant in the short run but negative and significant in the long run.

DOI: 10.4018/979-8-3693-1746-4.ch007

1. INTRODUCTION

Tunisia has undergone a democratic transition characterized by a peaceful succession of governments and numerous political parties ranging from Islamists to liberals to perceived freedom of expression. According to the Global Democracy Rankings Report (2015), Tunisia gained points on the democracy scale (+32 points) between 2010 and 2014. However, the influence of democracies on economic growth remains a matter of debate (Barro 1997). In fact, political instability, which external shocks have reinforced, has contributed to the country's economic difficulties and has revealed the extent to which many problems have worsened. In addition, contagious corruption remains among Tunisia's main complications and is costing the country about 4% of its GDP.

In 2017, Tunisia obtained a score of 42/100 and occupied 74th place out of 180 countries in the world. It has gained one point compared to 2016. But it lost 15 places between 2010 and 2017, the day before the fall of the supposedly very corrupt Ben Ali regime. In contrast, the country has supposedly become a democracy, a democracy more corrupt than a dictatorship.

In this index edition, Denmark and New Zealand shared the first position and recorded a high score of 90 Tunisia arrives, thus, at the head of the Maghreb countries since Morocco is ranked 81st (40 points), Algeria points to 112th place (33 points), Mauritania the 143rd place (28 points) and Libya the 171st place (17 points) but, Syria (178th), South Sudan (179th) and Somalia (180th) close the march of this TI index. Transparency International (2018).

On the other hand, according to Meddeb (2018), the percentage of citizens reporting that the level of corruption has increased "a lot" increased from 42% in 2015 to 55% in 2018, an increase of 13% in three years. In 2019, with a score of 43, Tunisia remained at a standstill on the CPI.

The ambiguous situation that occupied Tunisia in 2019 shows the extent of corruption that has plagued the country's machinery and public administrations, which operate in an uncontrolled environment. Mismanagement, waste and all types of smuggling and trafficking take place in the "black market" and are prevalent in all sectors.Corruption is a major problem facing humanity, destroying lives and communities, nations and institutions. It can also provoke popular anger, further destabilize society and fuel violent conflict.

The first section reviews the literature on the impact of corruption on economic growth. The second section presents the specification of the models and methodological issues. The third section provides a critical discussion of the empirical results. Finally, the "Conclusions" section summarizes the results and policy implications for future research.

In order to achieve the above objective, this chapter is organized as follows: The first section is the introduction. The second section presents the theoretical background related to the literature. The third section presents the empirical methodology (sources and description of variables, model specification and estimation strategy). The fourth section deals with the possible interpretation of the empirical results. The fifth section presents the study's conclusions and recommendations.

2. LITERATURE REVIEW

Based on endogenous growth theory, several adverse effects of corruption on countries' economic growth are widely recognized in the economic literature. Corruption diverts investors, reduces the productivity of public spending, distorts the allocation of resources and reduces economic growth; the idea is confirmed in the publications of Pellegrini, L., & Gerlagh, R. (2004). and Méon, P. G., & Sekkat, K. (2005).

In this context, Mauro (1995) article considered the first empirical assessment highlighting corruption with many economic, social and political variables. In his article, Mauro explained, over a period from 1960 to 1985, the adverse effect of corruption on private investment. The idea is confirmed by Campos, N. F., Estrin, S., & Proto, E. (2010) , Zhou, J. Q., & Peng, M. W. (2012).

Similarly, Zakharov N. (2019) studied the relationship between corruption and fixed capital investment in Russian regions from 2004 to 2013. He addressed the problem of endogeneity of corruption using the instrumental variables approach. The results showed that the breakdown of investments by ownership type revealed that only private investments are affected by corruption, but not investments made by state-owned enterprises. The author concluded that the negative effect is larger for firms with full or partial foreign ownership.

In the case of African countries, Baliamoune Lutz and Ndikumana (2009) studied a panel of 33 sub-Saharan African countries from 1982-2001. The results show that corruption negatively affects economic growth through investment. In the same context, Ouattara (2011) used time series data to obtain the impact of corruption on public and private investment in Côte d'Ivoire and its effect on GDP growth during 1998-2009. It estimated a simultaneous equation model using the double least squares (DLS) estimator. The estimation results show that corruption is an overestimating factor of private investment in Côte d'Ivoire and that corruption negatively affects GDP growth. On this basis, the author recommends that political and economic actors be made more aware of the harms of corruption.

Indeed, corruption can be a barrier for new investors due to the significant increase in entry and operating costs for multinational enterprises. As a result, Jingtao Yi et al. (2019) verified the results of previous studies, showing that corruption hurts FDI, as business activities in the host country lead to increased costs and uncertainties for multinational firms. For this reason, multinational firms always try to choose their locations strategically and not randomly; during the selection process, they must balance the costs and benefits of investing in a country with low corruption.

For his part, Cuervo-Cazurra, (2016) analyzed corruption in international trade; he argued that corruption creates a laboratory for expanding international trade studies because it's illegal nature and the variation in the enforcement of anti-corruption laws across countries challenge some of the assumptions on which the arguments were based, namely that managers can choose appropriate actions without major legal implications.

Mallik and Saha (2016) examined the relationship between growth and corruption in a sample of 146 countries from 1984-2009 using the generalized method of moments (GMM). The estimated results show a negative relationship between corruption and growth.

The results of the empirical literature show that corruption does not always have a negative effect on growth. Indeed, for some countries, it contributes to increased growth, which supports the idea that corruption helps to "grease the wheels."

As Moser (2008) work on Madagascar shows, corruption decreases the quality of public investment. In this sense, the choice of public investment is guided by the personal gains expected by decision-makers and not by the public interest.

Finally, corruption also affects existing infrastructure, particularly its ability to be used optimally due to the lack of maintenance. For this reason, Tanzi and Davoodi (1997) have explained that increased capital expenditure automatically leads to a reduction in the resources available for operating expenditure, particularly for the maintenance of old investments, which nevertheless allow existing equipment to continue to function.

Tanzi and Davooodi (2000) and Gupta et al. (2002) confirm the idea of Gray and Kaufmann (1998), who showed that public sector corruption is the main obstacle to the growth of wealth in countries because it changes the composition of government spending and thus determines its growth. As for Huang and al. (2015), fighting corruption theoretically leads to a decrease in capital investment and further affects economic growth.

Using cointegration and panel error correction models from 2002 to 2016, Song, C. Q.et al. (2021) studied the relationship between corruption, economic growth, and financial development in 142 countries in the long run. They used the FMOLS method to justify that corruption has a negative effect on economic growth. Thus, they relied on the VECM method to show the existence of long-run causal relationships between the variables in the model to be estimated.

Ghoneim and Ezzat (2016) studied the relationship between corruption and economic growth in the Arab world. To this end, they estimated a model with random effects panel data to determine the impact of corruption on economic growth in 15 Arab countries from 1998 - 2009. The study's results showed that corruption's direct impact on GDP growth depends strongly on other variables, including governance structure.

The study by Zangina, S. and Hassan, S. (2020) aims to analyze the time series from 1984 to 2017. They used the non-linear autoregressive distributed lag (NARDL) bounds test technique to investigate Nigeria's asymmetric relationship between corruption control and foreign direct investment (FDI). The estimation results show that corruption hinders the massive inflow of foreign direct investment and that corruption control has asymmetric effects on FDI inflow in Nigeria. In other words, strengthening corruption controls encourages FDI inflows to Nigeria, but decreasing corruption controls has a negligible effect.

Similarly, corruption destroys the vital purpose of education. Indeed, in an education system characterized by high levels of corruption, students are not provided with the skills and knowledge that will enable them to contribute expressively to their country's economy. However, over time, they learn that a lack of integrity is a permissible aspect that constantly develops into the social norm.

In this context, several studies have shown the negative effect of corruption on human capital. For example, Seka (2013) explained how corruption discourages young talent from pursuing a long education. Indeed, he developed a theoretical model that highlights the impact of detours that corruption had on students by forcing them to abandon long studies to find a job, but with a high bribe yield. This detour of skills reduces the availability of expertise needed for innovation to improve supply, increasing demand.

Padhan, Hemachandra, and al. (2022) examined how corruption can play an important role in the progress of the domestic economy in India and what the degree of response of foreign capital inflow to economic growth might be in the short and long run.

Therefore, the study examined the effects of foreign capital inflows on economic growth by controlling for corruption, government final consumption expenditure, and trade balance from 1995-96 to 2016-17. They used advanced econometric models such as autoregressive distributed lag (ARDL) and Bayer- Hank (B-H). The results showed that external capital inflows, corruption, trade balance, and government consumption expenditures are all associated with economic growth for long-term development.

Swaleheen, M. (2011) examined the effect of corruption on economic growth on panel data from 170 countries from 1984 to 2007. He based on the generalized method of moments. The estimation results explain that corruption does not decrease

GDP growth at all levels and can significantly increase it even at higher levels of corruption. Indeed, rejecting Shleifer and Vishny's (1993) hypothesis that corruption acts like sand in the wheels of growth seems important.

On the other hand, Murphy and al. (1991) observed that corruption diverts skills from productive sectors of the economy with low opportunity for bribes to less productive sectors with high potential for bribes. In other words, the ease of gain derived from corrupt practices in low-design administrative tasks attracts individuals with the potential to innovate, which slows down firms' ability to advance technologically. Based on a panel of 14 countries covering 2002 to 2018, Haseeb, M., & Azam, M. (2021) used the ARDL approach and showed that increased corruption discourages economic growth.

Nsor-Ambala, R. and Coffie, C.P.K. (2022) aim to observe corruption effect on foreign direct investment (FDI) inflows in Ghana. They used a time series econometric model covering the period 1984-2019 based on the non-linear ADRL approach to estimate data from the World Bank and the International Country Risk Guide.

Anas, Judges et al. (2020) note the phenomenon of corruption in Tunisia in terms of its impact on economic growth. They used a distributed autoregressive model (ARDL) over a study period from 1995 to 2014. Empirical results show that corruption has a negative impact on economic growth in Tunisia. This direct effect of corruption is justified by the low level of long-term growth, by close to 1%, after a 1% increase in the level of corruption. The results also indicate that corruption has indirect effects via transmission channels, such as investment in physical capital, which is positively significant in the presence of corruption.

The study uses annual time series data from 1998 to 2018. It aims to study the impact of corruption on economic growth in Tunisia to know whether it is a direct or indirect effect.

2.1 Definitions of Variables and Data Sources

The main variables of interest are:

Dependent variable: GDP per capita: Economic growth is generally quantified as GDP per capita. The data is in current U.S. dollars. Therefore, it is noted as "GDP." This series is taken from the World Bank database for 2018 (WDI, 2018).

Independent variables:

- Total population: is based on the de facto definition of population, which counts all residents regardless of legal status or citizenship. It is noted as "POP". Numerous empirical studies (Barro and Sala-i-Martin, (2004) Sachs, (2008). Headey and Hodge (2009) and Dao (2012) have estimated that economic growth is negatively affected by increasing population growth. This series is taken from the World Bank (2018) database.

- Inflation: is measured by the annual growth rate of the implicit GDP deflator; it takes into account the qualitative aspect of policies implemented in the countries in question, noted "INF". (Bruno, (1998), Kremer and Bick, (2013). Paldam (2002). This series is taken from the World Bank (2018) database.
- Human capital is measured by the gross enrollment ratio, the total enrollment in secondary education, regardless of age. It is rated "Kh". Among the empirical studies, human capital has a significant positive effect on economic growth. Lucas, (1990), Bergheim, (2005), Howitt, (2005), This series is taken from the World Bank (2018) database.
- Private investment: this is measured by the gross fixed capital formation in expenditure and is used to measure private sector investment. It is noted as "INVP. Seka (2013), Othmani. A et al., (2015), etc... This series is taken from the World Bank (2018) database.
- Government Expenditures: Government expenditures include all government payments in exchange for goods and services used to produce marketed and non-marketed goods and services. It is denoted as "PA". Gupta et al. (2002). This series is taken from the World Bank (2018) database.
- Corruption Perception Index: measures the perception of corruption in the public sector. This index varies between [0 and 10]: the closer it is to 10, the less corrupt the country, and the closer it is to 0, the more corrupt the country. It is denoted "CORR". (Gyimah-Brempong et al. 2006) (Agostino et al. 2016), Njoya, and Aman, N. (2017); Cieślik and Goczek 2018); Bação, 2019); Gründler et al, 2019). This series is taken from the non-governmental organization "Transparency International (2018).

2.2. Model Specification

The empirical objective of the study is to present an econometric model to study the impact of corruption on economic growth in Tunisia, based on a review of recent theoretical literature.The complete formulation of econometric model is based on the following previous studies: Hemachandra Padhan et al. (2021), Tsanana et al. (2016), Gyimah-Cieślik and Goczek (2018). We can write

$$GDP_{it} = \beta_0 + \beta_1 CPI_{it} + \sum \beta_2 Z_{it} + W_{it} + \varepsilon_t \qquad (1)$$

β0, β1, β3: Represent the set of coefficients indicating the partial impact of explanatory variables on growth, the vector Z reflects the direct impact of corruption on economic growth. Note that all variables are expressed in logarithm, except for the corruption.

$$GDP_{it} = \beta_0 + \beta_1 CPI_{it} + \beta_2 INVP_{it} + \beta_3 KH_{it} + \beta_4 INF_{it} + \beta_5 DP_{it} + \beta_6 POP_{it} + \mu_i + \varepsilon_t \quad (2)$$

Thus W reflects the indirect impact of corruption on each factor of production.

Interaction between human capital and corruption

$$GDP_{it} = \beta_0 + \beta_1 INVP_{it} + \beta_2 (CPI_{it} * KH_{it}) + \beta_3 INF_{it} + \beta_4 DP_{it} + \beta_5 POP_{it} + \mu_i + \varepsilon_t \quad (2.1)$$

Interaction between corruption and private investment

$$GDP_{it} = \beta_0 + \beta_1 KH_{it} + \beta_2 (CPI_{it} * INVP_{it}) + \beta_3 INF_{it} + \beta_4 DP_{it} + \beta_5 POP_{it} + \mu_i + \varepsilon_t \quad (2.2)$$

Interaction between corruption and total public expenditure

$$GDP_{it} = \beta_0 + \beta_1 INVP_{it} + \beta_2 (CPI_{it} * DP_{it}) + \beta_3 INF_{it} + \beta_4 KH_{it} + \beta_5 POP_{it} + \mu_i + \varepsilon_t \quad (2.3)$$

2.3 Estimation Strategy

In this subsection, we start with the analysis of the descriptive statistics of the variables, as well as the study of the stationarity and, finally, the estimation of the model.

2.3.1. Descriptive Statistics

Table 1 presents summary statistics on the variables in the model: the corruption index, economic growth and human capital, private investment, public expenditure, population, and inflation. The standard deviations are generally low for the different series. This observation can be explained by the logarithmic transformation of the series, which attenuates the variances between the values of the variables. Generally, the measure of corruption ranges from 0 to 10. From 1998-2018, Tunisia's corruption index is significantly more widespread, and its level varies between 5.2 (Maximum) and 3.8 (Minimum). Corruption has a mean of 4.495 and a standard deviation of

0.480, which shows that most of the population corruption is not far from the sample average, reflecting the severity of the corruption problem in Tunisia. The descriptive statistics of the endogenous variable and the explanatory variables, are presented in the following table:

Table 1. Descriptive statistics of the data

	Maximum	Minimum	Average	Standard deviation
GDP	3.634191	3.344751	3.521790	0.105464
KH	1.967856	1.834421	1.929060	0.041270
INVP	1.403549	1.268106	1.349189	0.041876
INF	0.839322	0.323719	0.580891	0.128834
DP	0.935077	0.639357	0.767452	0.107682
POP	7.063153	6.978174	7.018945	0.026037
CPI	5.300000	3.800000	4.495238	0.480079
CPI_KH	9.981450	7.393262	8.655616	0.768600
CPI_INVP	7.438812	4.931570	6.076029	0.775049
CPI_DP	4.930733	2.429557	3.489598	0.818594

Source: Author's estimate

2.3.2. Correlation Study

To detect a possible relationship between the different variables, we will present the different correlation coefficients in Table 2. Generally, values greater than or equal to 0.50 indicate that the variables are strongly positively or negatively correlated depending on the effect of the variable under consideration on the other. Indeed, the simple correlation matrix between the variables below shows two significant correlations between the dependent variable (GDP) and the explanatory variables. In addition, there is a strong correlation between human capital, total population, and public expenditure on goods and services (0.85 > 0.50 and 0.63 > 0.50). It may be possible that the importance of human capital creates more opportunities for increased economic growth in our country. However, there are weakly correlated correlations and others that are negative between the explanatory and explained variables. The well as the correlations between the different variables, are presented in the following table.

Table 2. Correlation matrix

	GDP	KH	INVP	INF	DP	POP	CPI	CPI_ KH	CPI_ INVP	*CPI_ DP*
GDP	1									
KH	**0,906**	1								
INVP	0,456	-0,577	1							
INF	0,402	0,484	-0,552	1						
DP	-0,675	**0,632**	**0,753**	-0,552	1					
POP	0,759	**0,856**	-0,825	0.594	-0,855	1				
CPI	-0,888	-0,846	0.579	-0,31	**0,806**	-0.846	1			
CPI_KH	-0,837	-0,763	0.552	-0,252	0,814	-0.763	0,990	1		
CPI_INV	-0,863	-0,854	0.725	-0,391	0,856	-0,913	0,981	0,965	1	
CPI_DP	-0,812	-0,766	0.703	-0,466	0,960	-0,891	0,936	0,935	0,955	1

Source: Author's estimate

2.3.3. Unit Root Test

The stationarity of the series is examined using the ADF and AZ unit root test. The ADF tests were performed under the three possible specifications of the model, namely with constant, with constant and trend, and withoutconstant and trend. The decision rule is that if the ADF or AZ value is less than the critical value, the null hypothesis of the presence of a unit root is rejected, and the hypothesis (H1) of the series stationarity is accepted. Otherwise, we accept the hypothesis of the non-stationarity of the series. The results are summarized in Table 3. This table shows that the statistical value of the ADF test associated with the different variables is higher than the critical value at the 5% threshold. Following the decision rule of the ADF and AZ test stated earlier, these results lead us to accept the null hypothesis of the presence of a unit root. This implies that our time series is non-stationary.

We note that public expenditure and the interaction variable between corruption and private investment are integrated of order 1 (stationary after the first difference). At the same time, inflation remains stationary at the level (without differentiation). But the other variables were differentiated twice to be stationary. In this context, the variables are either integrated or stationary at different orders, allowing us to choose the ARDL approach for estimating our model.

Table 3. Unit root test

Variables	ADF	Zivot and Andrews (1992)		Stationarity
	T-stat	T-stat	Time break	
GDP	-3.541	-6.626	2009	I(2)
KH	-4.964	-5.449	2014	I(2)
INVP	-6.595	-6.758	2014	I(2)
INF	-3.565	-5.499	2007	I(0)
DP	-6.041	-6.228	2015	I(1)
POP	-8.118	-9.155	2016	I(2)
CPI	-5.583	-6.784	2007	I(2)
CPI_KH	-5.580	-8.114	2010	I(2)
CPI_INV	-6.062	-7.404	2014	I(1)
CPI_DP	-6.151	-7.544	2011	I(2)

Source: Author's estimate

2.3.4. Testing Co-Integration

To test cointegration, it is important to: determine the optimal lag (AIC, SIC) and use Fisher's test to test for cointegration between series.

A. Optimal Shift and ARDL Model Estimation

We will use the Schwarz Information Criterion (SIC) to select the optimal ARDL model that provides statistically significant results with the least parameters. Table 4 shows globally significant results. For this, we assume that the selected ARDL approach is appropriate to avoid the uncertainties created by the unit root test and can obtain better estimates on small sample sizes (optimal estimation) to make the series stationary in the same order. Thus, we find that the coefficients associated with the recall force or the adjustment coefficients in all the estimated models are statistically significant and carry negative signs. This guarantees the existence of an error correction mechanism that increases the possibility of finding long-term relationships between the variables. But the adjustment coefficients in the sub-model3 are positive and insignificant even at the 10% threshold. This weakens the possibility of finding long-run relationships between corruption and human capital.

B. Short-Term Dynamics

The results of the short-term coefficient study are interpreted in the following paragraphs.

Table 4. Impact of corruption on short-term economic growth

Variables	Modele (1)	Modele (2.1)	Modele (2.2)	Modele (2.3)
GDP	0.695401 0.0003***	1.130366 0.0000***	0.581293 0.0008***	0.637429 0.0002***
KH	(1.584203) 0.0162**	-	(1.287194) 0.0304**	(1.558594) 0.0100**
INVP	(-0.592274) 0.0607*	0.160284 0.6778	-	
INF	(-0.149629) 0.0095***	(-0.234081) 0.0462**	(-0.164916) 0.0055***	(-0.440519) 0.0676*
DP	(-0.311148) 0.0206**	(-0.396019) 0.1187	(-0.240816) 0.0707*	-
POP	(-2.541027) 0.0085***	(0.900029) 0.4703	(-1.931148) 0.0187**	(-0.151739) 0.0036**
CPI	(0.036878) 0.3749			
CPI_KH		(0.034521) 0.3119		
CPI_INV			(-0.010370) 0.7044	
CPI_DP				(-0.037429) 0.0288**
R^2	0.987923	0.969886	0.981211	0.984759
R^2 adjusted	0.974505	0.942783	0.967547	0.973675
F- Stat	73.62312	35.78549	71.80717	88.84411
Probability	0.00000	0.000002	0.00000	0.000000
DW	2.605102	1.657213	2.004048	2.645234
ECM t-1	-0.304599 (0.0350)	0.130366 (0.4419)	-0.41870 (0.0071)	-0.36257 (0.0105)
Specification	1.277 [2911]	3.5306 [0.0635]	4.604 [0.0575]	0.776 [0.398]
Autocorrelation	1.755 [0.2053]	0.298 [0.5978]	0.064 [0.8051]	4.034 [0.072]
Heteroscedasticity	1.755 [0.2053]	0.644 [0.7395]	0.2434 [0.972]	0.697 [0.6886]
Normality	0.0850 [0.958]	0.919 [0.631]	0.971 [0.615]	0.636 [0.727]

Source: Authors' calculation of ARDL model using Eviews9 **Note**: Values in parentheses represent the coefficients of the estimated parameters, ***, **, * represent the significance of the coefficients at 1%, 5% and 10%, respectively. F-statistic values of the ARDL model.

Appropriate lag length (k) is chosen for each model.

C. Robustness Tests of the Estimated ARDL Models

To test the robustness of our model, it is important to apply tests that help diagnose the estimated ARDL models: the error autocorrelation test, the heteroskedasticity test, the error normality test, and the Ramsey test. Based on the results found, the Ramsey specification test reveals that the probabilities and Fisher statistics associated with the four models are greater than 5%, so we accept the null hypothesis, which means that there is no lack of variables and the models are well specified.

The normality test of the errors reveals that the probabilities associated with the models presented are greater than 5%, which implies accepting the null hypothesis and showing that the errors of the four models follow the normal distribution.

On the other hand, time series often carry error autocorrelation, so the Breusch-Godfrey autocorrelation test is necessary. The displayed results indicate that the probabilities of all the models presented in our study are higher than 5%. Then we accept the null hypothesis of the absence of autocorrelation. Statistically, the null hypothesis is accepted for all these tests. Thus, the models are validated.

2.3.5. Study the Cointegration of Pesaran et al. (2001)

Following the automatic procedure on Eviews 9, the Pesaran et al. (2001) cointegration test requires that the ARDL model be estimated beforehand. The computed test statistic will be compared to the critical values (which form bounds) as follows:

- If Fisher value > upper bound; Co integration exists
- If Fisher value < lower bound; Co integration does not exist

Table 5. Results of the Pesaran et al. (2001) cointegration test

Level of significance	Lower bounds	Upper bounds
1%	3.15	4.43
5%	2.45	3.61
10%	2.12	3.23

F-Stat 4.104056

The results of the Co-integration test confirm the existence of a Co-integration relationship between the variables studied. The F-calculated (4.104056) is higher than the largest value of Pesaran et al. (2001) at 5% (3.61).

A. Long-Term Elasticities

The long-run elasticities between corruption and the other variables are summarized in the table below.

Table 6. Impact of corruption on long-term economic growth

Variables	Model 1	Model 2	Model 3	Model 4
KH	(6.169752) 0.0263**		(3.643377) 0.0025***	(3.925773) 0.0015***
INVP	-0.867588 0.3775	-1.229487 0.7043		(-1.214986) 0.1519
INF	(-0.797980) 0.1170	2.593905 0.3721	(-0.509017) 0.1058	(-0.491307) 0.0741*
DP	(-1.021499) 0.0734*	1.096080 0.5355	-0.575143 0.0732*	
POP	(-8.342198) 0.0558*	-6.903853 0.5592	(-4.612172) 0.0157**	(-7.372888) 0.0298**
CPI	0.121071 0.4612			
CPI_KH		-0.424738 0.2902		
CPI_INVP			-0.024768 0.6950	
CPI_DP				(-0.103233) 0.0116***

Note: *Values in parentheses represent estimated parameter coefficients, ***, **, * represent significance of coefficients at 1%, 5%, and 10% respectively.*

3. DISCUSSIONS AND RECOMMENDATIONS

The results will be interpreted model by model, following the short-term and long-term relationships.

3.1. Corruption and Economic Growth

One of the most important results for our study is the link between corruption and economic growth and the corruption coefficient. Indeed, considering the ARDL estimates, we note that:

The coefficient on human capital is positive and significant at the 5% level. Indeed, this factor, represented by the total enrollment in secondary education, is one of the explanatory variables of the increase in economic magnitudes. Thus, in this context, Lucas (2015) claims the need to place human capital at the centre of economic growth since it contributes to increasing the GDP in the long and short run. This result is also consistent with the theories developed by Romer (1987) and Lucas (1988), who identify human capital formation and its externalities as the true sources of economic growth in the long run.

The coefficient associated with the population growth rate (POP) is negative (-2.54102) and significant at the 1% level (0.0085) in the short term as well as in the long term. The estimation results show that in Tunisia, when the population increases by 1%, all other things being equal, the economic growth rate decreases by 0.08% in the short term and by 0.05% in the long term, and vice versa. This value is highly significant at the 10% and 5% threshold. The sign obtained is consistent with our expectations and has been found in the work of Bloom, Canning Malaney, Dao (2012) and (Barro and Sala-i-Martin (2004) Sachs (2008). As a result, Headey and Hodge (2009) and others have revealed that an increase in population leads to a decrease in the level of capital per worker, negatively affecting economic growth.

In Tunisia, population growth during the period 1998-2018 had a negative impact on GDP per capita. This result is explained by the fact that investments in physical capital do not follow population growth. In addition, unemployment rates are still very high in our country. Therefore, it will be necessary to facilitate possible measures and conditions for investment in the private sector so that this high population growth positively impacts economic growth.

Generally speaking, for population growth to stimulate economic growth in Tunisia, the public authorities must facilitate the creation of private enterprises (which reduces unemployment and the dependence of the population), as well as make FDI more attractive (more flexible tax policy to facilitate the establishment of companies),. Etc. All these measures would contribute to the acceptable use of a qualified workforce and a great improvement of the economic wealth of Tunisia.

Second, private investment has a negative and significant coefficient at the 10% level in the short run. But negative and significant in the long run. In other words, private sector investment does not affect GDP, which implies that investment by private firms does not contribute to economic growth in Tunisia. This conclusion is contrary to our predictions. From an empirical point of view, our results contradict those of Mlambo and Oshikoya (1999), who find a positive effect of private investment on economic growth in a sample of 18 African countries. However, these results confirm the observations of the WB reports on economic growth in the world, echoed by Sackey (2007). These reports show that Africa is the slowest growing region in the world because private capital investment is low and does not contribute to growth. In the case of Tunisia, this observation could be explained by the weakening of commodity prices, which has led to a decline in investment in countries that export these products. In addition, the ambiguity related to economic decisions and the political game can contribute to the decline of private investment in Tunisia. And the concomitant slowdown of economic activity following idiosyncratic shocks. (2008 crisis, and 2011 revolution).

We also note that the coefficient of inflation in the short run is negative (-0.14962) and significant at the 1% threshold (0.0095); thus, in the long run, this coefficient remains negative (-0.797980) but not significant. In many empirical studies, the results suggest that the inflation rate has a negative impact on economic growth. In this context, a high level of inflation leads to an arbitrary distribution of public wealth. In addition, it increases the level of corruption in the country, which increases volatility and uncertainty, resulting in a shift to less productive activities. At this level, the results are consistent with the findings of Paldam (2002), Khan and Senhadji (2001), Burdekin et al. (2004) and Kremer and Bick (2013). However, Inflation is considered the main threat to the Tunisian economy; it was established at 7.5% for the whole year 2018, 6.4% in 2017, and 4.2% in 2016.

Indeed, due to these main factors, the competitiveness of the Tunisian economy is deteriorating, and foreign trade is penalized because of the fall in the price of imported products compared to the rise in the price of local products. Thus, inflation penalizes savings through the loss of the value of the money saved, which subsequently hinders the increase of economic growth.

Concerning public expenditure, we can conclude that in the long term as well as in the short term, the coefficient of total public expenditure on goods and services is negative and significant at the 5% threshold. Thus, we note that public spending is negatively related to economic growth in Tunisia, so that a decrease of 1%, all things being equal, in spending on goods and services leads to a decrease of 0.07% of GDP per capita in the long run and a decrease of 0.02% in the short run. At this level, the public sector and its external factors do not effectively constitute a factor of growth of the Tunisian economy as in other countries because the main failure of public finance management lies in the lack of control of public spending. Thus, the control system overspending and budgetary procedures play an important role in the fiscal adjustment process. However, in practice, Tunisia has not yet been able to put in place an effective system because of administrative restrictions and the lack of better allocation of state resources.

Finally, the link between corruption and economic growth is one of the most important results for the purpose of our study relates to the coefficient on corruption. Indeed, considering the estimates by the ARDL approach, we note that corruption presents a positive and insignificant coefficient even at the 10% threshold in the short run than in the long run. These results suggest that the coefficient obtained means that in the long run, corruption and economic growth are positively related so that an increase in the level of corruption causes an increase in GDP per capita. On the other hand, both the short-run and long-run estimates demonstrate the absence of a direct effect of corruption on economic growth.

At this stage, the findings of modelling the direct effect of corruption on economic growth in Tunisia are also consistent with the results found by Huang (2016), who studies the effect of corruption on economic growth in 13 Asia Pacific countries over a period from 1997 to 2013. Thus, the same results are found by Tsanana et al. (2016) and Ondo, A. (2017).) However, these findings are in contrast to the work of other authors who found different results, namely Gyimah-Brempong et al. (2006) or Gründler and Potrafke (2019) and, Cieślik and Goczek (2018), d'Agostino et al. (2016), Bação (2019).

To conclude, we note that corruption does not directly affect economic growth in Tunisia. Still, it can be passed through human capital, private investment or public spending to indirectly explain the negative impact on the dynamics of GDP in Tunisia.

The coefficient of determination (R2) is of the order of 0.987923, indicating a very strong positive relationship between the dependent variable (GDP) and the explanatory variables and that the model explains 98.8%.

Furthermore, a brief look at the adjusted R-squared value (97.45%) indicates that after removing the insignificant effect of the estimator (explanatory variable), about 1.14% of the variation in real GDP is still accounted for by the independent variables.

The Durbin-Watson statistic is a statistic used to detect the presence of autocorrelation. Generally, if DW is less than 2, the successive error terms are correlated; if DW is greater than 2, there is no autocorrelation. For our case, the value of the Durbin-Watson statistic for the model is 2.605102, so there is no autocorrelation.

3.2. Corruption and Economic Growth Through Human Capital

This regression tests the hypothesis of the existence of an indirect effect of corruption on economic growth in Tunisia through human capital formation. To this end, we start from the idea that human capital is one of the determinants of economic growth, in line with the literature (Becker 1993, Lucas 1988). We, therefore, seek to quantify the indirect impact of corruption on this variable.

In the long run, the results show once again that the signs of the parameters and their significance are not the same as those in the short run for government spending and inflation. However, we note that the interaction variable has a positive and insignificant coefficient even at the 10% level. Moreover, after estimating the ARDL method, the interaction between the level of corruption and the number of students enrolled in secondary school reduces GDP in the long run. Still, it has no effect in the short run. These latter findings, therefore, also indicate the absence of an indirect effect between corruption and human capital in the short run; this result is consistent with the results found by (Njoya, N., & Aman, N. (2017) in a study conducted on Cameroon.

In the same context, Outtara (2007) clarified how corruption could handicap human capital formation by distressing and discouraging young people from undertaking too long an education, which could have a negative impact on long-term growth. Similarly, Chkir and Allaoui (2010) presented an empirical application in panel data on a sample of 25 developing countries from 1984 to 2005. The results found by the latter show that corruption negatively affects the accumulation of human capital, hindering the growth of these countries. Seka (2013), Othmani. A et al., (2015), etc...

Indeed, the prevalence of corruption in our country may be due in part to the number of students who leave universities prematurely without having a complete and appropriate education that will enable them to obtain decent work. Therefore, to reduce corruption in education, it is necessary to focus on the cult of completion in school and the best possible reward for intellectual effort to increase the incentives for skill acquisition and the reduction of poverty so that families find the means to enrolment their children in school.

The hypothesis that corruption affects growth through its negative effect on human capital formation is at the heart of several articles and is even a secondary objective to achieve our main goal, which is summarized in the above theoretically and empirically. But in our study on Tunisia, this hypothesis is rejected in the short run and accepted in the long run.

3.3. Corruption and Economic Growth Through Private Investment

The regression conducted elsewhere attempts to examine the presence of indirect effects of corruption through private investment. To this end, we test for the direct effect of corruption and slip an interaction variable between the level of corruption and private investment.

The results allow us to understand that the coefficients associated with public spending are negative and significant at the 10% level in the long run. Thus, we notice that the parameter of human capital formation is positive and significant at the 1% level. This implies that a 1% increase in total secondary school enrollment, all else being equal, increases the economic growth rate by 0.02% and vice versa. Inflation also negatively affects economic growth through a 0.1% decline in the country's GDP in the event of a 1% increase in the inflation rate.

In both the short and long run, the coefficients associated with the interpreted variables have the same signs and are all significant. The results we are particularly interested in are related to the influence of corruption on private investment and growth. In this context, the coefficient obtained by the ARDL approach shows that the interaction between corruption and private investment has a negative sign (-0.010370) and is not significant even at the 10% level. In other words, investment in the private sector does not affect the increase in the country's GDP.

However, corruption is high in private firms and negatively affects their performance through bribes and bureaucratic inefficiency, as well as the political risks that exist in the country.

As a result, the influence of corruption on private initiatives tends to reduce GDP in the long run, indicating a negative indirect effect of corruption on economic growth through the level of the private capital stock.

The results of our estimation attest to the fact that corruption demoralizes and discourages private investment, suggesting that it increases costs for firms while intensifying uncertainty about the perceived return on investment. Our findings support the idea that corruption undermines the level of economic growth. This result is consistent with the expected signs and aligns with several works. Campos, Estrin, and Proto (2010), Zhou and Peng (2012), Jingtao Yi et al., (2019) and N. Zakharov (2019).

3.4. Corruption and Economic Growth Through Public Spending

The last regression seeks to test the hypothesis of indirect effects of corruption on economic growth in Tunisia through public spending.

To this end, we carry out the estimations controlling for the direct effect of corruption and introduce an interaction variable between corruption and public spending on goods and services. The results show that in the long and short run, the signs of all the variables included in the latter model are consistent with the expected signs already reported in the literature.

However, we note that the interaction variable has a negative coefficient of (-0.440519) and is significant at the 5% level in the short run; the estimation shows that the coefficient obtained reveals that the interaction between corruption and public spending also has a negative effect of (-0.103233) on GDP and significant at 1%. Thus, the impact of corruption on public spending leads to a reduction in GDP in the long run. However, there is a negative indirect effect of corruption on economic growth through the interaction between the level of corruption and public spending.

We build on the idea of Scott (1972) to certify that the increase in the proportions of corruption is greater when the size and scope of the public sector are more important questions in the economic circuit. This regression thus centrally confirms the existence of a negative indirect effect of corruption on Tunisia's GDP per capita. Corruption impedes the positive externalities of the public sector on economic growth. This finding is consistent with the expected signs and close to the findings of Tanzi and Davoodi (1997), Mauro (1998), d'Agostino, Dune, and Pieroni (2012). Njoya, and Aman, N. (2017).

4. CONCLUSION

In this empirical study, we tried to contribute to the resolution of the fundamental question: is there a link between the corruption of a country and the economic growth it achieves? To solve this problem, we have used an endogenous growth model in the case of Tunisia from the period 1998-2019. Furthermore, in the same context, we tested our variables' stationarity, Co-integration and the long-run relationship from this empirical study.

Finally, based on the estimation of the time series data of Tunisia, which are related to the period 1996- 2019, and the use of the ARDL method, The use of this type of model aims to study the existence of a long-term relationship between the dependent variables as well as the direct and indirect impact of corruption on economic growth in Tunisia the key findings from this empirical analysis reveal the following conclusions:

Our estimation results attest that corruption demoralizes and discourages private investment in the short and long run, suggesting that it increases costs for firms while intensifying uncertainty about the perceived return on investment.

The results also reveal that in the long and short run, the indirect impact of corruption is negative and insignificant for public expenditures. The results found in this study consolidate the conclusion reached in the empirical literature by several authors. However, the interaction between human capital and the corruption perception index is positive and insignificant in the short run but negative and significant in the long run.

We conclude, without confirming, that the analysis of this article has allowed us, even partially, to show the absence of a direct effect and then that it is a positive relationship between corruption and economic growth. Indeed, after detecting certain channels through which the effects of corruption on the performance of the Tunisian economy could pass, we note that it is an indirect effect transmitted through public spending and private investment.

This way, we will proceed with the analyses conducted in the following articles. But the following idea will attempt to empirically analyze the role of governance in the fight against corruption and improving economic growth in Tunisia.

As with any research work, the results of this article also set out some important implications that need to be taken into account in future research. With regard to the Corruption Perceptions Index, it is important for the global organization Transparency International to specify the practice or form of corruption measured by its indicator

(CPI). However, the CPI is characterized by a complex methodology that can lead to problems of interpretation. It is considered a general measure, but in reality, it takes into account the results of polls and surveys based on the statements of experts and businessmen. On the other hand, the main problem still to be solved is the inaccurate and imperfect measurement of corruption. Another potential problem facing Tunisia is that the country is characterized by a lack of accessible empirical data on corruption-related issues, probably due to a general lack of willingness for such an examination. Thus, the absence of data on macroeconomic variables seems to be important in the estimated model. Finally, we believe that there are many avenues of research in this area. They concern the introduction of the role of governance between fighting corruption and improving economic growth in this country.

REFERENCES

Anas, A Q., Azzouz, Z., & Mostafa, E. (2020). Does corruption adversely affect economic growth in Tunisia? ARDL approach. *Journal of Money Laundering Control, 23*(1), 38-54. doi:10.1108/JMLC-12-2018-0076

Bação, P., Gaspar, I., & Simões, M. (2019). Corruption and economic growth: The case of Portugal. *Notas Económicas*, (49), 11–33. doi:10.14195/2183-203X_49_2

Baliamoune-Lutz, M., & Ndikumana, L. (2009). Corruption and growth: Exploring the investment channel. *Economics Department Working Paper Series, 33.*

Bardhan, P. (1997). Corruption and development: A review of issues. *Journal of Economic Literature, 35*(3), 1320–1346.

Barro, R., & Sala-i-Martin, X. (2004). Economic growth (2nd ed.). Academic Press.

Bergheim, S. (2005). *Human capital is the key to growth-success stories and policies for 2020.* Deutsche Bank Research Current Issues Working Paper.

Bruno, M., & Easterly, W. (1998). Inflation crises and long-run growth. *Journal of Monetary Economics, 41*(1), 3–26. doi:10.1016/S0304-3932(97)00063-9

Campos, N. F., Estrin, S., & Proto, E. (2010). *Corruption as a barrier to entry: Theory and evidence*. Academic Press.

Cieślik, A., & Goczek, Ł. (2018). Control of corruption, international investment, and economic growth–Evidence from panel data. *World Development, 103*, 323–335. doi:10.1016/j.worlddev.2017.10.028

Cuervo-Cazurra, A. (2016). Corruption in international business. *Journal of World Business*, *51*(1), 35–49. doi:10.1016/j.jwb.2015.08.015

d'Agostino, G., Dunne, J. P., & Pieroni, L. (2012). Corruption, military spending and growth. *Defence and Peace Economics*, *23*(6), 591–604. doi:10.1080/10242694.2012.663579

D'Agostino, G., Dunne, J. P., & Pieroni, L. (2016). Government spending, corruption and economic growth. *World Development*, *84*, 190–205. doi:10.1016/j.worlddev.2016.03.011

Dao, M. Q. (2012). Population and economic growth in developing countries. *International Journal of Academic Research in Business & Social Sciences*, *2*(1), 6.

Ghoneim, A. F., & Ezzat, A. M. (2016). Growth and Corruption in Arab Countries: What Type of Relationship Connects Them? *Journal of Economics and International Finance*, *8*(5), 44–55. doi:10.5897/JEIF2015.0675

Gründler, K., & Potrafke, N. (2019). Corruption and economic growth: New empirical evidence. *European Journal of Political Economy*, *60*, 101810. doi:10.1016/j.ejpoleco.2019.08.001

Gupta, S., Davoodi, H., & Alonso-Terme, R. (2002). Does Corruption Affect Income Inequality and Poverty? *Economics of Governance*, *3*(1), 23–45. doi:10.1007101010100039

Gyimah-Brempong, K., & de Gyimah-Brempong, S. M. (2006). Corruption, growth, and income distribution: Are there regional differences? *Economics of Governance*, *7*(3), 245–269. doi:10.100710101-005-0008-2

Haseeb, M., & Azam, M. (2021). Dynamic nexus among tourism, corruption, democracy and environmental degradation: A panel data investigation. *Environment, Development and Sustainability*, *23*(4), 5557–5575. doi:10.100710668-020-00832-9

Headey, D. D., & Hodge, A. (2009). The effect of population growth on economic growth: A meta-regression analysis of the macroeconomic literature. *Population and Development Review*, *35*(2), 221–248. doi:10.1111/j.1728-4457.2009.00274.x

Howitt, P. (2005). Health, human capital, and economic growth: A Schumpeterian perspective. *Health and economic growth: Findings and policy implications, 1*, 19-40.

Huang, C. J. (2016). Is corruption bad for economic growth? Evidence from Asia-Pacific countries. *The North American Journal of Economics and Finance*, *35*, 247–256. doi:10.1016/j.najef.2015.10.013

Kremer, S., Bick, A., & Nautz, D. (2013). Inflation and growth: New evidence from a dynamic panel threshold analysis. *Empirical Economics*, *44*(2), 861–878. doi:10.100700181-012-0553-9

Lucas, R. E. Jr. (1988). On the mechanics of economic development. *Journal of Monetary Economics*, *22*(1), 3–42. doi:10.1016/0304-3932(88)90168-7

Mallik, G., & Saha, S. (2016). Corruption and growth: A complex relationship. *International Journal of Development Issues*, *15*(2), 113–129. doi:10.1108/IJDI-01-2016-0001

Mauro, P. (1995). Corruption and growth». *The Quarterly Journal of Economics*, *110*(3), 681–712. doi:10.2307/2946696

Méon, P. G., & Sekkat, K. (2005). Does corruption grease or sand the wheels of growth? *Public Choice*, *122*(1), 69–97. doi:10.100711127-005-3988-0

Moser, C. (2008). Poverty reduction, patronage or vote-buying? The allocation of public goods and the 2001 election in Madagascar. *Economic Development and Cultural Change*, *57*(1), 137–162. doi:10.1086/590458

Murphy, K. M., Shleifer, A., & Vishny, R. W. (1991). The allocation of talent: Implications for growth. *The Quarterly Journal of Economics*, *106*(2), 503–530. doi:10.2307/2937945

Njoya, N., & Aman, N. (2017). *Corruption et croissance économique au Cameroun: de l'effet direct et des effets indirects à travers la répartition des dépenses publiques* (Doctoral dissertation, Rennes 1).

Nsor-Ambala, R., & Coffie, C. P. K. (2021). Non-linear ADRL estimation of corruption and FDI inflow to Ghana. *Journal of Financial Crime*.

Othmani, A., Bakari, S., & Slimani, S. (2015). *Impact Direct et Indirect de la Corruption sur le Commerce Extérieur en Tunisie: Étude Descriptive*. Academic Press.

Ouattara, W. (2011). Corruption, investissements et croissance économique en Côte d'Ivoire. *Savings and Development*, *35*(1), 55–73. doi:10.2307avideve.35.1.55

Padhan, H., Behera, D. K., Sahu, S. K., & Dash, U. (2022). Does Corruption Hinderance Economic Growth Despite Surge of Remittance and Capital Inflows Since Economic Liberalization in an Emerging Economy, India. *Journal of the Knowledge Economy*, 1–24.

Paldam, M. (2002). The cross-country pattern of corruption: Economics, culture and the seesaw dynamics. *European Journal of Political Economy*, *18*(2), 215–240. doi:10.1016/S0176-2680(02)00078-2

Pellegrini, L., & Gerlagh, R. (2004). Corruption's effect on growth and its transmission channels. *Kyklos*, *57*(3), 429–456. doi:10.1111/j.0023-5962.2004.00261.x

Pesaran, M. H., Shin, Y., & Smith, R. J. (2001). Bounds testing approaches to the analysis of level relationships. *Journal of Applied Econometrics*, *16*(3), 289–326. doi:10.1002/jae.616

Romer, P. M. (1987). Growth based on increasing returns due to specialization. *The American Economic Review*, *77*(2), 56–62.

Sachs, J. D. (2008). The African green revolution. *Scientific American*, *298*(5), 42–43. doi:10.1038cientificamerican0508-42 PMID:18444321

Seka, P. (2013). Corruption, croissance et capital humain: Quels rapports? *Africa Development. Afrique et Developpement*, *XXXVIII*(1&2), 133–150.

Shleifer, A., & Vishny, R. W. (1993). Corruption. *The Quarterly Journal of Economics*, *108*(3), 599–617. doi:10.2307/2118402

Singh, A., Sharma, S., Singh, A., Unanoğlu, M., & Taneja, S. (2023). Cultural Marketing and Metaverse for Consumer Engagement. In *Cultural Marketing and Metaverse for Consumer Engagement*. IGI Global. doi:10.4018/978-1-6684-8312-1

Song, C. Q., Chang, C. P., & Gong, Q. (2021). Economic growth, corruption, and financial development: Global evidence. *Economic Modelling*, *94*, 822–830. doi:10.1016/j.econmod.2020.02.022

Swaleheen, M. (2011). Economic growth with endogenous corruption: An empirical study. *Public Choice*, *146*(1), 23–41. doi:10.100711127-009-9581-1

Taneja, S., Kaur, S., & Özen, E. (2022). Using green finance to promote global growth in a sustainable way. *International Journal of Green Economics*, *16*(3), 246–257. doi:10.1504/IJGE.2022.128930

Taneja, S., & Ozen, E. (2023). Impact of the European Green Deal (EDG) on the Agricultural Carbon (CO2) Emission in Turkey. *International Journal of Sustainable Development and Planning*, *18*(3), 715–727. doi:10.18280/ijsdp.180307

Taneja, S., & Sharma, V. (2023). Role of beaconing marketing in improving customer buying experience. In *Enhancing Customer Engagement Through Location-Based Marketing*. IGI Global. doi:10.4018/978-1-6684-8177-6.ch012

Tanzi, V., & Davoodi, H. (1997). *Corruption, Public Investment, and Growth.* IMF Working Papers 97/139, International Monetary Fund.

Tanzi, V., & Davoodi, H. R. (2000). *Corruption, growth, and public finances.* Academic Press.

Transparency International. (2018). *Indice de perception de la corruption 2018.* https://www.transparency.org/cpi

Transparency International. (2019). *Indice de perception de la corruption 2019.* https://www.transparency.org/cpi

Tsanana, E., Chapsa, X., & Katrakilidis, C. (2016). Is growth corrupted or bureaucratic? Panel evidence from the enlarged EU. *Applied Economics*, *48*(33), 3131–3147. doi:10.1080/00036846.2015.1136395

Yi, J., Meng, S., Macaulay, C. D., & Peng, M. W. (2019). Corruption and foreign direct investment phases: The moderating role of institutions. *Journal of International Business Policy*, *2*(2), 167–181. doi:10.105742214-019-00024-x

Zakharov, N. (2019). Does corruption hinder investment? Evidence from Russian regions. *European Journal of Political Economy*, *56*, 39–61. doi:10.1016/j.ejpoleco.2018.06.005

Zangina, S., & Hassan, S. (2020). Corruption and FDI inflow to Nigeria: A nonlinear ARDL approach. *Journal of Financial Crime*, *27*(2), 635–650. doi:10.1108/JFC-09-2019-0116

Zhou, J. Q., & Peng, M. W. (2012). Does bribery help or hurt firm growth around the world? *Asia Pacific Journal of Management*, *29*(4), 907–921. doi:10.100710490-011-9274-4

Chapter 8
A Study on Rural BPL Households' Perception Towards Financial Inclusion Schemes

Harvinder Singh
Chandigarh University, India

Kaushal Kishore Mishra
https://orcid.org/0000-0001-6466-0575
Chandigarh University, India

M. P. Singh
Graphic Era University (Deemed), India

ABSTRACT

The chapter aims to study the respondents' perceptions regarding financial inclusion schemes launched by the government of India. The provision of financial services at affordable prices to significant portions of economically underprivileged and low-income populations is known as financial inclusion. The union government and central banks worldwide have made financial inclusion their main priority to promote inclusive growth. It is crucial to look at respondents' opinions of different financial inclusion programs because doing so will pave the way for improving financial services. The study found that the perception level of PM-Jan Dhan Yojana and PM-Jan Arogya Yojana is more assessable and affordable; however, PM-Mudra Yojana and PM-Jan Arogya Yojana are adequate in both states.

DOI: 10.4018/979-8-3693-1746-4.ch008

INTRODUCTION

Every nation must establish an inclusive financial system in order to provide for fundamental needs and eradicate the ills of poverty, illiteracy, malnutrition, and unemployment. (Crisil report, 2018). The demand base constraints related to customers must be examined in order to apply corrective measures and meet the goal of FI. Despite offering a variety of financial products like savings, credit, and insurance, banks and other financial institutions are unable to help people escape poverty on their own (C Rangarajan, 2008). In order for financial inclusion projects to be successful, consumers must use these products in ways that improve their financial situation (Thorat, U., 2007). To truly help underprivileged people and small farmers use the formal banking system, financial inclusion products and services must take into account the cognitive traits of consumers. This study aims to examine respondents' perceptions of the suitability, affordability, and accessibility of various financial inclusion programs.

REVIEW OF LITERATURE

Kaur (2022) evaluated the awareness and usage regarding Ayushman Bharat Yojana among the people residing in particular locations of Punjab's Distt. Tarn Taran. Two hundred adults were chosen using convenience sampling, and structured questionnaires were used to gather the information. The study's findings showed that individuals knew of the Ayushman Bharat Yojana on average. Pandey et al. (2021) stated the difficulties in service adoption in a setting of universal healthcare. The researcher examined in this study how the principle of service adoption was used in a system of universal health care. The study places special emphasis on performance expectations, convenience of service access, beneficial societal influence, and conducive conditions for Ayushman Bharat service delivery. Kumar (2018) conducted this research in order to determine the satisfaction with and awareness of the services given regarding the PMJDY account. Secondary data has been gathered by a questionnaire from the Coimbatore district of Tamil Nadu. Simple percentage and Friedman rank tests were performed. According to the report, the account holders are happy with the services offered and are aware of the characteristics of their accounts (Dahiya & Taneja, 2023; Taneja et al., 2023).

Singh (2018) analyses the PM Mudra Yojana, its current status, and appropriate advice. The absence of financial provision from the organized segment, according to the researcher, is the main obstacle in the development of micro-level business. MUDRA Banks is playing a significant role in raising living standards, expanding employment opportunities, raising national income, and decreasing poverty by offering financial help. Joshi and Rajpurohit (2016) stated how well-informed rural clients were about financial inclusion programs (PMJDY). In gathering secondary data, different statistical tools such as the 'chi-square test' were used for analysis. According to the findings of this study, the program was only partially successful in raising public awareness of the new PMJDY compared to the previous 'Swabhimaan program,' and the government is still unable to significantly change the level of rural customers' financial inclusion program awareness. Verma and Garg (2016) quantify financial inclusion; they use three criteria: availability, affordability, and usability of those services. The study's findings indicated that there is still a long road to travel until financial untouchability is truly eradicated from our nation. Ahmed (2013) studied the perceptions regarding the Indian insurance industry. The outcome of the research showed that a large number of target audiences in rural areas were completely unaware of the insurance products and services. However, the section that had some knowledge did not know the difference between life insurance, general insurance, and other types of insurance products. The study also revealed that the insurance industry's shift from a product-focused approach to a customer-focused approach has also led to fewer innovations in product designs, and hence, there are hardly any major differences between products being offered by various insurers. Also, since all products are designed by keeping urban customers in mind, the rural masses are devoid of any affordable insurance coverage.

RESEARCH METHODOLOGY

It is crucial to look at respondents' opinions of different financial inclusion programs because doing so will pave the way for improving financial services. Statements that incorporate the availability, expense, and sufficiency of particular financial inclusion programs are used to examine respondents' perceptions. In the present study, descriptive research design is applied to study the perception of rural BPL households regarding financial Inclusion schemes.

Research Objectives

1. To analyze the perception level of respondents with reference to selected financial inclusion schemes on the basis of accessibility, affordability, and adequacy.
2. To compare the perception level between peoples of Haryana and Punjab regarding selected financial inclusion schemes.

Research Hypothesis

H_0 There is no substantial difference in the perceptions of respondents from Punjab and Haryana regarding the accessibility, affordability, and adequacy of Financial Inclusion products.

H_a There is a substantial difference in the perceptions of respondents from Punjab and Haryana regarding the accessibility, affordability, and adequacy of Financial Inclusion products.

Data Collection

The primary data has been collected from the rural areas of Punjab and Haryana. A multi-stage sampling method was used for collecting this data. An organized questionnaire was developed for the primary data collection. The sample size of this study was 502 respondents (270 from Haryana and 232 from Punjab). On the basis of the CRISIL Inclusix scores issued by CRISIL in February 2018, three districts from each state have been chosen. As a result, Ambala, Sonipat, and Nuh districts were selected from Haryana. Whereas from the Punjab region, Rupnagar, Faridkot, and Fazilka districts were selected. While selecting the households, only those who were under the criteria of Below Poverty Lime (BPL) according to the 'Socio-Economic Caste Census (SECC) 2011 statistics were considered.

Data Analysis and Interpretation

Respondent perceptions are analyzed through statements that include accessibility, affordability, and adequacy of selected financial inclusion initiatives, which are scored on a five-point scale. Descriptive Statistical tools like independent sample t-tests and ANOVA tests have been used to make the comparison of perception levels between the states of Punjab and Haryana regarding selected financial inclusion schemes.

Accessibility of Financial Inclusion Schemes

Financial services accessibility is a vital aspect in the growth of all segments of society. This necessitates the creation of an ecosystem to provide varied financial inclusion services to all segments of society (Germana & Luisa, 2017). Accessibility Indicators provide information about how all families can obtain a range of financial products at a fair cost (Verma & Garg, 2017). Some statements were designed with the accessibility of selected financial inclusion schemes provided by various financial institutes in mind, which were graded by respondents on a 'five-point Likert scale' and a comparison between the two states was made using descriptive statistics and an independent sample t-test.

Table 1. Result of 'descriptive statistics' for accessibility of financial inclusion schemes

	Name of State	N	Mean	Std. Deviation	Std. Error Mean
Accessibility PMJDY	Haryana	270	3.46	0.64118	0.03902
	Punjab	232	3.4784	0.66649	0.04376
Accessibility PMMY	Haryana	270	3.3762	0.71255	0.04336
	Punjab	232	3.4138	0.73936	0.04854
Accessibility PMJAY	Haryana	270	3.0717	0.55488	0.03377
	Punjab	232	3.0108	0.64125	0.0421

As per Table 1.1, the mean scores indicating respondents' perceptions of PMJDY accessibility in Haryana and Punjab are 3.46 and 3.48, respectively. The Mean scores of PMMY regarding accessibility are 3.38 and 3.41 for Haryana and Punjab, respectively. The Mean scores of PMJAY regarding accessibility are 3.07 and 3.01 for Haryana and Punjab, respectively.

Table 1.2 reveals that the "independent sample t-test" applied to the perception of respondents from Haryana and Punjab about the accessibility of selected Financial Inclusion products. The null hypothesis has been formulated as follows:

H_0: There is no substantial variation in the perceptions of respondents from Punjab and Haryana regarding the accessibility of Financial Inclusion products.

The result of "Levene's test" of variance equality was determined to be 0.81 in the case of PMJDY, which is greater than the assumed value of 0.05; hence, the assumed values of variance equality were taken into account. In this situation, the p-value estimated for the t-test was 0.752, which means that the null hypothesis is accepted, indicating that there is no statistically substantial variation in the perception of respondents from Punjab and Haryana regarding the accessibility of PMJDY. The fact that the mean difference is -0.018, which is negative and very minor, indicates that Punjab is better than Haryana in terms of access to PMJDY services.

Table 2. Result of 'independent samples t-test'

		'Levene's Test for Equality of Variances'		't-Test for Equality of Means'						
		F	Sig.	T	DF	'Sig. (2-Tailed)'	'Mean Difference'	'Std. Error Difference'	'95% Confidence Interval of the Difference'	
									Lower	Upper
Accessibility PMJDY	'Equal variances assumed'	0.061	0.805	-.316	500	.752	-.01845	.05846	-.13330	.09640
	'Equal variances not assumed'			-.315	482.47	.753	-.01845	.05863	-.13365	.09675
Accessibility PMMY	'Equal variances assumed'	0.147	0.701	-.579	500	.563	-.03757	.06491	-.16510	.08996
	'Equal variances not assumed'			-.577	482.78	.564	-.03757	.06509	-.16547	.09032
Accessibility PMJAY	'Equal variances assumed'	2.726	0.099	1.141	500	.254	.06092	.05338	-.04396	.16581
	'Equal variances not assumed'			1.129	460.26	.260	.06092	.05397	-.04514	.16698

The score of 'Levene's test' of variance equality was found to be 0.70 in the instance of PMMY, which is greater than the assumed value of 0.05; hence, the assumed values of variance equality were taken into account. Here, the p-value was 0.563. It suggests that the null hypothesis is accepted, indicating that there is no statistically substantial variation in the perspective of respondents from Punjab and Haryana regarding the accessibility to PMMY. Because the mean difference is -0.038, which is negative, it means that Punjab is better than Haryana in terms of the accessibility of PMMY services.

The p score of "Levene's test" of variance equality was determined to be 0.099 in the case of PMJAY, which is greater than the presumed value (0.05), so the values of 'equal variance assumed' were used. In this situation, the p-value calculated for the t-test was 0.254, which suggests that the null hypothesis is accepted, indicating that there is no statistically substantial variation in the perception of respondents from Punjab and Haryana regarding the accessibility of PMJAY. The mean difference is 0.061, indicating that Haryana is more accessible to PMJAY services than its counterparts in Punjab.

Affordability of Financial Inclusion Schemes

In a price-sensitive market like India, Financial products must be affordable. Credit, insurance, remittance, and transaction costs must be kept low in order to include impoverished and disadvantaged areas, as well as lagging sectors, in order to foster growth and decrease income gaps. Prolonged and continuous financial exclusion of a major sector of the population due to the inability to afford financial products would result in a drop in investments and could also result in social tensions, resulting in social exclusion.

Table 3. 'Descriptive statistics' for affordability of financial inclusion schemes

	Name of State	N	'Mean'	'Std. Deviation'	'Std. Error Mean'
Affordability PMJDY	Haryana	270	3.3511	.70830	.04311
	Punjab	232	3.3448	.75252	.04941
Affordability PMMY	Haryana	270	3.4926	.77270	.04702
	Punjab	232	3.5366	.75754	.04974
Affordability PMJAY	Haryana	270	2.9689	.61523	.03744
	Punjab	232	2.9405	.73602	.04832

As a result, the government is working to develop cheap financial solutions for the underserved. Some statements were created with the affordability of various financial inclusion products/services in mind, and a comparison between the two states was made using "descriptive statistics, independent sample t-tests, and the ANOVA test".

According to Table 1.3, the mean scores indicating respondents' perceptions of PMJDY accessibility in Haryana and Punjab are 3.35 and 3.34, respectively. The Mean scores of PMMY regarding accessibility are 3.49 and 3.53 for Haryana and Punjab respectively. The Mean score of PMJAY regarding accessibility is 2.96 and 2.94 for Haryana and Punjab, respectively.

The "Independent sample t-test" applied to respondents' perceptions of the affordability of various Financial Inclusion products in Haryana and Punjab.

Ho2: There is no substantial variation in respondents' perceptions of the affordability of Financial Inclusion schemes between Punjab and Haryana

The score of "Levene's test" of variance equality was determined to be 0.183 in the case of PMJDY, which is greater than the expected value of 0.05; hence, the assumed values of variance equality were used. In this situation, the p-value estimated for the sample t-test was 0.752, which means that the null hypothesis is accepted, indicating that there is no statistically substantial variation in the perception of respondents from Punjab and Haryana regarding the affordability of PMJDY. The fact that the mean difference is -0.018, which is negative and very minor, indicates that Punjab is better than Haryana in terms of affording PMJDY services.

The value of "Levene's test" of variance equality was found to be 0.708 in the instance of PMMY, which is greater than the supposed value of 0.05; hence, the assumed values of variance equality were taken into account. In this situation, the value of the sample t-test was 0.521, which suggests that the null hypothesis is accepted, indicating that there is no statistically substantial variation in the perspective of respondents of the two states regarding the affordability of PMMY. The fact that the mean difference is -0.038, indicating a negative number, indicates that Punjab is better than Haryana in terms of affording PMMY services.

The value of "Levene's test" of variance equality was determined to be 0.025 in the case of PMJAY, which means the values of 'equal variance not assumed' were used. In this situation, the p-value calculated for the t-test was 0.643, which suggests that the null hypothesis is accepted, indicating that there is no statistically substantial variation in the perception of respondents from two states regarding the affordability of PMJAY. The mean difference is 0.061, indicating that Haryana is more affordable to PMJAY services than its counterparts in Punjab.

Table 4. Result of 'independent samples t-test'

		'Levene's Test for Equality of Variances'		't-test for Equality of Means'						
		F	Sig.	T	DF	'Sig. (2-Tailed)'	'Mean Difference'	'Std. Error Difference'	'95% Confidence Interval of the Difference'	
									Lower	Upper
Affordability PMJDY	'Equal variances assumed'	1.774	.183	.096	500	.923	.00628	.06527	-.12195	.13451
	'Equal variances not assumed'			.096	478.459	.924	.00628	.06557	-.12255	.13512
Affordability PMMY	'Equal variances assumed'	.140	.708	-.643	500	.521	-.04405	.06855	-.17873	.09063
	'Equal variances not assumed'			-.644	491.392	.520	-.04405	.06845	-.17853	.09044
Affordability PMJAY	'Equal variances assumed'	5.083	.025	.470	500	.638	.02837	.06031	-.09013	.14687
	'Equal variances not assumed'			.464	451.792	.643	.02837	.06113	-.09176	.14851

Adequacy of Financial Inclusion Schemes

Adequacy refers to the sufficiency of FI products. Better and broader adequacy of financial products is a critical prerequisite for scaling up the existing demand of prospective clients. The adequacy of credit, remittance, and insurance coverage provided by financial inclusion programs has been assessed. Implementation of appropriate methods, goods, services, and technology, as well as systematic regional initiatives, are required to increase the impact of Financial Inclusion products (Bindal & Singh, 2022). The following statements were created with the sufficiency of various financial inclusion products/services in mind, and a comparison between the two states was made using "descriptive statistics and the independent sample t-test and ANOVA test."

Table 5. 'Descriptive statistics' for adequacy of financial inclusion schemes

	State Name	N	'Mean'	'Std. Deviation'	'Std. Error Mean'
Adequacy PMJDY	Haryana	270	3.3548	.76184	.04636
	Punjab	232	3.3983	.76118	.04997
Adequacy PMMY	Haryana	270	3.3269	.71291	.04339
	Punjab	232	3.3599	.71569	.04699
Adequacy PMJAY	Haryana	270	3.1000	.68215	.04151
	Punjab	232	3.0463	.78938	.05183

As per Table 1.5, the mean scores indicating respondents' perceptions of the adequacy of PMJDY in Haryana and Punjab are 3.35 and 3.40, respectively. The Mean scores of PMMY regarding adequacy are 3.33 and 3.36 for Haryana and Punjab, respectively. The Mean scores of PMJAY regarding adequacy are 3.10 and 3.05 for Haryana and Punjab, respectively.

Table 1.6 depicts the findings of an "independent sample t-test" used to respondents' perceptions on the appropriateness of chosen Financial Inclusion products in Haryana and Punjab. The following Null Hypothesis has been developed for the purposes of this study:

Ho3: There is no substantial variation in the perceptions of respondents from Punjab and Haryana regarding the adequacy of selected Financial Inclusion schemes.

Table 6. Result of "independent samples t-test"

		'Levene's Test for Equality of Variances'		't-Test for Equality of Means'						
		F	Sig.	T	DF	'Sig. (2-Tailed)'	'Mean Difference'	'Std. Error Difference'	'95% Confidence Interval of the Difference'	
									Lower	Upper
Adequacy PMJDY	'Equal variances assumed'	.064	.801	-.638	500	.524	-.04346	.06817	-.17740	.09048
	'Equal variances not assumed'			-.638	488.82	.524	-.04346	.06817	-.17740	.09048
Adequacy PMMY	'Equal variances assumed'	.006	.939	-.517	500	.605	-.03306	.06394	-.15868	.09255
	'Equal variances not assumed'			-.517	488.12	.605	-.03306	.06395	-.15872	.09260
Adequacy PMJAY	'Equal variances assumed'	2.368	.125	.817	500	.414	.05366	.06568	-.07537	.18270
	'Equal variances not assumed'			.808	459.94	.419	.05366	.06640	-.07683	.18415

The result of "Levene's test" of variance equality was determined to be 0.801 in the case of PMJDY, which is greater than the assumed value of 0.05; hence, the assumed values of variance equality were taken into account. Here, the p-value calculated for the t-test was 0.524, which suggests that the null hypothesis is accepted, indicating that there is no statistically substantial variation in the perspective of respondents of the two states regarding the sufficiency of PMJDY. Because the mean difference is -0.043, which is negative and very little, it means that Punjab is better than Haryana in terms of the adequacy of PMJDY services.

The result of "Levene's test" of variance equality was determined to be 0.939 in the case of PMMY, which is greater than the assumed value of 0.05; hence, the assumed values of variance equality were taken into account. In this situation, the p-value estimated for the t-test was 0.605, which suggests that the null hypothesis is accepted, indicating that there is no statistically substantial variation in the perception of respondents from two states regarding the adequacy of PMMY. Because the mean difference is -0.033, which is negative, it means that Punjab is better than Haryana in terms of the adequacy of PMMY services.

The p-value of Levene's test of variance equality was determined to be 0.125 in the case of PMJAY, which is greater than the assumed value of 0.05; hence, the assumed values of variance equality were taken into account. In this situation, the p-value calculated for the t-test was 0.414, which suggests that the null hypothesis is accepted, indicating that there is no statistically substantial variation in the perception of respondents from Punjab and Haryana regarding the appropriateness of PMJAY. The mean difference is 0.054, indicating that Haryana is superior to its peers in Punjab in terms of the adequacy of PMJAY services.

FINDINGS AND CONCLUSION

The results of the "Independent sample t-test" were applied to know the perception level of respondents of Haryana and Punjab regarding selected Financial Inclusion products. This result shows that 'there is no significant difference in the perceptions of respondents of two states in terms of accessibility, affordability, and adequacy of selected Financial Inclusion schemes.' In a scheme-wise comparison of perception, PMJDY and PMJAY are more assessable and affordable; however, PMMY and PMJAY are adequate in both states. The main reason behind the difference in respondent's perception is the geographic area of both states and state govt initiatives.

REFERENCES

Ahmed, A. (2013). Perception of Life Insurance Policies in Rural India. *Kuwait Chapter of Arabian Journal of Business and Management Review, 2*, 17 – 24.

Ajeet Kumar Sahoo, P. R. (2019). Performance of Pradhan Mantri MUDRA Yojana (PMMY): A Case Study of Haryana. *International Journal of Research in Social Science, 9*(5), 1–17.

Ayushman Bharat for a New India-2022, Announced. Press Information Bureau, Government of India, Department of Finance. (n.d.). Available from: http://www.pib.nic.in/newsite/PrintRelease.aspx?relid=176049

Ayushman Bharat Yojana. (n.d.). Available from: www.nap.gov.in

Bindal, A., & Singh, R. (2022). A study and review of Pradhan Mantri Mudra Yojana. *Journal of Education: Rabindra Bharati University, 23*(1), 309-315.

Chakrabarty, K. C. (2012). *Financial Inclusion – Issues in Measurement and Analysis.* Reserve Bank of India at the BIS-BNM Workshop on Financial Inclusion Indicators at Kuala Lumpur. http://www.rbi.org.in/scripts/BSSpeechesView.aspx?id=749

CRISIL, (2018). *An index to measure India 's progress on Financial Inclusion.* Report of CRISIL Inclusix.

Dahiya, K., & Taneja, S. (2023). To Analyse the Impact of Multi-Media Technology on the Rural Entrepreneurship Development. In Contemporary Studies of Risks in Emerging Technology (pp. 221–240). doi:10.1108/978-1-80455-562-020231015

Germana, C., & Luisa, C. (2017). Inclusive finance for inclusive growth and development. *Current Opinion in Environmental Sustainability, 24*, 19-23. doi:10.1016/j.cosust.2017.01.013

Hasan, M., Le, T., & Hoque, A. (2021). How does financial literacy impact on inclusive finance? *Financial Innovation, 7*(1), 40. doi:10.118640854-021-00259-9

Hussain, A. (2015). Pradhan Mantri Jan Dhan Yojana: A SWOT Analysis. *Journal for Advanced Research in Commerce and Management Studies, 2*(2), 84–94.

JoshiM.RajpurohitV. (2016), Pradhan Mantri Jan Dhan Yojana (The Financial Inclusion): A Study of Awareness doi:10.2139/ssrn.2816493

Kaur, H., & Singh, K. N. (2015). Pradhan Mantri Jan Dhan Yojana (PMJDY): A Leap towards Financial Inclusion in India. *International Journal of Emerging Research in Management &Technology, 4*(1), 26-27.

Kumar, R. (2018). A study on Pradhan Mantri Jan Dhan Yojana awareness and its satisfaction – A Financial inclusion initiative (With special reference to Coimbatore district). *International Journal of Research and Analytical Reviews, 5*(3).

OECD INFE. (2011). *Measuring Financial Literacy: Core Questionnaire in Measuring Financial Literacy: Questionnaire and Guidance Notes for conducting an Internationally Comparable Survey of Financial literacy*. OECD.

Pandey, N., Jha, S., & Rai, V. (2021). Ayushman Bharat: Service Adoption Challenges in Universal Healthcare System. *South Asian Journal of Business and Management Cases*, *10*(1), 35–49. doi:10.1177/2277977921991915

Pujari, B. (2019). *Promoting standard of living through Financial Inclusion: A study on Bargarh and Sambalpur districts of western Odisha* (Doctoral dissertation). Retrieved from http://hdl.handle.net/10603/284279

Rao, N. D. (2013). *Status of Financial Inclusion Among Rural Households in Andhra Pradesh. From Andhra University* (Doctoral dissertation).

Singh, K. R. (2018). Development of Micro, Small and Medium Enterprises through MUDRA Loans with Special Reference to Manipur. *Abhinav National Monthly Refereed Journals of Research in Commerce & Management*, *7*(1), 55–61.

Sriee G V VP, & Maiya GR. (2021). Coverage, utilization, and impact of Ayushman Bharat scheme among the rural field practice area of Saveetha Medical College and Hospital, Chennai. *J Family Med Prim Care, 10*(3), 1171-1176. . doi:10.4103/jfmpc.jfmpc_1789_20

Taneja, S., Bhatnagar, M., Kumar, P., & Rupeika-apoga, R. (2023). India ' s Total Natural Resource Rents (NRR) and GDP : An Augmented Autoregressive Distributed Lag (ARDL) Bound Test. *Journal of Risk and Financial Management*, *16*(2), 91. doi:10.3390/jrfm16020091

Thorat, U. (2007). *Financial Inclusion – The Indian experience Speech*. Academic Press.

Utpal Kalita. (n.d.). *Social Awareness Scale, 781 P, (SESS(R)–DSDV) Hindi/English.* National Psychological Corp.

Verma, Y., & Garg, P. (2016). Pradhan Mantri Jan Dhan Yojana (PMJDY): A step towards eradicating financial untouchability. *Indian Journal of Finance*, *10*(1), 56–64. doi:10.17010/ijf/2016/v10i1/85845

Chapter 9
Contribution of Disruptive Technologies in Computational Finance

Arvind Kumar Bhatt
https://orcid.org/0000-0002-2521-1942
G.L. Bajaj Institute of Management and Research, India

Anand Kumar Rai
G.L. Bajaj Institute of Management and Research, India

Rajesh Tiwari
https://orcid.org/0000-0002-5345-2508
Graphic Era University (Deemed), India

ABSTRACT

Disruptive technologies have ignited a profound transformation in the landscape of computational finance. As the realms of finance integrate cutting-edge technologies like quantum computing, artificial intelligence, blockchain, and big data analytics, the limits of financial possibilities are continually being pushed further. As artificial intelligence, blockchain, big data analytics, and quantum computing find their place in the financial realm, the boundaries of what is possible in finance are constantly expanding. This chapter explores the impact of these disruptive technologies on computational finance, dissecting their applications, benefits, challenges, and ethical considerations. By navigating this ever-evolving intersection of technology and finance, the authors gain insights into a future where financial services are more efficient, accessible, and adaptable than ever before. The chapter analyzes the tools for better understanding of the technology in finance domain and provide the trends of research in computational finance space using bibliometric analysis.

DOI: 10.4018/979-8-3693-1746-4.ch009

1. INTRODUCTION

The world of finance has always been an arena where innovation and technology collide. From the advent of double-entry bookkeeping in Renaissance Italy to the rise of electronic trading platforms in the late 20th century, each era has witnessed financial revolutions driven by technological advancements. In the 21st century, a new wave of disruptive technologies is sweeping through the realm of finance, fundamentally altering the way we approach and interact with financial systems. These technologies have the potential to reshape the landscape of computational finance, a field that has long been at the forefront of financial innovation.

Computational finance, also known as financial engineering, marries the principles of finance with mathematical modeling, statistical analysis, and computer science. It has traditionally been the engine driving risk management, asset pricing, portfolio optimization, and trading strategies. However, the introduction of disruptive technologies is redefining the boundaries of computational finance, enabling new frontiers in efficiency, accessibility, and innovation (Reepu et al., 2023; Singh et al., 2023; Taneja et al., 2023; Yadav et al., 2023).

In this chapter, we embark on a journey through the world of disruptive technologies in computational finance. We will delve into the key technologies that are reshaping the financial industry, exploring their applications and implications. Machine learning as well as Artificial intelligence are revolutionizing the way decisions are made, relying on data-driven insights. They're also transforming the landscape of automated trading, allowing transactions to occur at speeds that were once thought to be impossible just a few decades back. Block chain technology and cryptocurrencies are challenging traditional financial institutions with the promise of decentralized finance and smart contracts. Big data analytics is uncovering hidden insights in massive datasets, empowering better risk assessment and customer service. Quantum computing, while still in its infancy, holds the potential to revolutionize complex financial calculations.

However, as we navigate this brave new world, we must also confront challenges and ethical considerations. Data privacy, regulatory compliance and algorithm bias have been the issues putting the challenges before the entire world. Balancing innovation with accountability becomes paramount in this dynamic environment.

Through this exploration of disruptive technologies in computational finance, we tried to put a detailed overview of the current scenario and which will offer key insights for the future of finance. As we journey through the various facets of this transformation, we will gain a deeper understanding of how these technologies are not only disrupting but also enhancing the world of finance, ultimately shaping a more efficient, accessible, and adaptive financial ecosystem. However, this rapid transformation raises ethical concerns regarding data privacy, algorithmic bias, and regulatory compliance (Kroll et al., 2017). Navigating these challenges is crucial for maintaining trust in the financial system and ensuring equitable access to financial services.

As the landscape of finance undergoes a transformation driven by breakthrough technologies, this summary acts as a navigational tool in the journey towards a future where computational finance is characterized not only by its innovativeness but also by its commitment to responsibility and inclusivity.

2. LITERATURE REVIEW

Groundbreaking technological innovation along with rapid growth in digitalization of businesses, are occurring swiftly across sectors like global supply chains, high-tech manufacturing, logistics, finance, and healthcare. These cutting-edge technologies are set to profoundly influence Computational Finance and professional practices. Technological advancements such as decentralized finance (DeFi) platforms, smart contracts, digital currencies including cryptocurrencies and NFTs, cloud-based accounting, extensive data analysis, artificial intelligence, machine learning, and blockchain technology are key drivers of this change.

Various researchers, including Richins and others in 2017, and Andersen in 2019, have observed that the accounting sector is undergoing continuous transformation and adaptation due to the emergence and integration of technologies. These technologies include blockchain, AI, robotics, big data, and cloud computing. Ibrahim et.al. (2021) highlighted the role of big data, cloud technology, and AI in providing novel opportunities and solutions for accountants to enhance their capabilities in this fast-paced digital era.

A comprehensive survey by KPMG International in 2017, involving 580 participants from 16 countries, focused on the adoption trends of key disruptive technologies and their impact on business and investment strategies. According 77% respondent, big data and data analytics were considered as most impactful technologies, while 74% mentioned cloud computing as most impactful.

Deloitte conducted a study in 2018, where, more than 300 financial services executives were surveyed. The outcome of the study revealed that the blockchain, artificial intelligence, and robotics are the most rapidly emerging technologies in the financial services sector. Deloitte in 2018 itself released a report titled "Data is the new gold," that highlighted the potential and advantages of vast data reserves, cloud services and data analytics, in the accounting and auditing fields.

AICPA's webcast series "Go Beyond Disruption" features key figures in the accounting profession discussing the new challenges posed by disruptive technologies. The series emphasizes the impact of big data analytics, artificial intelligence and blockchain and robotic process automation on the accounting and finance profession. The consensus is that these technologies will fundamentally alter accounting practices and the professionals involved.

3. RESEARCH METHODOLOGY

Our study utilized co-word analysis to determine the publication volume of articles, specifically papers, by various entities and to track the trends and popularity of technologies from 2016 to 2020. The technique of bibliometric analysis, pioneered in the mid-20th century by E. Garfield, has become a widely accepted method in assessing scientific research. According to Abad-Segura & Gonzalez-Zamar, 2020, it employs mathematical and statistical approaches to evaluate literature and gauge the landscape of a particular scientific domain. According to Zupic & Čater, 2015, Co-word analysis, stands out as the solitary method for developing metrics of similarity that directly incorporate the text of the documents in question.

Initially, our qualitative examination within the literature review segment of our study highlighted the key disruptive technologies impacting the field of Computational Finance. This review also pinpointed the foremost professional firms, institutions, and scholarly publications that are most invested in dedicating resources for research and creating opportunities for disseminating work on Accounting and Management Information Systems associated with these technological advancements. Subsequently, we conducted a bibliometric analysis focusing on research papers listed in Scopus Indexed Journals.

Our thorough investigation, leveraging advanced search capabilities, was guided by select keywords with either or option: These keywords were "Computation Finance", "Artificial Intelligence", "Data Analytics", "Cloud", "Blockchain", and "Big Data". We analyzed a total of 705 articles, papers, and documents concerning disruptive technologies within Computational Finance, spanning the years 2016 to 2020.

4. BIBLIOMETRIC ANALYSIS

The upcoming section presents a comprehensive bibliometric assessment of literature on Disruptive Technologies in Computational Finance. This analysis is conducted in two primary phases. Initially, we focus on dynamic and influential factors, identifying key authors with significant contributions to Computational Finance. We spotlight the primary sources influencing the discourse across various themes within the field. We also outline the leading countries and their respective contributions to Computational Finance literature. The discussion then extends to the primary affiliations or institutions that are at the forefront of researching diverse Computational Finance topics. The pivotal contributions of top-tier documents are reviewed, and we pinpoint the predominant keywords within the Computational Finance body of literature.

In the second phase, our analysis constructs a conceptual structure. Here, we delve into the different themes and currents within the Computational Finance literature. This part aims to clarify the fundamental subjects of Computational Finance as they intersect with computer, social, and environmental sciences, while also forecasting potential future directions for Computational Finance technologies. We introduce " co-occurrence network" that interlinks "matrix of keywords", forming various clusters that illuminate the central themes. Additionally, we examine a thematic map that categorizes various topics into four distinct quadrants, each representing different attributes. Culminating this section, we identify emerging trends and developmental issues to suggest a research roadmap for future inquiries in Computational Finance literature.

4.1. Influential Aspects

4.1.1. Core Sources

Figure 1 delineates the ten most prominent sources influencing the domain of Computational Finance literature. At the forefront is the "Lecture Notes in Computer Science," a pivotal repository featuring studies on financial technology (fintech) innovations using patent data, the influence of information technology (IT) on the evolution of fintech business models, and the application of explainable fintech AI in assessing lending risk efficiency.

"Quantitative Finance" holds the position of the second key contributor to the field. This source is frequently the platform where new research within Quantitative Finance is unveiled.

The compilation of "ACM International Conference Proceedings" stands as the third essential source. It encompasses a range of cutting-edge research, including adaptable agile tailoring frameworks, sophisticated mechanisms for enhancing agricultural marketing, and the application of smart contracts through blockchain technology, as well as the employment of decentralized ledger technology in the context of financial derivatives markets.

Figure 1. Publication wise most relevant sources

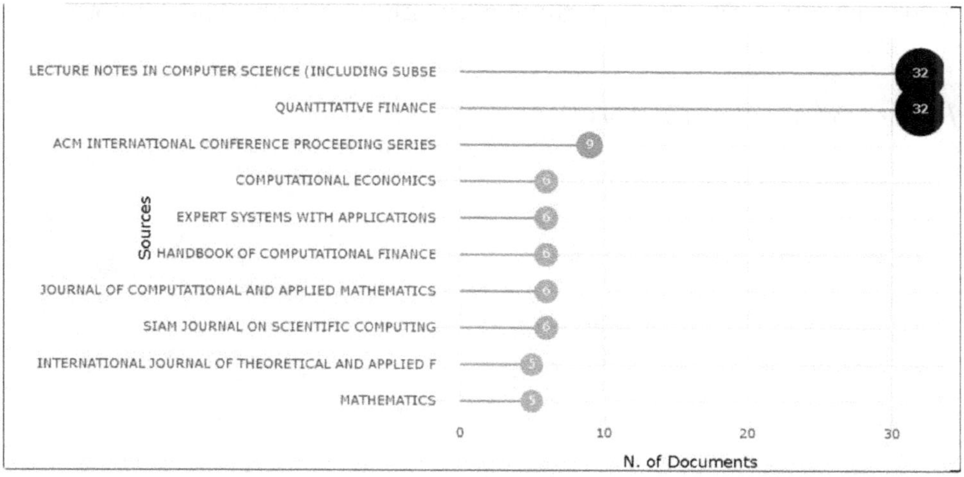

Table 1. Prominent Sources

Element	h_index	g_index	m_index	TC	NP	PY_start
Quantitative Finance	12	19	0.706	415	32	2007
Lecture Notes In Computer Science	7	12	0.304	172	32	2001
Expert Systems With Applications	5	6	0.333	96	6	2009
Acm International Conference Proceeding Series	4	8	0.222	65	9	2006
Computational Economics	4	5	0.667	33	6	2018
International Journal Of Theoretical And Applied Finance	4	5	0.2	64	5	2004
Journal Of Complexity	4	4	0.19	89	4	2003
Journal Of Economic Dynamics And Control	4	4	0.167	483	4	2000
Monte Carlo Methods And Applications	4	5	0.286	48	5	2010
2008 Workshop On High Performance Computational Finance, Whpcf 2008	3	3	0.188	57	3	2008

4.1.2. Most relevant Authors

In this section, we highlighted, the core authors who contributed significantly to computational Finance in the computer, environmental, and social sciences. Authors are graded according to total publications.

The most number of publications is done by Oosterlee CW, with 12 publication followed by Xiong X with 11 publication and Zhang Y with 10 publications.

Figure 2. Most relevant authors

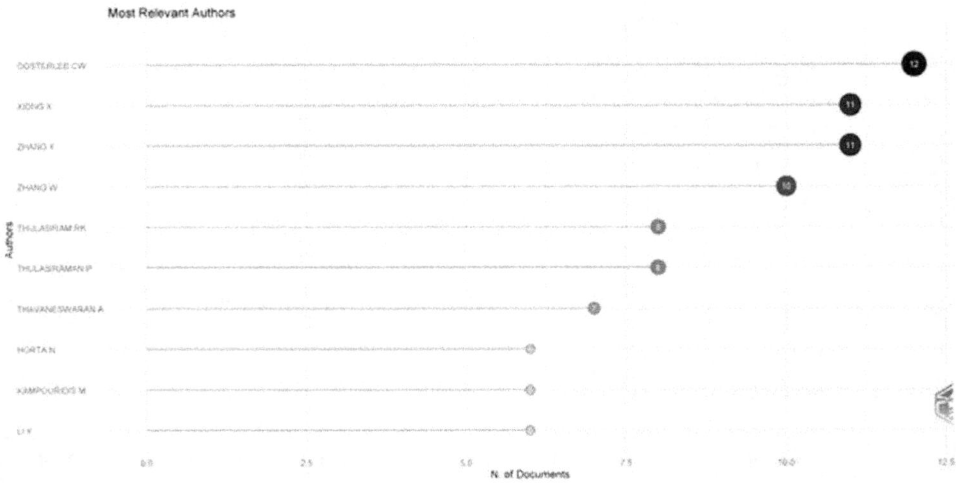

4.1.3. Influential Countries

Referring to Figure-3, the United States and the United Kingdom emerge as frontrunners in citation frequency. Notably, the United States boasts upwards of 850 citations, surpassing the United Kingdom's count by 22%. Additionally, the United States has produced some of the most compelling and frequently cited research in the field of financial technology, amassing a total of 855 citations. Singapore follows with a significant 477 citations, and Canada contributes 259 citations. Although the United Kingdom ranks third in the volume of publications, its scholarly work has garnered 394 citations. China and Germany claim the fourth and fifth spots, respectively, in citation rankings. Meanwhile, Portugal and Australia round out the list with the fewest number of citations.

Figure 3. Influential countries

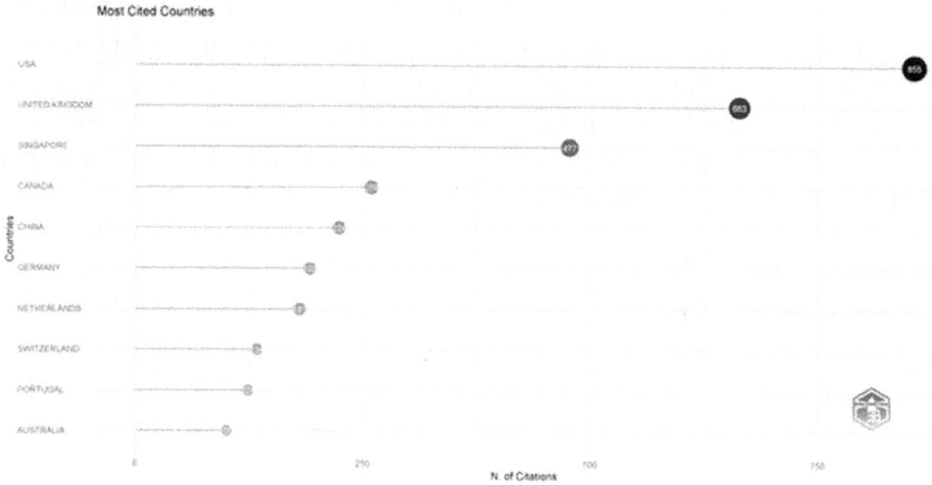

Table 2. Trending Topics

Particulars	freq	year_q1	year_med	year_q3
investments	52	2014	2018	2020
forecasting	35	2014	2018	2021
learning algorithms	12	2014	2018	2021
machine learning	16	2019	2020	2020
deep learning	10	2021	2022	2023
long short-term memory	8	2020	2022	2023

4.1.4 Thematic Map

In our research, we use a thematic map to categorize research topics based on four distinct quadrants. This classification, as outlined by Nasir and colleagues, relies on two key parameters: centrality and density. Centrality refers to the abundance of research within a particular theme, while density indicates the significance of that theme. The first quadrant highlights themes characterized by both low centrality and low density. Such themes are often in their nascent stages, evolving, or just emerging due to their limited research volume and importance. The second quadrant encompasses foundational themes that have a substantial volume of work (high centrality) but are not as crucial (low density). The third quadrant includes vital themes that, despite their importance, have not seen extensive research. These areas warrant significant discussion as they hold the potential to guide future research directions. Finally, the fourth quadrant contains themes that score high in both centrality and density.

Themes related to financial industry, digital economy, and internet of things, fall into the first quadrant. They are marked by both low centrality and density, indicating that they are either burgeoning areas likely to shape future research agendas or may fade from scholarly discussions in the future.

Figure 4. Thematic map

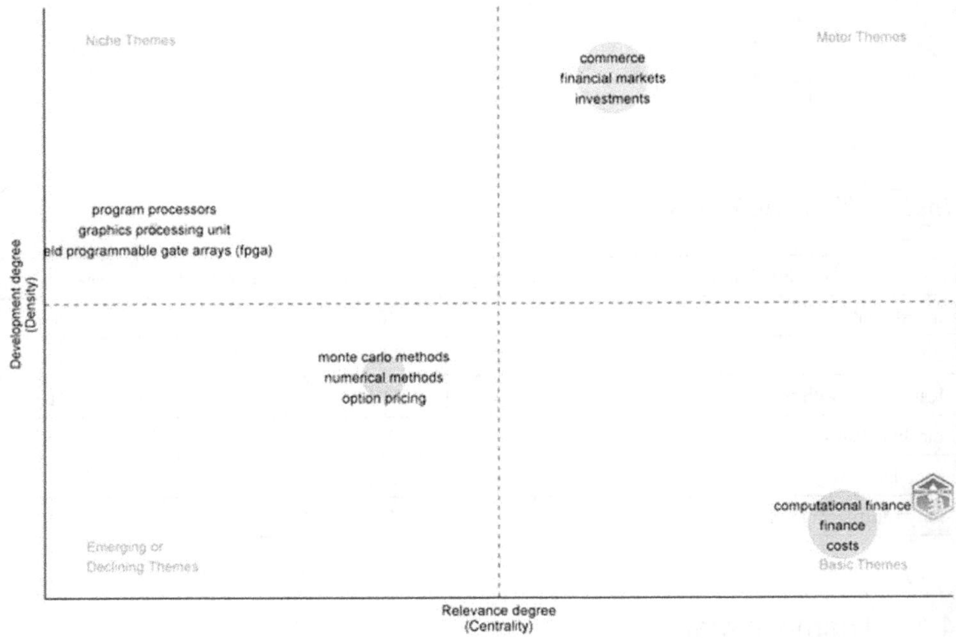

4.1.5 Keyword Analysis

Keywords play a pivotal role in literature search, and this is particularly true in the context of fintech research. Our study has identified critical keywords in this domain, which we've visually represented as word clouds in Figure 5. While 'fintech' itself is a primary keyword, our research delves deeper into other keywords that encapsulate a range of topics and fields. In the abstracts of fintech-related studies, 'financial' emerges as a frequently used term, often in conjunction with topics like technology, market, and blockchain.

The combination of keywords and authorship reveals authoritative topics within fintech, including financial services, investments, financial markets, artificial intelligence, blockchain, and electronic trading and commerce. Beyond this, the keywords alone also bring forth thematic topics in the field, like financial inclusion, financial technology, machine learning, blockchain technologies, fintech innovation and cryptocurrency.

Our findings indicate that author-specified keywords are more indicative of significant and authentic topics in fintech compared to other sources. These keywords encompass and scrutinize a broad spectrum of fintech subjects. By analyzing these author-designated keywords, one can identify and propose important themes and trends in fintech that span across computer, environmental and social sciences.

Figure 5. Keyword analysis

5. FUTURE RESEARCH

The study of fintech literature reveals key areas ripe for further investigation. Here are several suggestions for researchers, policy makers, educators, and IT professionals:

- Explore and apply diverse crowdfunding methods, including blockchain and bitcoin investments, while ensuring they adhere to appropriate regulations, to finance a variety of new ventures.
- Investigate the constraints and expand the scope of Industry 4.0 technologies, incorporating elements like digital transformation, blockchain and internet of things.
- Utilize FINTECH (Financial Technologies) to advance sustainable development goals, leveraging its potential to drive progress in this area.

- Integrate FINTECH tools within Islamic banking space to transform Islamic financial instruments such as Mudarabah, Musharakah, etc.
- In the development of fintech models and applications, particularly in blockchain technology, ensure adherence to standardized recording, reporting, and disclosure requirements for companies. This includes technological advancements in corporate governance-related documentation.

These recommendations aim to guide further exploration and implementation in the evolving field of financial technology.

6. CONCLUSION

The study indicates that fintech stands at the forefront of future business, economic progress, and technological advancements, and offers potential benefits for environmental conservation. Our exploration of the past decade's fintech literature has highlighted its key facets and influential elements. We've identified fundamental contributors to fintech's growing body of knowledge, noting the recent surge in related studies. Amongst these, "Quantitative Finance" emerges as the primary source of Computational finance literature, while "Electronic commerce research and applications" has the most significant impact within this domain. Oosterlee CW stands out as the most published author in the realm of Computational finance.

When we look at contributions by country, the USA, UK, and Canada emerge as top contributors, with the USA leading both in solo and collaborative publications. Our analysis also includes a co-occurrence network and thematic map that delve into the conceptual side of Computational finance literature. This investigation has helped isolate three main research directions:

1. Montecarlo simulation intertwined with financial technology.
2. The relationship between financial instruments, markets, and regulatory technology (regtech).
3. The intersection of artificial intelligence, deep learning and machine learning, with finance.

To distill the extensive fintech literature, these streams provide a clearer lens. Our study also categorizes fintech topics based on their developmental stage: emerging, foundational, isolated, and pivotal. For instance, subjects like financial inclusion, cryptocurrency and blockchain, artificial intelligence, and big data-centric topics occupy a central position in discussions but are sparse, indicating they might be saturated areas of research. E-commerce, despite being a hot topic, is distinct due to its low centrality and dense coverage. Finally, areas like the internet of things, digital economy, fintech are both upcoming and receding themes in the literature.

REFERENCES

Aria, M., & Cuccurullo, C. (2017). bibliometrix: An R-tool for comprehensive science mapping analysis. *Journal of Informetrics, 11*(4), 959–975. doi:10.1016/j.joi.2017.08.007

Bhatt, A. K., Verma, A. K., & Gaur, R. (2020). Consumer Cognizance about Forex Card in Digital Epoch. *2020 International Conference on Computation, Automation and Knowledge Management (ICCAKM),* 493-498. 10.1109/ICCAKM46823.2020.9051547

Bose, I., Chen, X., & Wang, W. (2018). Enhancing credit scoring models with social network information: A survey and future directions. *European Journal of Operational Research, 268*(2), 626–637.

Erosa, V. E. (2018). Online Money Flows: Exploring the Nature of the Relation of Technology's New Creature to Money Supply—A Suggested Conceptual Framework and Research Propositions. *American Journal of Industrial and Business Management, 8*(02), 250–305. doi:10.4236/ajibm.2018.82017

Gandomi, A., & Haider, M. (2015). Beyond the hype: Big data concepts, methods, and analytics. *International Journal of Information Management, 35*(2), 137–144. doi:10.1016/j.ijinfomgt.2014.10.007

Kroll, J. A., Davey, I., & Felten, E. W. (2017). The economics of Bitcoin mining, or Bitcoin in the presence of adversaries. *Proceedings of WEIS.*

Kumarathunga, M., Calheiros, R., & Ginige, A. (2020, May). Towards Trust Enabled Commodity Market for Farmers with Blockchain Smart Contracts. In *Proceedings of the 2020 Asia Service Sciences and Software Engineering Conference* (pp. 75-82). 10.1145/3399871.3399891

Legowo, M. B., Subanidja, S., & Sorongan, F. A. (2021). Fintech and bank: Past, present, and future. *Jurnal Teknik Komputer AMIK BSI, 7*(1), 94–99. doi:10.31294/jtk.v7i1.9726

Legowo, M. B., Subanija, S., & Sorongan, F. A. (2020). Role of FinTech mechanism to technological innovation: A conceptual framework. *International Journal of Innovative Science and Research Technology, 5*(5), 1–6.

Li, W., Bao, R., Harimoto, K., Chen, D., Xu, J., & Su, Q. (2021, January). Modeling the stock relation with graph network for overnight stock movement prediction. In *Proceedings of the twenty-ninth international conference on international joint conferences on artificial intelligence* (pp. 4541-4547). Academic Press.

Martínez-Plumed, F., Gómez, E., & Hernández-Orallo, J. (2021). Futures of artificial intelligence through technology readiness levels. *Telematics and Informatics*, *58*, 101525. doi:10.1016/j.tele.2020.101525

McAfee, A., Brynjolfsson, E., & Davenport, T. H. (2017). Big data. *MIT Sloan Management Review*, *55*(2), 1–4.

Mougayar, W. (2016). *The business blockchain: Promise, practice, and application of the next internet technology*. Wiley.

Nasir, A., Shaukat, K., Hameed, I. A., Luo, S., Alam, T. M., & Iqbal, F. (2020). A bibliometric analysis of corona pandemic in social sciences: A review of influential aspects and conceptual structure. *IEEE Access : Practical Innovations, Open Solutions*, *8*, 133377–133402. doi:10.1109/ACCESS.2020.3008733 PMID:34812340

Nüesch, R., Alt, R., & Puschmann, T. (2015). Hybrid customer interaction. *Business & Information Systems Engineering*, *57*(1), 73–78. doi:10.100712599-014-0366-9

Oprea, S. V., Bâra, A., & Andreescu, A. I. (2020). Two novel blockchain-based market settlement mechanisms embedded into smart contracts for securely trading renewable energy. *IEEE Access : Practical Innovations, Open Solutions*, *8*, 212548–212556. doi:10.1109/ACCESS.2020.3040764

Paulson-Luna, M., & Reily, K. (2020, May). The Financial Derivative Ecosystem is Old-Decentralized Ledger Technology is its Fountain of Youth. In *Proceedings of the 2020 Asia Service Sciences and Software Engineering Conference* (pp. 105-112). 10.1145/3399871.3399904

Puschmann, T. (2017). Fintech. *Business & Information Systems Engineering*, *59*(1), 69–76. doi:10.100712599-017-0464-6

Rabhi, F. A., Mehandjiev, N., & Baghdadi, A. (2020). State-of-the-art in applying machine learning to electronic trading. In *Enterprise Applications, Markets and Services in the Finance Industry: 10th International Workshop, FinanceCom 2020, Helsinki, Finland, August 18, 2020, Revised Selected Papers 10* (pp. 3-20). Springer International Publishing. 10.1007/978-3-030-64466-6_1

Reepu, T. S., & Singh, A. (2023). *Context aware computing. In Big Data: A Road-Map for Successful Digital Marketing*. Nova Science Publishers, Inc. https://www.scopus.com/inward/record.uri?eid=2-s2.0-85172698675&partnerID=40&md5=dfe437743a3d43d55acac9e4849f23f7

Salameh, A., & Bass, J. M. (2020, April). Heterogeneous tailoring approach using the spotify model. In *Proceedings of the 24th International Conference on Evaluation and Assessment in Software Engineering* (pp. 293-298). 10.1145/3383219.3383251

Singh, A., Sharma, S., Singh, A., Unanoğlu, M., & Taneja, S. (2023). Preface. In *Cultural Marketing and Metaverse for Consumer Engagement*. IGI Global. https://www.scopus.com/inward/record.uri?eid=2-s2.0-85162657422&partnerID=40&md5=1490c94e51004158cb0b33e2dffedda8 doi:10.4018/978-1-6684-8312-1

Taneja, S., Dangwal, A., Kaur, S., Ozen, E., & Kukreti, M. (2023). An evaluation of the operational and regulatory aspects of using blockchain in the insurance industry. In *The Application of Emerging Technology and Blockchain in the Insurance Industry*. River Publishers. https://www.scopus.com/inward/record.uri?eid=2-s2.0-85175665567&partnerID=40&md5=fa6499e497e6fb8a5f1510ffccd27bb6

Veilleux, M., Sénécal, S., Demolin, B., Bouvier, F., Di Fabio, M. L., Coursaris, C., & Léger, P. M. (2020). Visualizing a user's cognitive and emotional journeys: A fintech case. *Design, User Experience, and Usability. Interaction Design: 9th International Conference, DUXU 2020, Held as Part of the 22nd HCI International Conference, HCII 2020, Copenhagen, Denmark, July 19–24, 2020 Proceedings, 22*(Part I), 549–566.

Yadav, N., Taneja, S., Özen, E., Singh, A. B., & Vida, I. (2023). A Bibliometric Survey on Sustainable Finance: Research Patterns and Trends. *Acta Polytechnica Hungarica, 20*(10), 109–125. doi:10.12700/APH.20.10.2023.10.7

Chapter 10
Organizational Citizenship Behavior and Employee Retention

Shaina Arora
Chandigarh University, India

Nilesh Arora
https://orcid.org/0000-0002-8901-2205
Chandigarh University, India

ABSTRACT

The study measures organizational citizenship to retain bank employees. The banking sector is a crucial growth driver in our service-based economy. Young bankers work in a proper environment, so they can handle their obligations and responsibilities successfully. Banks plan a large functional outlay based on growth, retention, and performance. This study collected data from 322 public and private bank employees using irregular examinations. Smart PLS Software 3.3.3 employed partial least squares for reliable review results. The model shows a positive relationship between employee retention and altruism, courtesy, conscientiousness, sportsmanship, and civic virtue. This study covered solely bank employees; thus, findings may vary. More research is needed to help companies retain top talent. Today, it's important to keep employees pleased and from looking elsewhere. Retention and organizational citizenship increase representational performance. The results show the impact of organizational citizenship on banking employee retention and performance growth.

DOI: 10.4018/979-8-3693-1746-4.ch010

INTRODUCTION

The term Organizational citizenship behavior (OCB) was instituted in the last part of the 1980s after modifications. With the progress of organizational citizenship behavior, and the study of various factors among employees' attitudes organizations are required to be conscious for employee retention and performance. OCB suggests whatever specialists choose to do, quickly and intentionally, which often lies outside of their predefined definitive responsibilities. Organizational arrangements incorporate exercises that merge task performance and contextual performance of the employees. Progressive development by analyzing job performance can be considered as a state of connection that people working in organizations. Business Organizations have come to comprehend those moral values and beliefs that are very important for the employees with respect to ethical means (Scott, 2002). Accordingly, businesses accept an imperative part in shaping the viewpoint of developing business pioneers who understand the need to focus not simply on maintaining the social and mental environment where the task and contextual performances take place. This change of focus is inciting the appraisal of what can propel Organization Citizenship Behavior (OCB) among future business leaders. Business specialists are getting pieces of information from neuroscience to grasp the justification for why outstanding leaders oftentimes make terrible decisions. In some organizations, there are risks of abatement in organizational resources like time, energy, the lack of work/work components, and nonattendance of monetary resources augmentation delegates' bet taking and push them to partake in Immoral behaviors (Elshaer *et al.*, 2022).

In view of blended thoughts, there is growing thought with respect to an element of investigation made under the heading of 'care' with inputs from Human Psychology, Organization Science, Education Science, and related brooks of data. The growing realization of OCB helps business managers to understand the interpersonal behavior skills in the organization (Dangwal, 2022). Employees are all around likely to perform better and go past their allotted tasks. Many employees are also ready to help each other in unbelievable circumstances also (Chandra and Mathur, 2021).

The extant literature emphasizes the phases and importance of organizational citizenship be behavior retention of the employees. Various constructs including altruism, courtesy, conscientiousness, sportsmanship, and civic virtue play a vital role with respect to a dependent variable which is employee retention (Paillé, 2013a). While the ways to deal with acting have been and will keep on being gigantic, there are changes in the work environment that could maybe modify what kinds of OCBs will stay tremendous for affiliations later on, as well as what sorts of chances for OCB exist for delegates (Harvey *et al.*, 2018). The commitment to the real approach can be fanned out in the improvement processes among embellishments, in preparing, rules, and blueprints (Rosario Núñez *et al.*, 2020).

This observed that organizational trust and retention depend only on the variables like altruism and organizational learning capability (Emilisa, 2019). It has taken only altruism as a variable of OCB to study their performance at different levels and ignored the other variables (Örtqvist, 2020). It is quiet about gender differences, and no examination has been done on contrasts in instructive capabilities and other segment factors (Mallick *et al.*, 2014). It considered only personal factors of government bankers (Sriboonlue and Peemanee, 2014). Therefore the current study reports the gaps in the study of organizational citizenship behavior dimensions where the effects have been studied with the focus on employee retention. In some organispect towardzations, employees also lead towards incentives for individual growth and development with the prospective to match their growth with organizational growth. With this, the OCB five dimensions identify the importance for employee retention and performance. Therefore, this study will analyze the impact of OCB measurements on employee retention.

This study is as important as OCB literature. It combines the factors of OCB altruism, courtesy, conscientiousness, sportsmanship, and civic virtue into a model to assess the impact of employee retention. The next part reflects the review of the literature associated with employee retention, OCB components, and the banking sector. Based on this, the research conceptual framework was proposed and hypotheses have been framed in the succeeding section. This is followed by the result analysis, discussion, theoretical and practical implications, and limitations of the research direction of the future study.

CONCEPTUAL FRAMEWORK

Organizational Citizenship Behavior

OCB is something like an unforced behavior that a person does out of his job. Every person is unique in their way depending upon their culture, values, ethics, trust, and many other characteristics. at the point when workers are given satisfactory administrative help, inconceivable sidekick relationship, and different evened out help, they will be more drawn in with the association and will, generally speaking, remain with a similar association for a long run (Kundu and Lata, 2017). Long-term success is the main aim of every individual and it could be possible with the implementation of OCB in our work for the sake of organizational growth and development as well (Gupta, 2023). The way that pioneers should depend upon a few subordinates for extra-authentic bits of the gig is exceptionally tremendous in times when the dynamism in the climate renders fixed work definitions unfit.

Simultaneously, secluding a work unit into close friends and out-pack individuals is stacked with negative results (Bhal, 2006).

Different Interpretations of OCB Dimensions

Altruism can be perceived with respect to psychology, human behavior, evolution, economics, and more (Saksa, 2015). Altruism also predicts unselfishness in the minds of the people (Duncan, 2004).It has also been portrayed that generosity is a rule that dependably thinks about the assistance to the co-workers in an organization (Yuniawan *et al.*, 2018). In like manner, the Altruism gathered can work with the withholding team and also helps in creating an amicable work environment (Organ, 1990). Courtesy alludes to the signs that assist others in withholding social issues back from occurring, for instance, giving prior warning of the arrangement for completing work to someone who is in a tough situation, guiding others preceding taking any actions that would impact them. This estimation is a kind of supporting behavior, yet one that attempts to hold issues back from arising. It also joins the word's demanding significance of being polite and sort of others stated by Organ, D. W. (2006).

Conscientiousness the most intense non-cognitive indicator of word occupational performance (Wilmot & Ones, 2019). This has been found in their examination that, principles was fundamentally identified with every one of the five kinds of OCB (Konovsky and Organ, 1996). Conscientiousness' alludes to optional practices that go past the essential necessities of the work as far as submitting to work rules, participation and occupation execution (Redman and Snape, 2005). Administrative assessments of execution were discovered to be coordinated by Altruism and Conscientiousness comparatively as by target work execution stated by (Lowery and Krilowicz, 1996). It states civic virtue is, to incorporate oneself carefully in and being stressed over the presence of the association (Borman, 2001). 'Civic virtue' alludes to practices which show a dependable worry for the picture and prosperity of the association (Redman and Snape, 2005). This contends that civic virtue was more confined in their association with legitimate sufficiency; for instance, the more the affiliation is amazing the chances of improvement of this social point are the most (Coole, 2003).

Sportsmanship was defined as being "a willingness to tolerate the inevitable inconveniences and impositions work without complaining" (Organ, 1990b). This states that extraordinary sportsmanship would overhaul the certainty of the work bundle and along this decrease worker turnover (Podsakoff, P. M. 1997). It's been depicted sportsmanship as the lead of liberally enduring through the aggravations that are an unavoidable piece of basically every authentic setting stated by Organ (1988).

Employee Retention

Human resource management considerations like efficient effective leadership, profiling of employees, good correspondence will ultimately lead to strategic financial achievements that result in retention of the employees in an organization (Munish & Agarwal, 2017). Anyway, the term expert help is depicted in various ways, it fundamentally infers that different measures are taken by relationship to animate its representative so they stay with it for a more drawn out span (Singh, 2019). If people will find suitable jobs as per their skills, interest, and knowledge they are more likely to retain in an organization (Janet Chew & Entrekin, 2005). Retention of the employees can also be influenced by the capacity of organizations to keep their manpower for a longer period (Mishra & Sahoo, 2018). Employee retention can be portrayed as the exertion by a business to keep up appealing workers in charge to meet business objectives (Fredric D. Frank & Taylor, 2004). Environmental performance plays a very significant role in employee retention. Their exploration depicts esteem harmoniousness as a significant component in job fulfillment, representative maintenance, positive results, and improved execution (Omotayo Olubiyi & Melaragno, 2019). Therefore, Employee retention matters, as, progressive issues like getting ready time and theory, over-the-top candidate search, etc. are incorporated. Therefore, failing to hold a key specialist is an over-the-top idea for any affiliation (Mathimaran & Kumar, 2017). Employees always fear about their security and long-term success, so if organizations will help them in building up their strength then there are more chances to retain the employees in an organization. Human resources needs to move their fixation to the vigorous responsibility that diminishes the objective to leave and increases definitive citizenship conduct. Also, the connection between stacked with feeling commitment and self-assessed and peer-reviewed different leveled out citizenship lead were clashing (Lau et al., 2016).HRM practices under concentrate positively impact accommodating help of representatives, in any case, their master status: fulfillment with an aware and enabling workplace, fulfillment with preparing and improvement, fulfillment with innovative advantages and fulfillment with main impetus pay endlessly out increment significant upkeep of laborers.

Theoretical Framework

Organizational Citizenship Behaviour Theory

The current study considers the OCB theory to formulate the framework of the model. Presenting a theoretical basis to explain the constructs that were therein the previous parts as organizational citizenship behavior (OCB), as well as related structures like pertinent execution, are of late exceptional (Organ, 2005).In light of the conversation on OCB aspects, the idea of OCB has been enunciated. From that *point*, a host of forerunners for OCB was distinguished and equipped with these predecessors a hypothetical structure for OCB is proposed (Jahangir *et al.*, 2004). The continuous work becomes our thinking on OCBs that can occur outside the organization. These external approaches to retaining can influence organizational employees (Benuyenah, 2021).

A Valuable Involvement: OCB

One of the important segments of OCB is the path regardless of the way that it is consistently seen, perceived, and compensated by administrative staff.

As of now, the most notable assessments used to quantify OCB are found in the 5-factor model (Organ, 1988):

i. Altruism: to be supportive
ii. Courtesy: to be respectful as well as polite; forestall struggle
iii. Conscientiousness: accomplishing something beyond the base; scrupulousness
iv. Civic Virtue: showing interest and association (for example staying up with the latest) with the organization; shield authoritative arrangements and practices
v. Sportsmanship: enduring not exactly ideal conditions; tolerating changes and performing demands without grievances.

As an influence of OCB on employee retention that also supports social and psychological support system in relation to helping the business persons/managers/ leaders for knowing the Behaviour of the employees for design framework of job, allocating on position, retaining for the profile, role & responsibility to assigned one, etc. in regard of explaining the psychological context.

Formulation of Hypothesis

With this, the approach of OCB towards employee retention in organizations has benefits for social causes as awareness and shield from unemployment and efforts for economic growth. The level of increasing the retention rate depends upon the knowledge of the business officials to understand the psychology of employees and to put efforts into society for the growth rate. Below is a discussion of research conducted in this area, the theories underpinning the hypothesis formulated for the present study, and the model explaining how OCB dimensions impact employee retention.

Hypothetical Establishment of the Study

Altruistic Behavior and Employee Retention

The power of learning gets improved with the altruistic behavior of the employees in an organization. So in every sense, the altruistic behavior of employees helps them to retain them in an organization (Guinot *et al.*, 2015). Altruistic behavior leads to effective and kind leadership which will show a very supportive and optimistic behavior of employees toward an organization (Hazzi, 2018). Employees or workers with altruistic conduct help each other in the association which prompts a solid relational relationship that ultimately leads to the retention of the employees for a longer time (Olendo and Muindi, 2017). Selfless behavior of the employees also helps them to retain in an organization (Paillé, 2013b). Out of all the other measurements of OCB, altruism shows positivity with employee retention (Mossholder, 2005). In the study of Chen et al. (1998), altruism was most important which helps to create a coordination among workers, continuously prepared to help some assistance to those around the person in question, and eagerly gives of their chance to help other people who have business-related issues. Basic Leadership Skills for a Disrupted World looks at the basic authority ideas of Altruism, Compassion, and Empathy (ACE) (Jenkins, 2021).Toward the day's end, leader humbleness propels charity and, along these lines, firm imaginativeness which assists the employees to retain in the organization (Mallén *et al.*, 2019).

The above discussion signifies the hypothesis

H1 - Altruistic behavior of employees has a significant influence on employee retention.

Courtesy and Employee Retention

Results of Tian et al., 2020 show that employees' authentic graciousness or courtesy toward collaborators, considerably under the most tiring business or in hectic circumstances, which assists with upgrading OCB. Additionally, this examination expounds that if employees enthusiastically help each other then it will increase their retention in an organization. Courtesy is about preventing problems by recognizing choices that may affect employees in your organization (Farooq, 2015). Analysis of Deotale (2018) stated that courtesy is successful in generation of positive work environment where employees complain very less and that will lead to employees' retention. Employees exit insistently impacts data upkeep. Also, the definitive plan doesn't immediately let the employees to exit and helps them more in their retention (R. Farooq, 2021).

The above discussion signifies the hypothesis.

H2- Courtesy among employees has a significant influence on employee retention.

Conscientiousness and Employee Retention

Conscientious employees would go much above customers assumptions and would likely retain more (Koys, 2001). Conscientiousness will highlight the power of a relationship's motivating potential. High conscientiousness should help to amplify employee retention and work engagement (Gupta and Agarwal, 2018). Ethical people will in general be more engaged and objective-oriented, they may think that it's simpler to succeed. This could improve their retention (Jain and Rizvi, 2020). Conscientiousness leads to path-goal leadership in an organization which will benefit the long-term success of the employees (Hazzi, 2018). The supportive consequences of employees' support information were ensured to increase their retention. The employees who share things with each other and fit in the organization their conscientious efforts would likely to retain more (Esmaeelinezhad and Afrazeh, 2018).

The above discussion signifies the hypothesis.

H3- Conscientiousness among employees has a significant influence on employee retention.

Sportsmanship and Employee Retention

With the help of sportsmanship in the working environment, there are very few disputes between the employees and which a leading factor to retain them (Deotale, 2018) As per the study of Walz and Niehoff, 1996 sportsmanship leads to good financial results which makes organization employees happier one. Sportsmanship would establish a positive environment among employees that spills over to clients and employees (Koys, 2001).One huge outcome identifies with the part of sportsmanship in worker maintenance, demonstrating that employee maintenance corresponding to the business and the calling relies to a great extent upon the degree of personal resistance to extreme work requests (Paillé, 2015). Sportsmanship makes the work environment the best work environment for and helps in representative retention (Dash & Pradhan, 2014). Revelations of showed that the coordinating effect of quest for work on the association between capable obligation and mean to leave a calling is higher at a low level of sportsmanship and lower when sportsmanship is high (Paillé and Valéau, 2019).

The above discussion signifies the hypothesis.

H4- Sportsmanship among employees has a significant influence on employee retention.

Civic Virtue and Employee Retention

Civic virtue is the obligations of workers which he receives in its contribution in the association world of politics and leads to retention of employees (Farooq, 2015) Financial results ad satisfaction in an organization will get improved when employees perform civic virtue behaviour in an organization (Walz and Niehoff, 1996). Civic virtue does not let the employees leave the organization (Paillé, 2015) There is always positivity among the employee's and it reduces their chances to leave an organization (Popescu *et al.*, 2015). Civic Virtue practices show workers' interest and worry about the existence of the organization, for example, taking an interest in gathering and which will increase their retention as well (Kasinathan and Rajee, 2017).

The above discussion signifies the hypothesis.

H5- Civic virtue among employees has a significant influence on employee retention.

PROPOSED FRAMEWORK

Figure 1 presents the research conceptual model in this study.

METHODOLOGY

To evaluate the research results of this study, we have used primary data and worked on observational method of data collection. The research is based upon the empirical study and tries to find out the results based on some factors. These factors are underlying the areas of dependent and independent variables. A study of dependent variable is centered on Employee Retention and independent variable is centered on OCB – Organization Citizenship Behavior. In relation to analyze the study based on the hypothesis considering OCB dimensions – Altruism, Courtesy, Sportsmanship, Conscientiousness, and Civic Virtue. In order to validate the hypotheses, the following approach was undertaken: "Analyze whether the literature review supports the hypotheses. Data collection and contrasting correlations in between the variables suggested in the hypotheses."

Figure 1. Proposed model

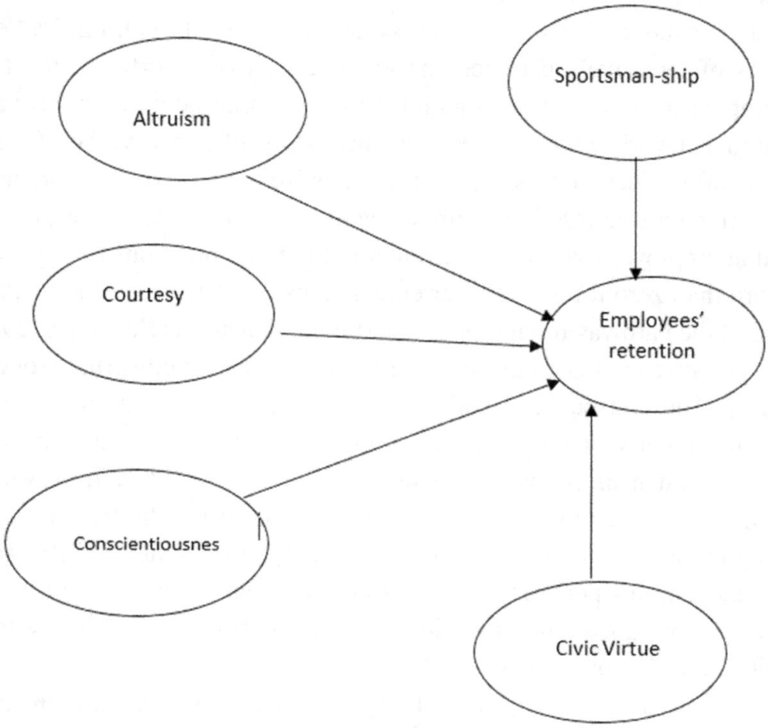

The study is based on primary and secondary data. This collection of primary data was performed in the following ways: The data were collected from top public and private sector banks of India, a count of 322 employees through a reliable source of online platform. And to obtain reliable results, structural equation modeling through the least squares method was used to evaluate the data (with Smart PLS Software 3.3.3).

An online review was finished with purposive sampling to gather information using a questionnaire. A 5-point Likert scale method is used to obtain the results of the questionnaire (1 = "strongly disagree" to 5 = "strongly agree").

RESULTS

From survey results of altruism, courtesy, conscientiousness, sportsmanship, civic virtue, it can be concluded that OCB leads to enhancement in retention of the banking sector employees. In this study altruism, and civic virtue is much correlated to the retention of the employees in an organization. This has also been identified that OCB is identified with the pursuit of employment and expectation to leave the business what's a more, expectation to leave the calling (Paillé, 2015). This focus of tentatively certified the great impact of assortment the board on agents' impressions of brimming with feeling a commitment to the affiliation and responsibility at work, which consequently decidedly influence workers OCB (Bizri, 2018). The aftereffects of this exploration likewise work on our comprehension of the connection between OCB and employee retention. In some studies, it is also not easy to that employees will leave or remain in the organizations (Parry, 2008). Q^2 value more than zero for a particular endogenous construct reflects the predictive relevance of the pathway model for that particular construct (Hair *et al.*, 2014). Our model has reported 0.421 as the value of Q^2 in the case of construct cross validity redundancy. The consequences of the conceptual reflection model showed that the relationship between employee retention and positive was found, and altruism, courtesy, sportsmanship, conscientiousness, and civic virtue played a very important role in employee retention. This examination is basic for the business world, is overseeing issues of holding the specialists which impacts their ability, worth and value. Organization's performance as a tool increases in regard of increasing the individual performance when individuals as an employees performing tasks at a satisfaction level (Gupta and Arora, 2022).

Table 1 shows the reliability and validity of model assessment interpret by Factor loadings, Average variance extracted, Cronbach's Alpha, Composite reliability, and Dijkstra and Henseler's RhoA. It has disclosed in a study that the minimum required value of factor loadings is 0.708 and all the factor loadings values are above the required value (Hair *et al.*, 2019). Also stated indicated that the outer loading of more than 0.50 is considered adequate for indicator reliability (Byrne & Fernald, 2016). The value of Cronbach's Alpha, Rho_A, and CR meet the best benchmark of 0.70 as suggested by (Hair *et al.*, 2019). The minimum requirement for AVE value is .50 (Fornell & Larcker, 1981b) Therefore our results also meets the threshold by Nunnally (1978) that Cronbach's Alpha values of above .70 are considered adequate and above .80 are preferable (DeVellis, 2003).

Table 2 shows that the entirety of the development meets Fornell and Larcker's rules as each build had a reasonable qualification from others. Thus, there is no discrimination validity issue. The study further investigated discriminated validity utilizing Fornell and Larcker's Criterion which expressed that the under the base of the AVEs of the inclining builds was higher than their between thing relationship esteems.

Table 1. Measurement model assessment: Reliability and validity

Constructs	Items	Loadings	Cronbach's Alpha	rho_A	Composite Reliability	Average Variance Extracted (AVE)
Altruism	ALT1	0.834	0.838	0.849	0.892	0.676
	ALT2	0.835				
	ALT3	0.897				
	ALT4	0.712				
Civic virtue	CIV1	0.824	0.864	0.865	0.907	0.71
	CIV2	0.849				
	CIV3	0.866				
	CIV4	0.831				
Conscientiousness	CON1	0.867	0.851	0.863	0.899	0.692
	CON2	0.852				
	CON3	0.858				
	CON4	0.745				
Courtesy	COU1	0.824	0.843	0.844	0.894	0.679
	COU2	0.867				
	COU3	0.858				
	COU4	0.745				
Sportsmanship	SPO1	0.746	0.807	0.83	0.873	0.633
	SPO2	0.844				
	SPO3	0.858				
	SPO4	0.728				
Employee	RET1	0.759	0.803	0.803	0.871	0.628
Retention	RET2	0.788				
	RET3	0.82				
	RET4	0.803				

Table 2. Fornell-Larcker

	Altruism	Civic Virtue	Conscientiousness	Courtesy	Employee Retention	Sportsmanship
Altruism	0.822					
Civic virtue	0.629	0.843				
Conscientiousness	0.503	0.611	0.832			
Courtesy	0.633	0.648	0.56	0.824		
Employee Retention	0.677	0.691	0.695	0.703	0.793	
Sportsmanship	0.61	0.619	0.637	0.61	0.686	0.796

Table 3. Heterotrait Monotrait (HTMT)

C	Altruism	Civic Virtue	Conscientiousness	Courtesy	Employee Retention	Sportsmanship
Altruism						
Civic virtue	0.738					
Conscientiousness	0.592	0.706				
Courtesy	0.757	0.757	0.658			
Employee Retention	0.81	0.826	0.835	0.843		
Sportsmanship	0.748	0.738	0.76	0.741	0.835	

Table 4. Hypothesis Testing of Relationships

Hypothesis	Relationship	Std. Beta (β)	Std. Error	T-Value	P-Values	Decision
H1	ALT-> RET	0.206	0.052	3.979	0.000	Supported
H2	COU -> RET	0.228	0.055	4.168	0.000	Supported
H3	CON-> RET	0.274	0.061	4.482	0.000	Supported
H4	SPO -> RET	0.154	0.055	2.806	0.005	Supported
H5	CIV-> RET	0.151	0.063	2.391	0.017	Supported

HTMT criterion has been used to evaluate discriminant validity. From the study of Henseler *et al.* (2015) and Rasoolimanesh *et al.* (2019) it has been analyzed that the HTMT ration should be less than 0.85. As per Gold *et al.* (2001) the permissible value of the HTMT ratio is 0.90. And our results that are shown in Table 3 show the relevant HTMT values.

Table 4 results revealed that ALT, COU, CON, SPO, CIV, has a positive and direct effect on d with. The p-value of all proposed hypotheses is 0.000 which is less than the required p-value of 0.05. The t-value of all proposed hypotheses is more than the required value of 1.96. Table 4 summarizes the results of hypotheses that revealed that H1, H2, H3, H4, H5 were supported.

Model

The conceptual reflective model shows the relationship of OCB constructs with employee retention. A total of 322 responses were received and used in a specific study using Partial Least Squares Structural Equation Modeling (PLS-SEM) in Smart PLS. PLS-SEM is considered the preferred strategy in this study because the calculated model includes altruism, courtesy, conscientiousness, athletic ability, civic virtue, and employee retention as dependent variables as OCB constructs. PLS-SEM in Smart PLS is a widely accepted multivariate analysis method as it offers greater adaptability (Hair et al., 2017).

Figure 2.

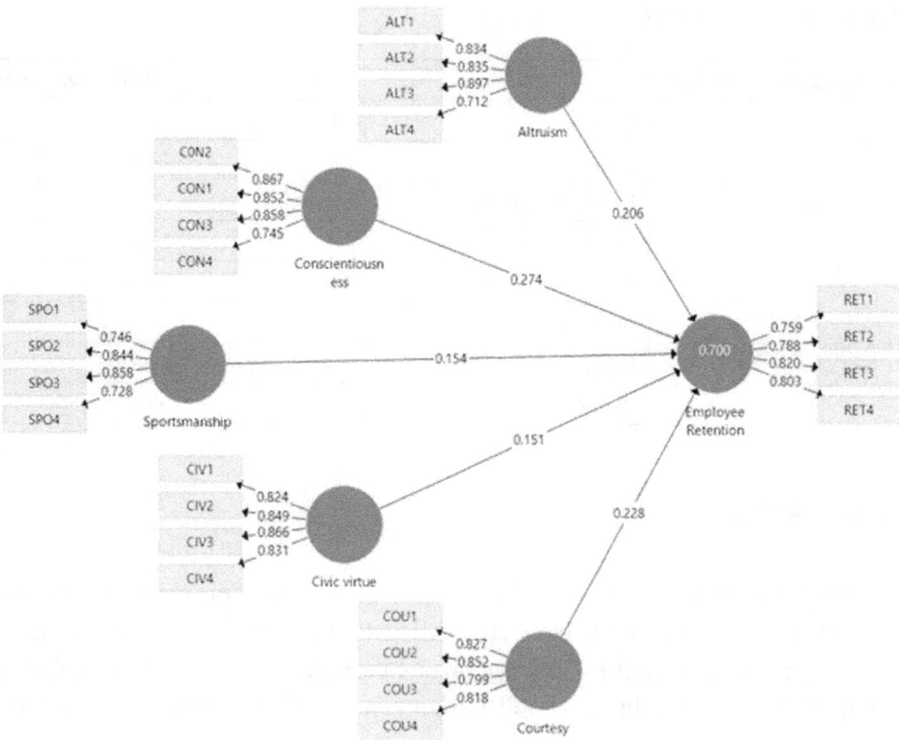

Model Fit Analysis

The admissible value for the SRMR index is between 0 and 0.08 as suggested by (Hu and Bentler, 1999) and as per our model fit analysis, the SRMR value has been tracked as 0.071 which is within the permissible range and which summarizes that model is fit. The R^2 value was, which was reported as 0.700 in the model and represents the intermediate degree of the dependent variable that can be explained by the explanatory variable. In many cases, the R^2 obtained for each intrinsic factor is greater than 0.1 and is considered satisfactory if necessary (Falk & Miller, 1992). In this study of PLS-SEM models, worldwide model fit files such as SRMR are essential to assess the integrity of the model fit (Hair *et al.*, 2020).

The demographic data included in this study are Gender, age, and type of industry shown in Table 1. It is to be interpreting from the table that the percentage of males was 75.16 and females was 24.84. The maximum of respondents fell under the age group of 21-40 years with 86.96% while 13.04% were under the age group of 41-60 years. Therefore, no respondent fell under less than 20 or above 60 years. Referring to the industry type 47.83% of the respondents as belonging to the public sector and on the other hand, 52.17% were from the private sector.

Table 5. Demographic data (N = 322)

Demographic Variables	Category	Frequency	Percentage% (100)
Gender	Male	242	75.16
	Female	80	24.84
Age	Less than or equal to 20	0	0
	21-40	280	86.96
	41-60	42	13.04
	Above 60	0	0
Industry type	Public	154	47.83
	Private	168	52.17

DISCUSSION

The aftereffects of this report show how OCB measures or plots emphatically affect worker maintenance in the financial area. All tests applied show very optimistic and convincing results. Structures are tested using complex system reliability, factorial loading, AVE, cross-loading, Fornell-Larker tests, and Heterotrait Monotrait Ratio (HTMT).

This describes that OCB plays a very greater role in productivity and retains more if employees foster some good attitude among themselves (María Zayas-Ortiz & Pablo Colón Gruñeiro, 2015). Those employees who are having an urge to go for organizational justice through their skills and knowledge will succeed in attaining competitive advantage. This discussed that motivation among the employees leads to satisfying jobs and which further results in an optimistic relationship with OCB measurements except for sportsmanship and civic virtue (Khadija Mushtaq & Warraich, 2014). It revealed that employees can support each other during their retention and which will lead to a reduction in the costs and higher profits in the organization, and for this employee, support is really very important and should be encouraged as a sense of responsibility (Azhagan & Thiagarajan, 2020). This identified the advantages of organizational citizenship conduct can be seen in usefulness, proficiency, decreased expenses, consumer loyalty, unit level turnover, and organizational effectiveness (Mahmood & Kareem, 2018). This will be helpful in employee retention and achieving a competitive advantage. It found that HR is seen as the main asset in associations have tracked down that the most significant factor and better playing out the allocated jobs and even extra-job obligations by HR is one of the genuine worries of the associations' directors (Khoshnammoghadam, 2017). Also recognized that transformational leadership is to be considered very effective in OCB (Almaqableh & Noor, 2017). OCB contains an introduction to help an outsider to get familiar with his/her character and the working environment, a partner who might be focused on targets, or electing to adjust changes. It revealed that OCB of bank employees shows a positive and critical impact on the authoritative execution, the board should consider the extraordinary consideration furthermore, treatment given to improve the recognized pointers that made the OCB variable and the hierarchical adequacy variable, to convey incredible assistance exhibitions to the bank clients(Das, 2020). The study revealed that includes work satisfaction and affiliation trust offer better citizenship direct grinding away by delegates (Habib-ur-Rehman Makhdoom & Khaliq, 2016). It stated that the bank employees need to stay with the bank and feel genuinely annexed to the work (Pahirathan, 2018). Most of the specialists show their tendency to spend the rest of the time with their bank.

MANAGERIAL IMPLICATIONS

The current scenario is expecting that many banking sector employees would like to stay in an organization if people will have OCB attributes. The importance of OCB has been revealed in this study. Once the employees have a better understanding of the factors, it will help them to build long-term relationships with a particular organization. The current research also suggests that it is very beneficial for the employees to follow OCB constructs which will increase their retention and also discovered that employee retention is strongly influenced by OCB constructs. Organizations work on the idea to be made to help the employees stay happy and don't look for a change. Execution of employee retention with the assistance of OCB estimations is a fruitful technique for guaranteeing that the crucial workers stay used while changing and keeping up work execution and handiness. Nobody can force anyone to adapt OCB; it is something internal and depends upon one's nature and liking towards work. Sometimes it is reflected by the time and with the characteristics of individuals. This is the reason behind recruitment of human assets in the organization instead of human resources and retaining them is again the most important task for every individual. In some organizations referring great employees also leads to generation of incentives for individual growth and development. Therefore, this study will analyze the impact of OCB measurements over the job performance ad employees' retention in Bank employees. Managers should make a conventional structure-wide assessment of the nature and kind of agents' OCB on Organizational obligation and occupation satisfaction, and subsequently return again to appropriate activities to work on here or continue to develop a by and large productive effort.

THEORETICAL IMPLICATIONS

The potential to contribute to a deeper understanding of Organizational Citizenship Behaviors and employee retention is the theoretical explanation for this work. The study is based on the "Organizational Citizenship Behaviors Theory". The study contributed to understanding the existing literature regarding organizational citizenship behavior measurements. The study demonstrates its greater validity by examining current trends in the field of OCB, its most important sources, authors, and articles, as well as contributing to the expansion of the literature. It also identifies the top nations where the majority of the research in this field is conducted. Employees must determine whether to accept OCBI that goes above and beyond their inherent responsibilities or required obligations. OCB is similar to unintentional conduct that someone engages in while at work. Depending on their culture, morals, ethics, trust, and many other qualities, each individual is different in their own particular way. Numerous academics have also observed that employees' uncompelled or voluntary behaviors have a favorable effect on their job and context-related performances. Long-term success is undoubtedly the goal of every person, and it may be achievable if we adopt OCB in our job for the benefit of organizational development.

LIMITATIONS AND FUTURE RESEARCH

The present study explored the organizational citizenship constructs with employee retention. This study was based on banking sector employees only so results may differ in different service sectors depending upon their perception. This has also considered OCB to retain employees and future research can be done on how OCB can be used to improve the performance of the employees as well. As results have been depicted on banking sector employees only so results may differ in different service sectors depending upon their perception. More future research should be done to help the powerful nature of the employees to retain in an organization. The current research offers accept to understand further studies to use this model and to take different facets of OCB. Also, cultural aspects can have a significant influence on the nature and personality of the employees. Organizational Citizenship Behaviors can be used to improve organizational performance, trust, leadership, and many more variables. This study explored the organizational citizenship constructs with employee retention. The current model framework may be used as a structure for mounting added research studies, which can further discover the employee behavior in the organizations.

REFERENCES

Benuyenah, V. (2021). Theorising an organisational citizenship behaviour model for managerial decision-making: From history to contemporary application. *Management Research Review*, *44*(8), 1182–1198. doi:10.1108/MRR-07-2020-0422

Bhal, K. T. (2006). LMX-citizenship behavior relationship: Justice as a mediator. *Leadership and Organization Development Journal*, *27*(2), 106–117. doi:10.1108/01437730610646615

Bizri, R. (2018). Diversity management and OCB: The connection evidence from the Lebanese banking sector. *Equality, Diversity and Inclusion*, *37*(3), 233–253. doi:10.1108/EDI-03-2017-0059

Chandra, Y., & Mathur, K. (2021). Organization Citizenship Behaviour and Work-Life Interface Practices: Exploring Entrepreneurial and Intrapreneurial Mindset. *Vision: The Journal of Business Perspective*, *25*(3), 361–372. doi:10.1177/09722629211010980

Chen, X., Hui, C., & Sego, D. J. (1998). The role of Organizational Citizenship Behavior in Turnover. *The Journal of Applied Psychology*, *83*(December), 922–931. doi:10.1037/0021-9010.83.6.922

Dangwal, A., Kaur, S., Taneja, S., & Ozen, E. (2022). A Bibliometric Analysis of Green Tourism Based on the Scopus Platform. In Developing Relationships, Personalization, and Data Herald in Marketing 5.0 (pp. 242-255). IGI Global. doi:10.4018/978-1-6684-4496-2.ch015

Dash, S., & Pradhan, R. K. (2014). Determinants and consequences of Organizational Citizenship Behavior: A Theoretical Framework for Indian Manufacturing Organisations. *International Journal of Business and Management Invention, 3*(1), 17–27.

Deotale, M. (2018). *Analytical study on impact of Organisational Citizenship Behaviour on Retention of employees working in IT industry*. Academic Press.

Duncan, B. (2004). A theory of impact philanthropy. *Journal of Public Economics, 88*(9–10), 2159–2180. doi:10.1016/S0047-2727(03)00037-9

Elshaer, I. A., Azazz, A. M. S., & Saad, S. K. (2022). Unethical Organization Behavior: Antecedents and Consequences in the Tourism Industry. *International Journal of Environmental Research and Public Health, 19*(9), 4972. doi:10.3390/ijerph19094972 PMID:35564367

Emilisa, N. (2019). *The Role of Altruism, Organizational Learning Capability and Organizational Trust: A Study from Online Motorcycle Drivers in Jakarta*. Available at: www.money.id

Esmaeelinezhad, O., & Afrazeh, A. (2018). Linking personality traits and individuals' knowledge management behavior. *Aslib Journal of Information Management, 70*(3), 234–251. doi:10.1108/AJIM-01-2018-0019

Farooq, K. (2015). Organization Citizenship Behaviour a Key for Employee Retention: An Empirical Investigation from Systematic Institutional Industry Pakistan. *Journal of Political Sciences & Public Affairs, 03*(02). Advance online publication. doi:10.4172/2332-0761.1000151

Farooq, R. (2021). Employee exit and its relationship with multidimensional knowledge retention: The moderating role of organizational structure. *VINE Journal of Information and Knowledge Management Systems*. Advance online publication. doi:10.1108/VJIKMS-06-2021-0093

Gold, A. H., Malhotra, A., & Segars, A. H. (2001). Knowledge management: An organizational capabilities perspective. *Journal of Management Information Systems, 18*(1), 185–214. doi:10.1080/07421222.2001.11045669

Guinot, J., Chiva, R., & Mallén, F. (2015). The effects of altruism and relationship conflict on organizational learning. *International Journal of Conflict Management, 26*(1), 85–112.

Gupta, M., Arora, R., & Taneja, S. (2023). Bibliometric Analysis on Employee Engagement and Human Resource Management. In Enhancing Customer Engagement Through Location-Based Marketing (pp. 185-205). IGI Global. doi:10.4018/978-1-6684-8177-6.ch013

Gupta, S., & Arora, N. (2022). Quality Management Practices and Organisational Performance A Study of Indian Manufacturing Organisations. *International Journal of Business and Globalisation, 1*(1), 1. doi:10.1504/IJBG.2022.10044486

Gupta, V., & Agarwal, U. A. (2018). Relationships between job characteristics, work engagement, conscientiousness and managers' turnover intentions: A moderated-mediation analysis. *Personnel Review.*

Hair, J.F., Howard, M.C., & Nitzl, C. (2020). Assessing measurement model quality in PLS-SEM using confirmatory composite analysis. *Journal of Business Research, 109*, 101–110.

Hair, J. F., Hult, G. T. M., Ringle, C. M., & Sarstedt, M. (2017). *A Primer on Partial Least Squares Structural Equation Modeling (PLS-SEM)*. Sage.

Hair, J.F., Risher, J.J., Sarstedt, M., & Ringle, C.M. (2019). When to use and how to report the results of PLS-SEM. *European Business Review.*

Hair, J. F., Sarstedt, M., Hopkins, L., & Kuppelwieser, V. G. (2014). Partial least squares structural equation modeling (PLS-SEM): An emerging tool in business research. *European Business Review, 26*(2), 106–121. doi:10.1108/EBR-10-2013-0128

Harvey, J., Bolino, M. C., & Kelemen, T. K. (2018). Organizational Citizenship Behavior in the 21 st Century: How Might Going the Extra Mile Look Different at the Start of the New Millennium? Academic Press.

Hazzi, O. A. (2018). Organizational Citizenship Behavior: A Holistic Review. Global Encyclopedia of Public Administration, Public Policy, and Governance, 1–12.

Henseler, J., Ringle, C. M., & Sarstedt, M. (2015). A new criterion for assessing discriminant validity in variance-based structural equation modeling. *Journal of the Academy of Marketing Science, 43*(1), 115–135. doi:10.100711747-014-0403-8

Hu, L. T., & Bentler, P. M. (1999). Cutoff criteria for fit indexes in covariance structure analysis: Conventional criteria versus new alternatives. *Structural Equation Modeling*, *6*(1), 1–55. doi:10.1080/10705519909540118

Jahangir, N., Akbar, M. M., & Haq, M. (2004). *Organizational citizenship behavior: Its nature and antecedents. BRAC University Journal, 1.*

Jain, N. R., & Rizvi, I. A. (2020). Impact of Corporate Citizenship on Organizational Citizenship Behaviour of Managers: A Study from Selected Indian Banks. *Global Business Review*, *21*(1), 294–311. doi:10.1177/0972150917749289

Jenkins, M. (2021). Altruism in the Workplace. In *Expert Humans: Critical Leadership Skills for a Disrupted World* (pp. 85–100). Emerald Publishing Limited. doi:10.1108/978-1-80071-260-720211009

Kasinathan, S., & Rajee, M. (2017). Interrelationship among factors of OCB in Service industry with respect to Information Technology. *An Empirical Study*, *6*(4), 120–126.

Koys, D. J. (2001). The Effects of Employee Satisfaction, Organizational Citizenship Behavior, and a Unit-Level, Longitudinal Study. *Performance Improvement*, *54*, 101–114.

Kundu, S. C., & Lata, K. (2017). Effects of supportive work environment on employee retention. *The International Journal of Organizational Analysis*, *25*(4), 703–722. doi:10.1108/IJOA-12-2016-1100

Lau, P. Y. Y., McLean, G. N., Lien, B. Y.-H., & Hsu, Y.-C. (2016). Self-rated and peer-rated organizational citizenship behavior, affective commitment, and intention to leave in a Malaysian context. *Personnel Review*, *45*(3), 569–592. doi:10.1108/PR-04-2014-0083

Mallén, F., Domínguez-Escrig, E., Lapiedra, R., & Chiva, R. (2019). Does leader humility matter? Effects on altruism and innovation. *Management Decision*, *58*(5), 967–981. doi:10.1108/MD-11-2018-1180

Mallick, E., Pradhan, R. K., Tewari, H. R., & Jena, L. K. (2014). Organizational Citizenship Behaviour, Job Performance and HR Practices: A Relational Perspective. *Management and Labour Studies*, *39*(4), 449–460. doi:10.1177/0258042X15578023

Mossholder, K. W. (2005). A Relational Perspective on Turnover Examing Strucutal. *Pdf*, *48*(4), 607–618.

Olendo, O. P., & Muindi, F. (2017). The Perceived Relationship between Employee Retention Practices and Organization Citizenship Behaviour at D.T.Dobie (K) Ltd. *International Journal of Scientific and Research Publications*, *7*(2), 320.

Organ. (2005). *OCB in the Context of Organization Theory*. Author.

Örtqvist, D. (2020). Performance outcomes from reciprocal altruism: A multi-level model. *Journal of Small Business and Entrepreneurship*, *32*(3), 227–240. doi:10.1080/08276331.2019.1661616

Paillé, P. (2013). Organizational citizenship behaviour and employee retention: How important are turnover cognitions? *International Journal of Human Resource Management*, *24*(4), 768–790. doi:10.1080/09585192.2012.697477

Paillé, P., Raineri, N., & Valeau, P. J. (2015). Retention : Examining The Relationships. *Journal of Applied Business Research*, *31*(4), 1437–1452. doi:10.19030/jabr.v31i4.9329

Paillé, P., & Valéau, P. (2019). I don't complain, but I am ready for any eventuality. *The International Journal of Organizational Analysis*, *27*(3), 566–581. doi:10.1108/IJOA-02-2018-1351

Parry, J. (2008). Intention to leave the profession: Antecedents and role in nurse turnover. *Journal of Advanced Nursing*, *64*(2), 157–167. doi:10.1111/j.1365-2648.2008.04771.x PMID:18990096

Popescu, A. M., Deaconu, A., & Popescu, T. (2015). Organization's Age and Organizational Citizenship Behavior (OCB), Performance Criteria at SMEs Level. Case Study – Bucharest – Ilfov Development Region. *Procedia Economics and Finance*, *22*(October), 645–654.

Rasoolimanesh, S. M., Taheri, B., Gannon, M., Vafaei-Zadeh, A., & Hanifah, H. (2019). Does living in the vicinity of heritage tourism sites influence residents' perceptions and attitudes? *Journal of Sustainable Tourism*, *27*(9), 1295–1317. doi:10.1080/09669582.2019.1618863

Rosario Núñez, A., Marquez, E., Zayas, M., & López, E. (2020). Relationship between organizational citizenship and commitment in Puerto Rico banks. *The International Journal of Sociology and Social Policy*, *40*(7/8), 643–658. doi:10.1108/IJSSP-02-2020-0028

Saksa, J. (2015), *An Investigation of Research on Altruism in Recent Literature of the Three Sectors: Public, Private, and Non-Profit*. Available at: https://scholarworks.gvsu.edu/honorsprojects/556

Scott, E. D. (2002). Organizational Moral Values. Business Ethics Quarterly, 12(1), 33–55. doi:10.2307/3857647

Singh, D. (2019). A Literature Review on Employee Retention with Focus on Recent Trends. *International Journal of Scientific Research in Science, Engineering and Technology*, 425–431. doi:10.32628/IJSRST195463

Sriboonlue, P., & Peemanee, J. (2014). Personal-organizational factors, OCB, and job performance: The governance bank employees. *International Journal of Strategic Management, 14*(2), 101–110. doi:10.18374/IJSM-14-2.9

Tian, H., Iqbal, S., Akhtar, S., Qalati, S. A., Anwar, F., & Khan, M. A. S. (2020). The Impact of Transformational Leadership on Employee Retention: Mediation and Moderation Through Organizational Citizenship Behavior and Communication. *Frontiers in Psychology, 11*(March), 1–11. doi:10.3389/fpsyg.2020.00314 PMID:32256424

Walz, S. M., & Niehoff, B. P. (1996). Organizational Citizenship Behaviors and Their Effect on Organizational Effectiveness in Limited-Menu Restaurants. *Proceedings - Academy of Management, 1996*(1), 307–311. doi:10.5465/ambpp.1996.4980770

Yuniawan, A., Udin, U., Abdurrahman, A., & Suci, R. P. (2018). *A Systematic Literature Review of Altruism: Challenges* (Vol. 21). Outcomes and Future Research Directions, European Research Studies Journal.

Chapter 11
User Experience and Interaction in Information Applications:
Advanced Human-Machine Interfaces

Reepu
Chandigarh University, India

Sanjay Taneja
https://orcid.org/0000-0002-3632-4053
Graphic Era University (Deemed), India

ABSTRACT

This chapter aims to explore the advancements and potential of human-machine interfaces (HMIs) in improving user experience and interaction in information applications. With the proliferation of digital technologies and the increasing reliance on information systems, the design and usability of interfaces play a critical role in enhancing user engagement and effectiveness. This chapter investigates the latest developments in HMIs, such as natural language processing, gesture recognition, augmented reality, and virtual reality, and examines their impact on information applications across various domains. It also highlights the challenges and opportunities associated with implementing advanced HMIs and provides recommendations for optimizing user experience and interaction. The findings of this research contribute to the understanding of how information applications can leverage advanced HMIs to deliver seamless and intuitive user interfaces that enhance productivity, accessibility, and overall user satisfaction.

DOI: 10.4018/979-8-3693-1746-4.ch011

INTRODUCTION TO USER EXPERIENCE AND INFORMATION APPLICATIONS

User experience refers to the overall interaction and satisfaction that users have when using a product or service. It encompasses the emotional, cognitive, and behavioral aspects of the user's interaction with the system.

Enhancing user experience and interaction in information applications has become crucial in today's digital landscape. As more and more people rely on information applications for various tasks and activities, it is essential to ensure that these applications are designed in a way that provides a seamless and enjoyable user experience. There has been a growing interest in both academia and industry regarding user experience, as reflected in the increasing number of publications and companies transitioning towards user-centric design (Dabouis et al., 2023).

User experience plays a vital role in the success of information applications. If the user experience is poor, users may become frustrated, lose interest, and be less inclined to use the application. To address this challenge, advanced human-machine interfaces have been developed to enhance user experience and interaction in information applications.

These interfaces utilize innovative technologies and design principles to create intuitive, efficient, and engaging user experiences.

Factors Affecting User Experience and Interaction

Several factors contribute to the overall user experience and interaction in information applications.These factors include branding, usability, and the interface design (Fajar & Legowo, 2018).

Branding plays an important role in shaping the user experience. It covers all elements related to the design and visual aspects of a website or application. A visually appealing and cohesive branding can create a positive impression on users and enhance their overall experience.

Usability is another critical factor in enhancing user experience and interaction. It refers to the ease of use of the application and how well it allows users to achieve their goals. A usable information application is intuitive, efficient, and minimizes the cognitive effort required of users. Effective usability involves factors such as learnability, appropriateness, recognizably, portability, user error protection, user interface aesthetics, and accessibility (Brdnik et al., 2022). The design and interface of an information application also significantly impacts user experience and interaction.

The design of an information application includes aspects such as layout, navigation, typography, color scheme, and visual hierarchy. These design elements should be carefully considered to ensure that they are visually appealing, easy to understand and navigate, and enhance the overall user experience. In addition to branding, usability, and interface design, the quality of information provided by the application is also crucial for user experience. The information architecture and content design of the application play a vital role in shaping users' perceptions of the credibility and quality of the application. Users rely on accurate and relevant information to make informed decisions or complete tasks efficiently. Without accurate and reliable information, users may become frustrated or lose trust in the application, leading to a negative user experience. In addition to these factors, there are 'deeper' aspects that can also significantly impact the user experience (Gibson & Martinez-Maldonado, 2017).

Understanding Human-Machine Interfaces

To enhance user experience and interaction in information applications, it is important to understand the concept of human-machine interfaces. Human-machine interfaces refer to the means by which humans interact with machines, such as computers or software applications. These interfaces can be physical, such as keyboards or touchscreens, or they can be virtual, such as graphical user interfaces or voice recognition systems. Research has shown that advanced human-machine interfaces can greatly enhance user experience and interaction in information applications. Studies have shown that advanced human-machine interfaces, such as natural language processing and gesture recognition, can make the interaction with information applications more intuitive and efficient. By utilizing advanced human-machine interfaces, information applications can provide a more natural and seamless user experience. Advantages of Advanced Human-Machine Interfaces include improved ease of use, increased productivity, and enhanced decision-making capabilities.

Improved Ease of Use: Advanced human-machine interfaces can simplify the interaction between users and information applications.

These interfaces can eliminate the need for complex commands or navigation, allowing users to interact with the application in a more intuitive and natural way.

Increased Productivity: Advanced human-machine interfaces can streamline tasks and processes, allowing users to complete them more quickly and efficiently. For example, the use of voice recognition technology in a virtual assistant application can enable users to perform tasks simply by speaking commands, eliminating the need for manual input or navigating through complex menus.

Enhanced Decision-Making Capabilities: Advanced human-machine interfaces can provide users with more relevant and actionable information, allowing them to make better decisions.

For example, a weather forecasting application with an advanced human-machine interface could provide real-time weather updates, personalized recommendations based on user preferences, and interactive visual displays of weather patterns.

The Role of Advanced Interfaces in Enhancing User Experience

Advanced human-machine interfaces play a crucial role in enhancing user experience in information applications. These interfaces provide users with a more intuitive and seamless interaction, leading to improved ease of use.

By incorporating natural language processing and gesture recognition technology, advanced interfaces can eliminate the need for complex commands or navigation, allowing users to interact with information applications in a more natural and effortless manner. This not only reduces the learning curve for new users but also enhances the overall usability of the application, leading to higher user satisfaction. Moreover, advanced interfaces also contribute to increased productivity. By streamlining tasks and processes, these interfaces enable users to complete their work more efficiently. For example, a healthcare information application with an advanced human-machine interface can simplify the process of accessing patient records and inputting data, allowing healthcare professionals to spend more time on patient care rather than administrative tasks. Furthermore, advanced interfaces can enhance decision-making capabilities by providing users with relevant and actionable information. For instance, a financial analytics application with an advanced human-machine interface can analyze complex financial data and provide users with interactive visualizations and personalized recommendations for investment strategies. Overall, advanced human-machine interfaces are essential for enhancing user experience and interaction in information applications (Lehoux, 2004).

Current Challenges in Information Application Interactivity

Despite the benefits of advanced human-machine interfaces, there are several challenges that need to be addressed in order to fully enhance user experience and interaction in information applications.

One of the key challenges is the need to make a quantitative economic case for designing and implementing advanced interfaces.Prospective industry users of these technologies often require concrete evidence of the return on investment before adopting advanced human-machine interfaces. This notion has gained impetus over the last 20 years with the growth of information technology and research into Human-Computer Interface. Research into Human-Computer Interface has shown that a well-designed interface can significantly impact workers' efficiency. Additionally, the development of new industrial service solutions brings about the need for advanced human-machine interfaces. These interfaces should not only improve user experience and interaction but also generate affect, efficiency, satisfactory interactions, and guarantee learning processes in complex systems like industrial machinery (Zabalo et al., 2018). Another challenge is ensuring that human-machine interfaces provide information in the most user-friendly way possible (Kari & Steinert, 2021). Studies have shown that users' perception of an interface's usability and ease of use greatly affects their overall experience and satisfaction. To address these challenges and enhance user experience and interaction in information applications, researchers and developers need to focus on several key areas.

Firstly, there is a need for further research and development in advanced human-machine interfaces to ensure their effectiveness and usability.

This can be achieved through the use of advanced technologies such as natural language processing, machine learning, and data visualization. These technologies can enable interfaces to better understand and respond to user input, adapt to individual preferences, and present information in a clear and intuitive manner. Furthermore, the design of advanced human-machine interfaces should also take into account the specific tasks, goals, plans, and problem domain of the users (Hou et al., 2011). By considering these factors, interfaces can be tailored to meet the needs of users and provide them with the most relevant and useful information. Secondly, the evaluation of advanced human-machine interfaces is crucial in determining their effectiveness and impact on user experience.

Research Methodology: Studying Interface User Interaction

To study the user interaction with advanced human-machine interfaces, a combination of research methodologies can be utilized. One possible approach is to conduct usability testing, where participants are given specific tasks to perform using the interface while their interactions and feedback are observed and recorded. Usability testing can provide valuable insights into how users navigate through the interface, whether they encounter any difficulties or frustrations, and how effectively they are able to accomplish their tasks. Another approach is to use eye-tracking technology, which can provide detailed information about where users look and focus their attention while interacting with the interface. This information can help identify areas of the interface that may need improvement or optimization.

Techniques for Improving User Interaction

There are several techniques that can be employed to enhance user interaction in information applications through advanced human-machine interfaces. One approach is the use of natural language processing to enable users to interact with the interface using their own words and sentences. This can make the interaction more intuitive and user-friendly, as users can communicate in a way that feels natural to them. Another technique is the incorporation of machine learning algorithms to adapt the interface based on user preferences and behavior. These algorithms can analyze user data and make personalized recommendations or adjustments to the interface, improving the user experience over time. Additionally, the use of advanced visualization techniques can also enhance user interaction. For example, the incorporation of interactive and dynamic visualizations can help users better understand complex information and make more informed decisions.

Evaluating the Effectiveness of Human-Machine Interfaces

The evaluation of the effectiveness of human-machine interfaces is crucial in ensuring that they meet the needs and expectations of users. There are several evaluation methods that can be utilized to assess the effectiveness of human-machine interfaces. One commonly used method is user-centered evaluations, which involves gathering feedback and insights directly from users. This can be done through techniques such as questionnaires, interviews, and observations of user behavior. Another approach is the use of cognitive psychology and interaction design principles to evaluate usability.

Case Studies: Successful Applications of Advanced Human-Machine Interfaces

There have been several successful applications of advanced human-machine interfaces in enhancing user experience and interaction in information applications.

One notable example is the use of gesture recognition technology in gaming consoles such as the Nintendo Wii. This technology allows users to control the game using natural gestures, making the gaming experience more immersive and enjoyable. Another successful application is in virtual reality systems, where users can interact with a simulated environment using a combination of gesture recognition, voice interaction, and haptic feedback. These advanced interfaces have revolutionized industries such as architecture, healthcare, and education by providing users with immersive and interactive experiences.

CHALLENGES AND FUTURE DIRECTIONS

While advanced human-machine interfaces offer great potential in enhancing user experience and interaction in information applications, there are still challenges that need to be addressed for further improvement.

One major challenge is the development of accurate and reliable gesture recognition systems. These systems need to be able to accurately interpret a wide range of gestures and differentiate between intended user actions and unintentional movements. Additionally, there is a need for more research on the usability and user experience of augmented reality interfaces. To overcome these challenges, researchers and designers need to collaborate and continue to explore innovative approaches. Furthermore, the evaluation of usability and user experience in advanced human-machine interfaces is an ongoing research area. There is a need for further research to develop effective methods of evaluating the usability and user experience of these interfaces.

FUTURE TRENDS IN HUMAN-MACHINE INTERFACE TECHNOLOGY

Future trends in human-machine interface technology are promising and hold great potential for enhancing user experience and interaction in information applications.

One of the future trends is the development of natural user interfaces that rely on intuitive and natural behaviors, such as gestures.

These interfaces allow users to interact with machines in a more intuitive and seamless way, mimicking human-human interaction. Another trend is the integration of multiple modalities in human-machine interfaces.

This includes combining gesture recognition, voice interaction, virtual reality, augmented reality, and haptic interaction to create a more immersive and interactive experience (Deebak & Al-Turjman, 2021). By incorporating these different modalities, users can interact with information applications in a more intuitive and natural manner. Furthermore, the use of haptic interfaces is also a future trend in human-machine interface technology. Haptic interfaces stimulate the human senses through touch sensations, allowing users to qualitatively perceive and manipulate virtual or remote environments (Pediredla et al., 2021).

IMPACT OF ENHANCED USER EXPERIENCE ON INFORMATION APPLICATION ADOPTION

The enhanced user experience and interaction facilitated by advanced human-machine interfaces have a significant impact on the adoption of information applications. When users are able to interact with information applications seamlessly and intuitively, they are more likely to engage with and adopt these applications. This, in turn, leads to increased efficiency and productivity in performing tasks and achieving desired outcomes. Moreover, the enhanced user experience also contributes to improved satisfaction and enjoyment, which can further encourage users to continue using the information applications. ## Challenges and Considerations in Designing Advanced Human-Machine Interfaces Designing advanced human-machine interfaces entails various challenges and considerations.

One challenge is the need to ensure compatibility and interoperability across different devices and platforms. As technology advances and new devices come into the market, it becomes essential for advanced human-machine interfaces to be compatible with a range of devices and platforms. Another challenge is the need to provide a realistic and immersive experience to users. This can be achieved through the use of technologies such as computer graphics, virtual reality, and augmented reality. However, the insufficiency of rendering various haptic modalities can limit the realism and effectiveness of these interfaces.

CONCLUSION: ADVANCING INTERACTION FOR BETTER USER EXPERIENCE

In conclusion, advanced human-machine interfaces play a crucial role in enhancing user experience and interaction in information applications.

These interfaces, such as gesture recognition, voice interaction, virtual reality, augmented reality, and haptic interaction, offer more intuitive and natural ways for users to interact with information applications. Through the use of advanced technologies like computer graphics, virtual reality, and augmented reality, these interfaces provide a more immersive and realistic experience for users in virtual or remote environments. Additionally, the design of effective and efficient human-machine interfaces is essential for overall system performance, as it allows users to quickly understand and interact with the technology in a smooth and efficient manner (Hou et al., 2011). Moreover, the design of advanced human-machine interfaces must prioritize compatibility and interoperability across different devices and platforms to ensure that users can seamlessly engage with these applications regardless of the device they are using. Furthermore, the challenges in designing advanced interfaces, such as ensuring compatibility and providing a realistic experience, must be addressed to maximize the benefits of these interfaces. Through addressing these challenges, the field of human-machine interfaces can continue to advance and provide users with a more intuitive, immersive, and satisfying experience. In today's rapidly changing world, the significance of accurate weather forecasts cannot be overstated. Overall, enhancing user experience and interaction in information applications through advanced human-machine interfaces is crucial for improving the usability and effectiveness of these applications.

In conclusion, advanced human-machine interfaces have the potential to greatly enhance user experience and interaction in information applications.

By utilizing technologies such as gesture recognition, voice interaction, virtual reality, augmented reality, and haptic interaction, these interfaces offer more intuitive and natural ways for users to interact with information applications. These interfaces provide a more immersive and realistic experience in virtual or remote environments, improving the overall user experience.

REFERENCES

A methodology for creating intelligent wheelchair users' profiles(2012*Proceedings of the 4th International Conference on Agents and Artificial Intelligence*. doi:10.5220/0003749701710179

Brdnik, S., Heričko, T., & Šumak, B. (2022). Intelligent User Interfaces and Their Evaluation: A Systematic Mapping Study. *Sensors (Basel)*, *22*(15), 5830. doi:10.339022155830 PMID:35957387

Dabouis, B., Boccara, V., & Yannou, B. (2023). Retrospective coding of the ux design process for ux design enhancement in design agencies. *Proceedings of the Design Society*, *3*, 3105–3114. doi:10.1017/pds.2023.311

Deebak, B. D., & Al-Turjman, F. (2021). Digital-twin assisted: Fault diagnosis using deep transfer learning for machining tool condition. *International Journal of Intelligent Systems*, *37*(12), 10289–10316. doi:10.1002/int.22493

Fajar, A. N., & Legowo, N. (2018). Services modeling based on soa and bpm for information system flexibility improvement. *Iranian Journal of Electrical and Computer Engineering*, *8*(4), 2451. doi:10.11591/ijece.v8i4.pp2451-2455

Gibson, A., & Martínez-Maldonado, R. (2017). That dashboard looks nice, but what does it mean? *Proceedings of the 29th Australian Conference on Computer-Human Interaction*. 10.1145/3152771.3156171

Hou, M., Zhu, H., Zhou, M., & Arrabito, G. G. (2011). Optimizing operator–agent interaction in intelligent adaptive interface design: A conceptual framework. *IEEE Transactions on Systems, Man, and Cybernetics. Part C, Applications and Reviews*, *41*(2), 161–178. doi:10.1109/TSMCC.2010.2052041

Kari, R., & Steinert, M. (2021). Human factor issues in remote ship operations: Lesson learned by studying different domains. *Journal of Marine Science and Engineering*, *9*(4), 385. doi:10.3390/jmse9040385

Lehoux, P. (2004). Patients' perspectives on high-tech home care: A qualitative inquiry into the user-friendliness of four technologies. *BMC Health Services Research*, *4*(1), 28. Advance online publication. doi:10.1186/1472-6963-4-28 PMID:15462682

Pediredla, V. K., Chandrasekaran, K., Annamraju, S., & Thondiyath, A. (2021). Design, analysis, and control of a 3-dof novel haptic device displaying stiffness, texture, shape, and shear. *IEEE Access : Practical Innovations, Open Solutions*, *9*, 72055–72065. doi:10.1109/ACCESS.2021.3079175

Zabalo, E. A., Erle, G. L., & Gerrikagoitia, J. K. (2018). *Evaluating the human machine interface experience in industrial workplaces*. Electronic Workshops in Computing. doi:10.14236/ewic/HCI2018.93

Chapter 12
Assessing the Impact of Quality and Internal Control on Academic Institutions' Performance:
A Case of Study of HIBAG

Amal Slimani
Higher Institute of Business Administration of Gafsa, Tunisia

Ali Ahmadi
https://orcid.org/0000-0002-2170-941X
Higher Institute of Business Administration of Gafsa, Tunisia

ABSTRACT

This study assesses the relationship of both quality and internal control on academic institutions' performance by using a case of study of the Higher Institute of Business Administration of Gafsa (HIBAG). The study uses mixed-methods research approach, including surveys, interviews, and document analysis, and it aims to examine the current state of quality and internal control practices at the higher institute subject to study and their impact on its overall performance. The findings highlight that a solid quality management system and an effective internal control have a crucial impact on ensuring academic institutions' performance. The interviews conducted with the managers and the institute director revealed that the internal control system has helped to enhance the efficiency and effectiveness of the institution's operations. The findings of the study highlight the importance of quality management and internal control systems in enhancing the performance of academic institutions.

DOI: 10.4018/979-8-3693-1746-4.ch012

1. INTRODUCTION

Brain drain is a pervasive issue in developing countries, and Tunisia is no exception. In recent years, the country has witnessed a significant migration of highly skilled professionals, including doctors, engineers, and scientists. This trend has adverse consequences on the Tunisian economy and society, as the loss of skilled human capital hinders the country's growth and development. In this context, academic institutions play a crucial role in mitigating the impact of brain drain by producing highly skilled graduates who can contribute to the country's development. However, the performance of academic institutions is not only essential for addressing the issue of brain drain but also for ensuring their sustainability and competitiveness in an increasingly globalized world.

The performance of academic institutions can be assessed through various indicators, such as research output, student satisfaction, academic success, financial stability, and social impact. To achieve and maintain high levels of performance, academic institutions need to adopt a systematic approach that involves quality management and internal control systems.

Quality management refers to the processes and practices used by organizations to ensure that their products and services meet or exceed customer expectations. In the context of academic institutions, quality management encompasses various aspects, such as curriculum design, teaching methods, assessment, and student support. Implementing a quality management system can help academic institutions to enhance the quality of their programs and services and, consequently, improve their performance.

Internal control systems, on the other hand, refer to the policies, procedures, and mechanisms used by organizations to ensure that their operations are efficient, effective, and compliant with relevant regulations and standards. In the context of academic institutions, internal control systems can help to enhance the transparency and accountability of their operations, mitigate risks, and improve their overall performance.

In light of the above, this paper aims to assess the impact of quality management and internal control systems on academic institutions' performance, with a case study of a higher academic institute that has implemented ISO9001:2015 and an internal control system.. Overall, this paper contributes to the literature on the performance of academic institutions by providing insights into the role of quality management and internal control systems in enhancing their performance.

Academic Institutions (AI) play a crucial role in shaping the future of individuals and society as a whole. These institutions are responsible for providing quality education, conducting research, and producing innovative ideas that drive progress and development. The performance of educational institutions is, therefore, of great importance in evaluating their contributions to the advancement of knowledge and society.

This study will explore the different measures and indicators used to evaluate the performance of AI, including rankings, funding, research output, student outcomes, and impact on society. It will also discuss the challenges and opportunities faced by these institutions in maintaining and improving their performance in an ever-changing and competitive global landscape. Ultimately, this study aims to provide insights into how AI can optimize their performance and fulfill their vital role in shaping the future.

Main questions

How can we evaluate our AI's performance?

So, how can the AI enhance its performance?

And to what extent does the quality and the internal control contribute in enhancing the overall performance?

The rest of this study is structured as below; section 2 presents an overview of the academic institutions and there performance. The section 3 focuses on Internal control Quality in AI. The section 4 presents a case study of HIBAG. And we will conclude by section 5.

2. ACADEMIC INSTITUTIONS AND THERE PERFORMANCE

Let us first identify the AI and discover Tunisian academic system. AI are known as entities, which their main purpose is providing instructional services or education-related services. Merely, an AI is each institution that provides a large variety of learning-pace and learning-environment to individuals at different age ranges.

2.1. Tunisian Academic System

In Tunisia, the ministry of education offers the possibility of establishing a variety of types of institutions:

- Early childhood care and Education (ECE)
- Basic education
- Secondary education
- Technical and vocational Track
- Higher Education

According to the statistics of 2021, there are up to 6315 AI in Tunisia, which among them 1242 are private ones.

Academic institutions' stakeholders: Each AI treats with several stakeholders:

Students: They are the reason for the A.I's existence. That is why they are considered as the privileged or the primary stakeholders.

Alumni: Once they finish their education at the institution, they can become a source of support, advocacy and funding.

Faculty and staff: These are the critical stakeholders of A.I. Their responsibilities are delivering quality education, providing administrative support and conducting research.

Government: plays the role of a regulatory body, a funding agency, a policymaker, etc. since it fixes up academic standards, provides budget for educating...

Employees: They are the army of each A.I.

Parents: Parents are concerned the quality of education that is offered for their children. So, the always play the role of control.

Community: The environment surrounding the institution is also a stakeholder since there are exchanges between them. For example, institutions' operations have an impact on community. This last can provide for them resources and opportunities for collaborations.

2.2. Academic Institutions' Performance

Now, after treating each concept alone: 'AI' and 'performance' let us study the relationship between both of them, we will firstly discover what the indicators that allow us to evaluate the performance of one AI are. Then, we will give some tips that enable every institution to enhance its performance.

The Importance of Evaluating AI's Performance

The answer on the question: Why to evaluate our AI is the following:

Transparency: By evaluating AI' performance, a transparency would be provided to the public about the quality of education and research being conducted at an academic institution.

Quality education: Performance evaluation helps institutions to evaluate their teaching quality, curriculum, facilities, and student support services, then to identify areas where they need to improve. This information is beneficial in terms of taking data-driven decisions. By regularly evaluating their performance, academic institutions can ensure that they are providing high-quality education that meets the needs of their students and stakeholders.

Accreditation: Evaluating the performance of academic institutions is often a requirement for accreditation, which is necessary both for institutions where it can receive federal funding and for students who become eligible to receive federal financial aid

Accountability: Institutions that receive public funding or donations are required to demonstrate their effectiveness and efficiency. By evaluating their performance, all stakeholders can ensure that they are using their resources in a responsible and effective manner.

Benchmarking: By evaluating the performance of an AI, it becomes easy to compare it with other institutions, which can provide insights into best practices and help identify areas where an institution may need to improve. Moreover, comparison can add a competitive sense between different institutions. Consequently, each one will try to make an added-value comparing with others.

Continuous improvement: AI that evaluate their performance can easily pick out weaknesses or dysfunctions, identify areas for improvement and then make necessary changes to better meet the needs of their stakeholders. Evaluating AI' performance is crucial for ensuring that they are providing high-quality education. This task promotes transparency accountability, and continuous improvement and other benefits that are essential for meeting the needs of different stakeholders and maintaining institutional sustainability. We notice that evaluating the AI' performance have a plenty of benefits. However, the question that can be asked here is the following:

How can we evaluate our AI's performance?

AI' Performance Indicators: Evaluating the performance of an academic institution is a crucial process that plays such a significant role in ensuring that it provides high-quality education, conducts impactful research, and contributes positively to society. The evaluation it's a complex task that requires consideration of various indicators because no single indicator can provide a complete picture of that institution's performance.

Actually, AI have educational and research missions; they primarily do not focus on financial profitability. Financial indicators, mentioned above, are broadly used to evaluate a company's profitability. These indicators are generally not relevant for measuring the performance of an

The purpose and mission of an AI are different from those of a business. Therefore, performance indicators for an AI should be linked to its educational and research objectives. In fact, there are several critters can be used to do that task; they vary depending on the specific institution and its goals.

3. INTERNAL CONTROL QUALITY IN AI

In this section, we will explore the importance of quality and IC in AI, and how they affect the overall performance of these institutions. We will delve into the many ways in which quality and IC contribute to the success of academic institutions. So, let's dive in and discover the crucial role of these factors.

QMS is composed of three key words, which are:

3.1. Overview on Quality

Quality has become increasingly a key variable for all businesses that offer goods or services. ISO defines quality as "The degree to which a set of inherent characteristics fulfills requirements". In other words, quality is "a measure of how well something performs its intended function and how well it meets the needs and expectations of its users".

Therefore, quality is not only about meeting a set of features but also if these features meet the users' requirements or not. In fact, ISO is not the only one who defined quality, many authors talked about this concept. The most popular definitions are the following:

- "Constancy of purpose".
- "Fitness of use".
- "The degree of satisfaction of the customer".
- "Zero defects".
- The characteristics through which the service meet the expectations of customers,
- And so on

The common point between all of these definitions is that quality requirements vary according to the needs of stakeholders and especially customer' wants.

Relevance of quality: Both AI and its stakeholders, especially students are beneficiaries from quality.

Funding and support: Quality is closely tied to financial success since it enables AI to obtain funds and support from different stakeholders such as donors, government agencies, etc. Furthermore, institutions that prioritize quality usually tend to have stable financial situations.

Faculty recruitment: Top faculty members are a key-factor to the success of any AI. High-quality institutions can easily retain them to work for her profit in exchange for providing them with necessary resources and support to excel in their teaching and research.

Brand and reputation: Quality is the strongest weapon for an AI to build a good brand and to gain a respectful reputation. That is undoubtedly that qualified ones are more likely to attract students.

Competitiveness: Qualified AI that have a good reputation may remain competitive in an increasable global and dynamic educational landscape.

Research success: The most successful AI in terms of making significant contributions to scientific fields by publishing scientific papers and securing research grants by its researchers are those that invest the ore in quality research infrastructure

For students: Student is the first stakeholder who can take advantage from quality in AI since it directly effects his education, professional life and his career prospects.

Students' outcome: A good education from a reputable academic institution enables students to develop the necessary skills, knowledge and competencies such as modern technology to succeed their professional as well as their personal life.

Personal development: Quality education facilitates the growth of students' soft skills such as communication, critical-thinking, time and stress management, problem solving, etc., which are valuable for personal growth and lifelong learning.

Networking opportunities: Providing students with opportunities to interact with professors and professionals from their academic life, help them a lot to take advantage from their experience. Moreover, these connections can be a great chance that may lead to future job opportunities.

Further education opportunities: The reputation of an academic institution can also influence students' opportunities for further education, research or even studying abroad. None can deny that Students from highly regarded institutions are more likely to be accepted into prestigious graduate programs or secure research grants.

Employability: High-quality education can certainly give candidates an edge when applying for jobs. Usually, employers seek those who are graduated from well-respected institutions, so quality plays the role of guarantee that the candidate will succeed his job effectively.

AI that make quality on their top priorities are the most likely to have positive effects first on themselves because it directly affects their reputation and ability to attract stakeholders, then on their stakeholders especially students in terms of improving their education, personal development, career prospects and overall success in life.

3.2. Quality Tools

Standardization: Now, we will explore some potential topics or questions that can be asked about standardization in order to make it as clear as possible.

Overview about Standardization: By answering the following questions: What?, when?, why? And how?, we can easily build knowledge about standardization. Standardization is the process that consists on creating, elaborating, implementing and developing standards. It is defined, according to ISO, as a framework of agreements because each standard should be approved and adhered by all relevant parties. These parties can belong to an organism of standardization, government, businesses, organizations, etc. That is to say that this mission requires such a respectful level of experience and a high sense of analyze.

A standard: Typically developed by standardization organization or committee, a standard is a document, which describes a set of guidelines or rules, specifications or requirements. By covering a wide range of topics and touching all specialities from performance to designing information system to management of environmental resources, standards can be classified into three categories:

Legal Standards: They consist on requirements and guidelines set by law or regulations. Consequently, any incompliance can cause legal penalties, for example the food safety laws.

Technical standards: They specify the technical requirements and characteristics of products, services or systems. As an example, we can mention the ISO 9001 standard.

Industry standards: Developed by industry organizations, they define the best practice for a specific sector.

Social standards: Usually developed by non-governmental organizations, social standards focus on the ethical and social impact of products and services. For example, the labor conditions, etc.

Aims of standardization: By studying this notion and its types, we can pick out the basic aims of standardization, which are as following:

Quality assurance: Standardization plays on the cords of customer satisfaction since it helps to increase his trust in products/ services that are subject to the standards because these standards guarantee a certain level of quality.

Increasing efficiency: Implementing standards helps in reducing production costs and supply chains, which lead to the performance increase.

Environmental sustainability: Standardization cares a lot about environmental cases. In order to protect natural resources, it imposes such rigorous guidelines that impose a rational use of that natural fortune and a maximum reduction of waste.

4. CASE OF STUDY OF HIBAG

Before diving into the depth of this case study, let us first identify the methodology and describe the research design, data collection, and data analysis methods used in the study. We found that the perfect way to rich our goal is to adopt a mixed-methods approach, involving both quantitative and qualitative data collection and analysis.

- The quantitative method would involve *documents analysis* and a *survey* administered to a specific range of stakeholders. The survey would collect data on performance indicators such as productivity metrics, financial indicators, customer satisfaction surveys and other.

- The qualitative method would involve *observation* and *interviews* with selected participants to provide more in-depth insights on the factors that influence academic performance.

So let us first present the hero of our case study. Let us present first our institute subject to study.

4.1. Presenting the HIBAG

We will define it from different aspects, including:

Background information: Created in 2003 by decree number 2003-1663 on August 4th, 2003, the HIBAG is a public institution with administrative character, endowed with civil personality and financial autonomy. The supervisory authorities under which the institution works are the University of Gafsa and Tunisian Ministry of Higher Education and Scientific Research. The organizational chart is the following:

Figure 1. HIBAG's organizational chart
Source: https://isaeg.rnu.tn/fra/contact

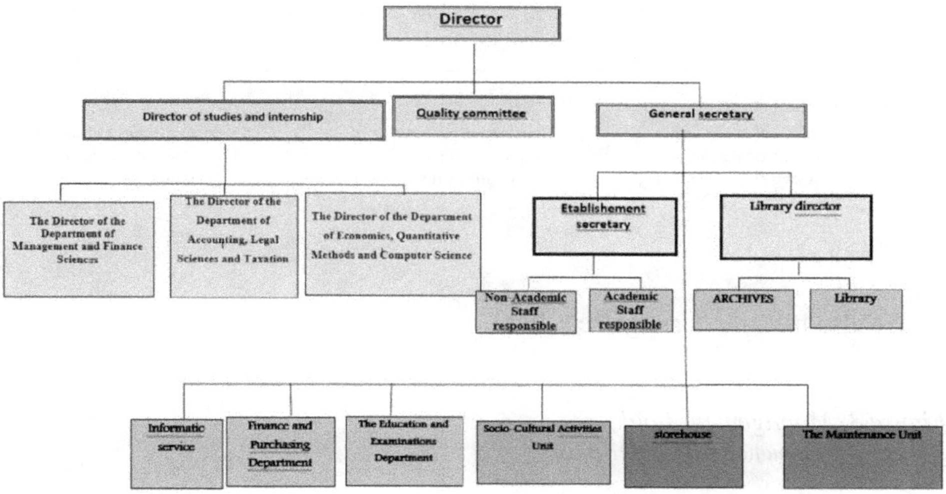

Here are the institution's contact details:
Address: Rue Houssine ben Kaddour Sidi Ahmed Zarroug - 2112 Gafsa
Telephone: 76 21 14 40

Fax: 76 21 14 50

Email: webmaster@isaeg.rnu.tn

Programs and courses: In the framework of the LMD system, the HIBA of Gafsa provides on-site higher education training leading to the obtainment of three License degrees, two research Master's degrees, and three professional Master's degrees as follow:

- Economics
- Management Science
- Computer Science in Management

In addition, the institute offers distance education in collaboration with the National Center for Continuing Training and Professional Promotion under the Ministry of Vocational Training and Employment, leading to the obtainment of two professional Master's degrees at a distance in the accounting Sciences and Management Science

The following figures clearly sum up the HIBA's programs and courses:

Figure 2. Business computing field
Source: Auto-evaluation report of HIBAG

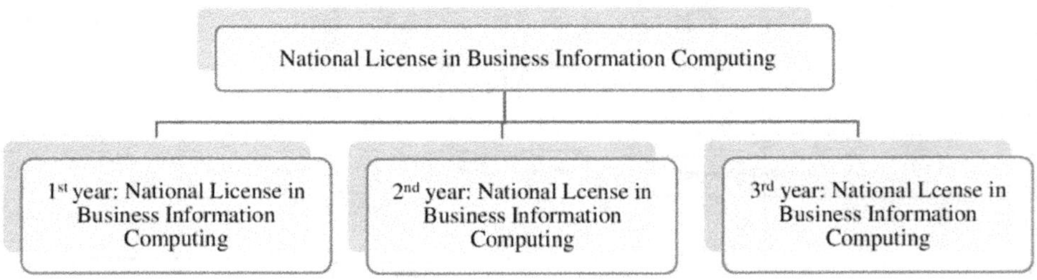

We also have the management field:

Figure 3. Management field
Source: Self-evaluation report of HIBAG

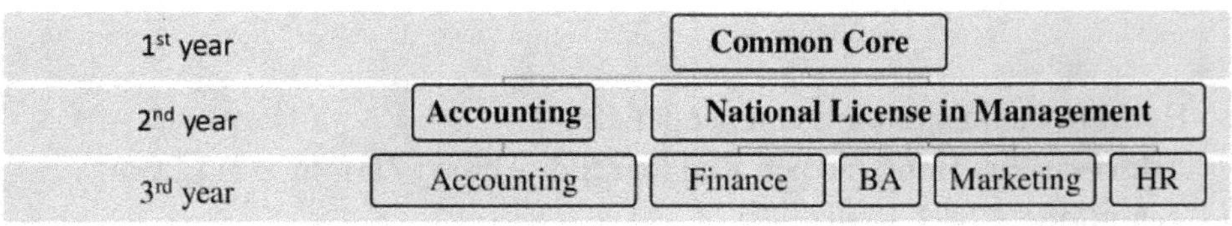

Then, we have economic field:

Figure 4. Economic field
Source: Self-evaluation report of HIBAG

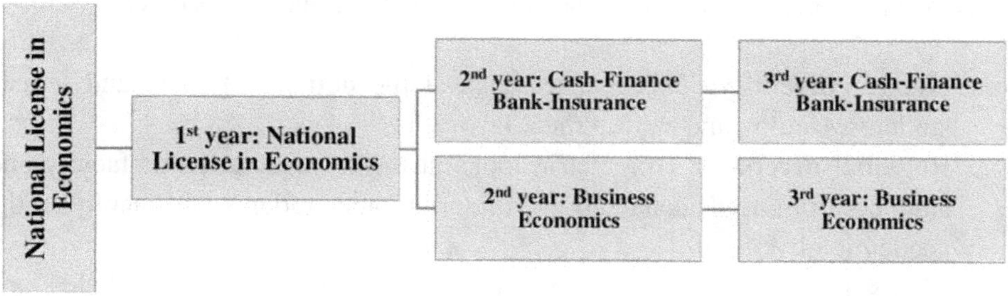

The institute provides a high-level scientific and technical education that is harmoniously developed across various fields including economics, management, and computer science. These specialties are integrated into different programs: money, finance and banking, finance, accounting, business administration, finance, marketing, and computer science.

Mission: The missions of HIBAG are:

- Contributing to the general dissemination of knowledge.
- Participating in the training of the necessary leaders for the development of the country.
- Providing high-quality education and training to students at the undergraduate and graduate levels.
- Conducting original research and contributing to the advancement of knowledge in various academic fields.
- Preparing students to become responsible and engaged citizens who can make meaningful contributions to society.
- Cultivating a culture of innovation and entrepreneurship that encourages the development of new ideas and technologies.
- Developing partnerships with other academic institutions, businesses, and community organizations

4.2 HIBAG's Performance Indicators

In this section, we will try to evaluate the performance of our academic institution subject to study. To accomplish this task, we will use several Keys Performance Indicators (KPI) to judge if this institute is a performing one or not.

Diversity indicator: Some of the common metrics that assess diversity are:

- **Gender diversity:** This metric looks at the number of male and female students, faculty, and staff in the AI.
- **Regional diversity:** This metric looks at the representation of faculty and students from all Tunisia and even international students and faculty in the academic institution.
- **Fields diversity:** when the institute offers a large range of fields and specialities in the same field, it can attract more stakeholders from faculty to students.

Faculty qualifications: To gather data about our institute faculty qualifications, we decided to make an interview with our institution's human resources department.

Table 1. Faculty number and qualifications before and after ISO 9001:2015 certification

	2021-2022	2022-2023
Faculty number	84	96
Certified Faculty number	08	48
Promoted Faculty number	02	04
Recruited Faculty number	00	14

Source: out-put of interview with HR' manager

These results show the changes in faculty number and qualifications before and after the ISO 9001:2015 certification in two academic years, 2021-2022 and 2022-2023. In the first academic year (2021-2022), there were a total of 84 faculty members, out of which only 8 were certified. Additionally, 2 faculty members were promoted during this period. After the ISO 9001:2015 certification, in the second academic year (2022-2023), there was a significant increase in the total faculty number to 96, which includes 48 certified faculty members. This indicates that the institution has made efforts to increase the number of certified faculty members, which is a positive sign in terms of meeting quality standards. Furthermore, 4 faculty members were promoted during the second academic year, and 14 new faculty members were recruited, indicating an expansion in the faculty base of the institution.

As a whole, these results suggest that the institution has made progress in enhancing the qualifications of its faculty and expanding its faculty base after the ISO 9001:2015 certification. The Resource allocation includes Student facilities, such as measured by the percentage of facilities provided for students such as computer labs, health services, and clubs. In fact, the HIBAG provide for its students, its faculty and its staff a well-equipped library, four computer labs, a share market room, a space for clubs and entertainment activities, a Wi-Fi system and a very well-equipped training room (4C).

4.3 The Impact of Quality on HIBAG's Performance

Now, we will examine the impact of quality on the performance of the institution subject to study. There are actually a lot of techniques that enhance quality in the context of AI. Thus, the HIBAG has engaged in more than one strategy to improve its quality such as ISO9001:2015 certification, PAQ-DGSE and PAQ-4C projects'. Indeed, and to examine the effect of quality on our institution's performance, we chose to talk about the ISO9001:2015 certification that it gained lately. That is to say that ISO9001:2015 is a QMS standard, which aims to achieve the stakeholders' satisfaction and to meet their needs and expectations. As known, all stakeholders are important but the privileged one for a high education institute is the student since it is the 'final product' of that entity. Therefore, the best tool to investigate about this topic is to conduct a survey about students' satisfaction with:

- **The quality of Education:**

The survey has shown the following results:

Figure 5. Student satisfaction
Source: Out-put Google Forms.

Results have shown that 63.6% are satisfied with the quality of education offered by the HIBAG while 9.1% agree that they are completely satisfied with. These results can be explained that HIBAG is performing well in their eyes of most of its students and this is great. However, we should never ignore the other point of views, which while 21.2% answered by rather than unsatisfied, 6.1% have expressed a complete non-satisfaction and this is harmful as far as the institute risk to lose 27.3% of their students.

- **The quality of Services**

Figure 6. How would you rate the effectiveness of academic programs in future career?
Source: Out-put Google Forms

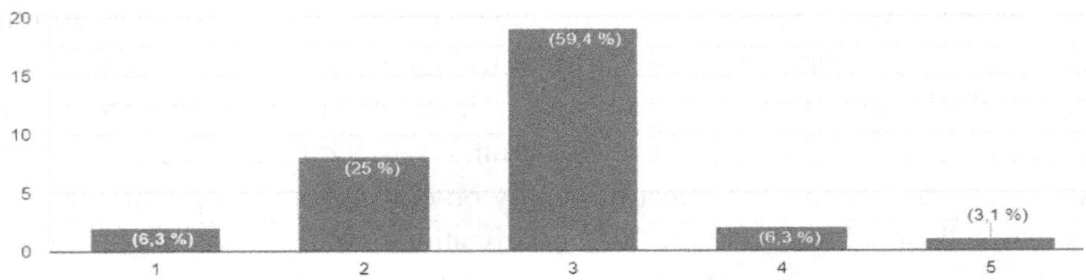

Based on those results, it seems that the majority of students (59.4%) rated the effectiveness of the HIBAG's academic programs in preparing you for their future career as 3 out of 5, with 25% rating it as a 2, and 6.3% each giving a rating of 1 or 4, and only 3.1% rating it as a 5. The fact that the majority of students rated the programs as 3 shows that the academic programs are performing well. Therefore, to enhance its performance and meet its student's needs, the HIBAG should pick out areas for improvement to satisfy the indicator of adequately prepare them for their careers.

Figure 7. How satisfied are you with trainings offered by our institution?
Source: Out-put Google Forms

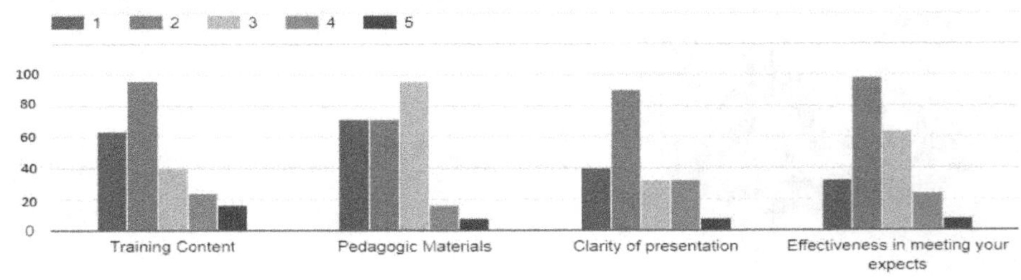

- **The quality of trainings**

Let us interpret each metric independently.

- **Pedagogic materials**

Table 2. Analyzing students' satisfaction towards pedagogic materials used in trainings

	5	20	60	70	95
1			✓	✓	
2				✓	
3					
4		✓			✓
5	✓				

Source: Out-put Google Forms

There still weakness and lack in providing well-equipped training rooms which can affect the overall performance of the HIBAG.

- **Clarity of presentation**

Table 3. Analyzing students' satisfaction towards clarity of training presentation

	5	36	40	83
1			✓	
2				✓
3		✓		
4		✓		
5	✓			

Source: Out-put Google Forms

Results show that 123 students from 200 are not satisfied either rather than unsatisfied with the clarity of presenting trainings.

Effectiveness in achieving students' expectations

Results show that 137 students from 219 confess that trainings offered by HIBAG do not meet their expectations.

Table 4. Students' satisfaction towards the effectiveness of trainings in students' expectations

	5	20	37	60	100
1			✓		
2					✓
3				✓	
4		✓			
5	✓				

Source: Out-put Google Forms

The quality of student service: We asked 300 students the following question: How satisfied are you with the availability and accessibility of our faculty and staff for academic support? Their answers were the following:

Figure 8. Analyzing students' satisfaction towards the effectiveness of services
Source: Out-put Google Forms

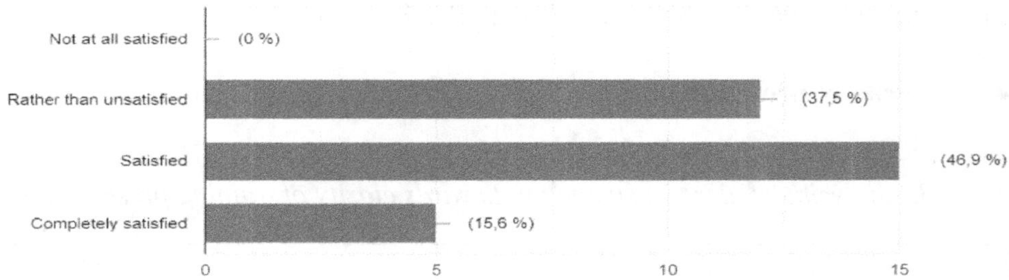

This diagram shows average results; 62.5% of students express high satisfaction, while it seems that only 37.5% sow some reservations towards the availability and accessibility of faculty's and staff for academic support. It is important to note that students' satisfaction with the services and availability of staff is likely to influence the overall experience and academic performance of the faculty. Thus, it should make improvements to get more satisfaction rates.

- **Quality of facilities**

Figure 9. Analyzing students' satisfaction towards the effectiveness
Source: Out-put Google Forms

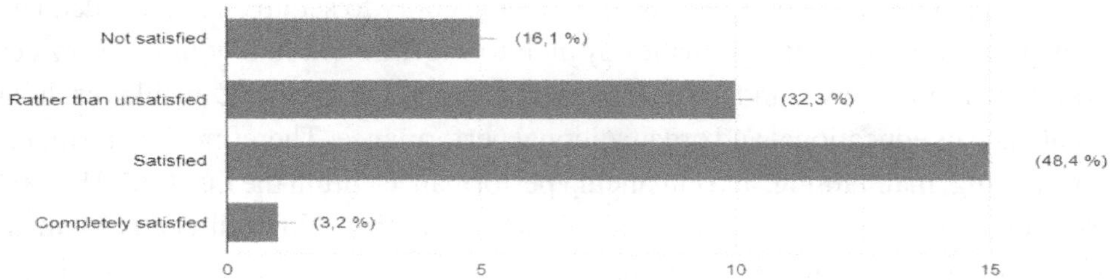

Based on the diagram, approximately 52% of students (3.2% completely satisfied + 48.4% satisfied) are satisfied with the facilities provided by your institution, while approximately 48% of students (32.3% rather than unsatisfied + 16.1% not satisfied) are unsatisfied with the facilities provided by HIBAG. We notice that some students are not that satisfied with many metrics, so HIBAG is probably weak at meeting some KPI. Their non-satisfaction can result by several causes, so we asked students, subject to survey, to write down their recommendations to better enhance HIBA's performance and then, their satisfaction. In this regard, they suggest to:

- Offer world widely recognized certifications such as TOEFL, TOEIC, IELTS, etc.
- Make deals with employers to hire the graduated students
- Provide scholarship to carry on studies abroad
- Work on introducing the applied teaching system
- Only if there is a way for the certificates presented by our institution to become recognized in our country as is the case in other states
- If scientific research in accounting can be studied
- They give us trainings in our fields
- Practical trainings is our specialities

While it is positive to see that the majority of students are satisfied or somewhat satisfied, it is important to address the concerns of the students who are not satisfied. In other words, the HIBAG have to interact actively with these feedbacks to make improvements, which will automatically enhance its performance.

4.4 Evolution and Contribution of Services and Departments in The Performance of The Institution

IC is important since it assumes various responsibilities in the educational context within colleges and universities. It may involve both reasonable assurance and/or advice on a wide range of topics as it allows the entity to set up clear and adequate work procedures, to avoid anomalies by monitoring different functions and services to system improvement, and to achieve its objectives. Therefore, IC enables each AI to enhance its educational and organizational performance. Therefore, it contributes to achieving, maintaining, and enhancing performance within the institute. The best proof on this thought is to conduct a unique dataset that allows direct assessment of outcomes that should be impacted by ICS and quality management in higher education. But we should, first refer to several studies such those of (DeSimone, & Rich, 2020; Sari, et al., 2017).

4.4.1 Data Collection

An empirical examination of the contributions of IC within Tunisian higher AI is important. In fact, CIS for colleges and universities are likely to be less mature than those for publicly traded companies (Sari, et al., 2017), that is why a more comprehensive understanding of CI in this sector is timely. Blackmore (2004) suggests that *internal academic audit inspection and quality control processes are close to the ISO 9001 guidelines* for auditing quality management systems but also sometimes fall short in the areas of quality assurance and TQM[1]. This study is an interview research. The data used are primary data. They are all collected from four services listed in the HIBAG. Research subjects are to the parties directly involved in public university of public service agencies and the internal control with the reason: they understand more about the duties and functions of internal control system who carry out the responsibilities given to them.

To do this, we refer for four services and department from our institution. The services and department concerned by this interview are listed as bellow: the HR Service; the financial and purchasing service; the library and the "4C" center of skills.

4.4.2 HR Service

The HR Service offers its expertise in all areas of HR management from recruitment, selection, payroll to retention. It can give advice related to social security, tax and stay authorization issues. Moreover, it does administrative tasks related to lecturer and visiting researchers. The organizational structure of the HR service of the HIBAG is as following HR team should satisfy some qualifications and characteristics that can be summarized into three categories.

- **Professional skills and technicality**

They are summarized on the: Mastery of "Wadhifa Plus" software; Knowledge of HRM practices and other key knowledge (Law, Economics, Group management, Entrepreneurship, Quality support projects (PAQ)…)

- **Contribution to the activity of the service**

It's related to the Team work, Work organization and Integration of IT tools.

- **Personal and relational qualities**

These qualifications are related to the team spirit, respect for hierarchy, active communication and ability to speak in public and active listening. We carried out an interview with the HR's service manager and we tried to gather the maximum possible of indicators, improvements that enable us to assess the performance of this service.

Table 5. Performance of HR's service

Question	Indicator	Performance Improvement	Performance Improvement
Operational processes and procedures	Rate of achievement of training actions.	We find a weak level and some needed training service for personals	Supervise, animate and coordinate the services of the HRS, promote communication and transversally and mobilize the skills of its employees and Guarantee the application of the statutory, legislative, regulatory or jurisprudential provisions and establish internal rules specific to the establishment.
Performance outcomes	Effectiveness rate of training actions.	Needed of pinpoint training for both of academic and non-academic staff	Define the orientations of the establishment's HR
Personal qualification	Personal Versatility Rate	Need for versatile employees to ensure absenteeism coverage and improve the overall performance of the institute	Implement continuous improvement Define the orientations of the HR & Participate in the definition of an HR policy (Digitization of activities within the service)
	Absence rate (unjustified) of staff	Good with continuation the guarantee the application of statutory, legislative and regulatory provisions from sensitization to sanction'	Establish internal rules specific to the establishment And implement continuous improvement of processes in terms of HR.

Source: Out-Put of interview with HR responsible

After receiving the recommendations of external audit, the HR service have add other actions to improve the quality of the above indicators, these actions are taken by the decision coordinately of Direction, direction of studies, general secretary and other department and services. According the result of getting ISO the auditor has requested the enhancement of some steps to facilitate and control and thus the performance of HIBAG.

For these reasons, and all instructions of the post of HR manager', he need to execute all the following tasks and he give proof of each task:

- Digital personnel management (Wadhifa plus software),
- Digital clocking management, (Electronic clocking),
- Communicate with the general secretariat and management via email (transfer of data and documents relating to teachers and staff)
- Disseminate information to teachers through email.
- Ensure the proper sharing of information for administrators and teachers as soon as possible and in the most precise and efficient manner. Meet periodically to assess and prepare the task execution schedule (election of the joint administrative and pedagogical committee,
    - Highlight the internal regulatory texts for the proper administrative functioning of the establishment (Internal notes, press release, letters, etc.) - Supervise the proper management of staff and teacher files (Organization, archiving, filing,)
    - Follow-up of letters sent and received from the university while respecting response times and consistency.
    - Monitoring the maintenance of computer applications
    - Drafting of periodic reports relating to the HR department and for the preparation of the institute's annual activity report.
    - Supervise the completion of the additional hours file for teachers for each end of the academic year (overtime and vacation).
    - Coordinate with the director of studies and the department directors for the signature of the final version of the timetables for the teachers (semester 1 and 2).
    - Ensure the digital sending of the convocations signed by the director of the establishment to the members of the scientific council and preparation of any other necessary documents.

According to the response of the interviewee, responsible of HR service, there is a good amelioration of the level of Personal Versatility, which gives the HIBAG some solution to enhancement of the quality service offered to the student, also the promotion of some of them. In the same point of view, the academic staff, a good evolution has seen in that last year, according to the recruitment of a high number of assistant professors and the promotion of the old professors and a high value of scientific publication in the top ranking journals.

4.4.3 The Financial and Purchasing Management

According to interview and instructions related to this post, the responsible of the financial and purchasing management service operate the following functions:

- Supervise, animate and coordinate the financial affairs department.
- Coordinate closely with the director and the SG for all financial operations.
- Manage Title 1 and 2 of the institution's annual budget.
- Ensure the proper functioning of the service at all levels.

To assess this service's performance, we gathered the information mentioned in the following table.

Table 6. The financial and purchasing management service's performance

Thematic	Indicator	Performance Level	Solution
Supervise, animate and coordinate the financial affairs department.	- Ensure the application of the internal regulations of the service financial and purchasing management and its implementation (manual of procedures and application of the texts). - Control the progress of the acquisition procedures and payment of suppliers.	Application of all needed rules	Continue with this good reputation of service, which can facilitate the internal control and the external coordination with the university supervisors and ministry supervisors
Coordinate closely with the Director and SG for all financial transactions.	- Regularly prepare the state of progress of the budget for periodic meetings with the Director and the SG - Ensure the regular follow-up of commitments,	Good coordination	Continue with this good reputation of service, which can facilitate the internal control and the external coordination with the university supervisors and ministry supervisors
Manage title one and two of the institution's annual budget.	- Intervene in the event of a malfunction to reveal the various administrative and technical obstacles, - Train and mentor subordinates for proper use system of financial management of the budget.	Good coordination	Continue with this good reputation of service, which can facilitate the internal control and the external coordination with the university supervisors and ministry supervisors

Source Out-Put of interview with financial and purchasing service responsible

Such as this service have a direct relationship and supervision of the director and according to the first visit report' of the external audit, we have taken information that there is no breaking of rules and instructions of this job. There just some minor revisions and requirements to office organization, and thus the result of getting ISO certification reflect the good application rules in the preparation and execution of the budget by the responsible of this service and the direction of the HIBAG. also all other partners such as the direction of studies, the head of departments have some interventions by the requesting of needed supplies or personnel needs from an year to another. As a result of this study we can said that the implementation of the internal control system can improve the facility of execution and t transparency of this service.

The financial and purchase service need some security and a high level of confidentiality and a good Internal control and SMQ function improve the resolution of the conflict which will lead to reduced agency cost that will ultimately improve the performance of the university towards good governance of HIBAG. Also this service gives our institution the opportunity to manage and to take the decision of development and finance some activities such as the training. For example the process of getting of the ISO 9001 has needed a high level of budget consecrated for the preliminary evaluation and the other rounds until getting this certification. Indeed the signature of this certification by international audit of ISO reflect that this service respect all rules and have a good reputation and coordination with all partners in the HIBAG, direction, head of departments, other services…

4.4.4 The Library

Library is integrated and engaged in teaching and learning. The library is not just a repository of books and resources, but it actively related and coordinate between students, professors, and staff across all discipline. Furthermore, it aims to enrich academic experiences by providing the resources needed from books to archives to rich databases, and the spaces for creation and cooperation.

The library service at the HIBAG is under the responsibility of library director. HIBAG has engaged in the TMQ approach, where all services, including library, have been affected by the QMS. Let us check if it has been affected either positively or negatively. The internal audit done to evaluate the effectiveness of the library's ICS has identified a set of weaknesses within the service. The table below mentions some of these weaknesses or risks and then identifies their origins:

To make it clearer, we should quantify these weaknesses. The following diagram does so:

Table 7. The IA results

Activity	Risk Identification	Origin
Enhancing quality services	Non-satisfaction of faculty and students towards the library services	Mediocre quality
Communication	Low student interaction with library services	Lack of communication and sensitization
Digitalization	Non-satisfaction regarding archive services	Bureaucracy in realizing services

Source: IA on library service

Figure 10. Library weaknesses
Source: IA results on library service

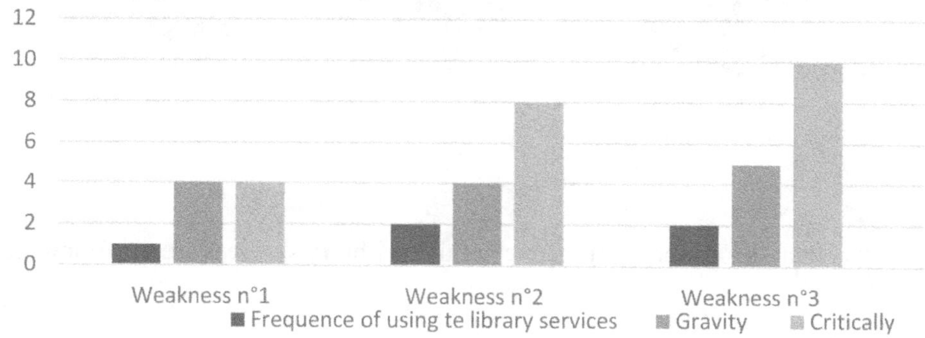

As a response to those weaknesses that threat achieving objectives, the library manager, in cooperation with the QMS service and based on the QMS requires, set goals and pick out measures, which aim to correct and to make improvement.

The table below describes each objective and each measure taken to correct each weakness.

Table 8. Objectives and corrections

Activity	Objective	Measure
1	Satisfying staff and students requirements	Setting a QMS specialized for the library's specificities
2	Increasing the rate of use of books and references offered by the library	Organizing journeys of sensitization to the students
3	Satisfying all stakeholders expectations	Setting a digitalized archive management system

Source: out-put interview with Library service

Now, let us assess the impact of the implementation of the improvement measures, which are, already based on the QMS requirements on the library's performance.

Figure 11. Assessing the impact of corrective measures on the library's performance
Source: Library service

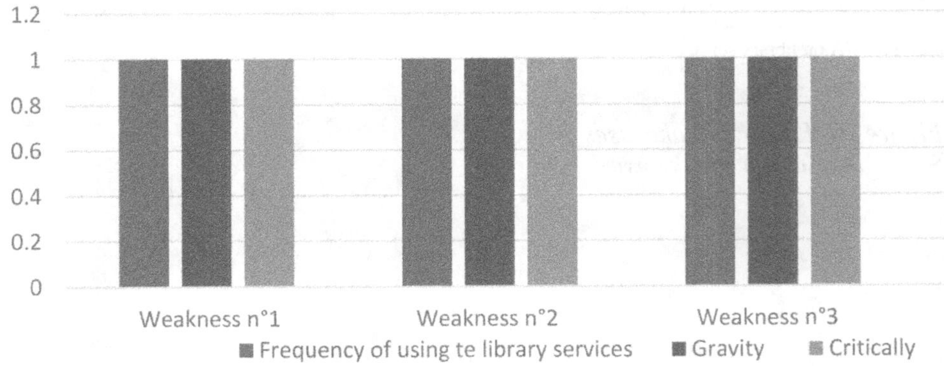

Given that, the critters of frequency of using library services are the followings:

Table 9. Frequency criteria

Once per year	1
At least once per month	2
At least once per week	3
At least once per day	4

Source: Out-put interview with Library service

-Of weakness gravity:

Table 10. Weakness gravity critters

No effect on the product conformity or the process	1
Product or process non conform but	2
Product or process non conform and non	3
Product or process non conform and non	4

Source: Out-put interview with Library service

-Of critically:

Table 11. Critically critters

No effect on the product conformity or the process	1
Product or process non conform but	2
Product or process non conform and non	3
Product or process non conform and non	4

Source: Out-put interview with Library service

We can conclude that library service has improved all its weaknesses and has succeeded in enhancing its performance.

4.4.5 The '4C' Center

In order to ensure a learning process in practical skills for the benefit of graduates and future graduates, to facilitate their integration into society and the professional world, the project will provide trainers, drawn from the teaching staff of the institute with necessary certifications (accounting techniques, banking techniques, tax operations, and statistical control of processes). The direction of the HIBA has two PAQs related to our institution to improve the quality of services and coordinate between them about the training services and the layout and equipment of the rooms (PAQ DGSE & PAQ 4C). For this reason the PAQ 4C titled: BEDER with the subject of Best Employability Development & Effective Responsibility have two aspect in the execution of his process: the first one is relation to the layout and equipment of the rooms nominated Room 4C, and this step it's done before getting the ISO' certification and the second step related to the subject of PAQ-4C project. Such was launched mainly to help solve the crucial problem of unemployment among HIBAG graduates, faced with an increased number of nationals. This project's approach to alleviating this burden is to achieve the following three outcomes:

- Training and certification of teachers and students of HIBA Gafsa in practical skills in accounting, finance and governance.
- The establishment and operation of a space for training and meetings with socio-economic actors allowing new graduates access to the job market and to build their own relationships with the business world.

- Guarantee a standardized quality to the administrative services of our establishment in order to adapt to a world of technical and organizational competition

Table 12. The 4C center criteria

Specific Objectives	Expected Results	Results & Indicators for Evaluation	Necessary Resources to Collect and Analyze the Indicator
Setting up a PAQ-4C space	Arrangement of the surface of the space	Furnished and equipped premises	Civil Engineering Equipment
Create a cell of teachers certified in practical skills	100% of trained teachers are certified	Percentage of teachers participated in certified training	Training of Trainers Teacher Certification Exam Result
Improving pedagogical tools and approaches	Integrate the content of the training into the university curriculum	Number of certifying modules integrated into academic courses	Course manuals
Train and certify graduates and future graduates in practical skills.	Above than a fixed level	Rate of certified students	Vouchers Preparation for exams Training
Certify the quality of the administrative framework	Diagnosis and implementation of a quality standardization system	Participation rate of administrative executives Auditor consultations	Obtaining the ISO 9001-2015 certificate

Source: Out-Put of interview with the director of 4C center

At the level of this overall objective, there is the risk of the small size and saturation of the job market at the regional level (weak economic and industrial fabric) and national level (increased number of graduates). To increase the chances of professional integration of young graduates the 4C coordinate with the direction of studies and internships, to enhance the Number of students who have benefited from training within the framework of the projects and who have been retained for jobs. But the Job offers are generally for categories of skilled workers, the graduates are obliged to accept such offers to guarantee their integration in the mean-time and waiting for their promotion can take a lot of time.

Specific objectives (that the project could achieve) are:

- Certify the teachers and non-academic staff in practical skills.
- Improve teaching tools and approaches.
- Train and certify graduates and future graduates in practical skills

Here and according to the statistics offered by the Center 4C, we see a high number of list of attendance at training and number of certificates obtained by participating students and graduates out of the total number of students. the percentage of teaching elements that can be integrated into the study plan directly related to the practical skills required by certified teachers (optional subjects 25% of the program); for example the practices of AI-Compta for accounting and taxation, the Deep learning for business computing students, the management innovation for students of leadership and management. These finding show a high level of competence of 4C to improve the quality of diploma of HIBAG. And here we need to refer to some statistics of PAQ DGSE, which have the initiative to finance the program of ISO qualification and to improve the evaluation of any training session in the institution. Also the PAQ DGSE have a high level of certification for student and the team of this PAQ give a very importance for soft skills, competitively of our graduated students.

There are a high number of certificates and certificates issued, optional teaching elements integrated into the study plan directly related to the practical skills required by certified teachers, and a high number of certified students and graduates. For example as a strategy with the main objective of remove the low presence and lack of interest of students and administrative staff, and attract them to training and certification exams. For this, it is important to intensify awareness and information days (via Facebook, emails, word of mouth, etc.). These findings show a good level of performance, and when we ask the responsible they said that the internal control and process of getting ISO 9001 help them to improve the quality of services. The agenda of the council will integrate the various activities of the project. In this way, the implementation will be supervised and controlled by a representative management. Internally, the project implementation monitoring strategy will be carried out by the team mentioned in the human resources table for project management.

4.4.6 Interview With the Director of HIBAG

We have arrived to the end but we have nothing finished.

We will finish by an interview carried out with the director of our institute, which aims to investigate about his attitudes, perspectives towards the internal control within his academic institution as well as his future plans in enhancing the ICS

By discussing each of his answers, we can conclude that:

- The director believes in the importance of internal control to his institution.
- The director has affected for each department head and service manager the IC of his function
- The director has organized each department tasks
- The director has put clear guidelines and work procedures in place

He communicated them to different departments/ services formally reported in internal service note and in job instructions.

- The director confesses that control instructions are subject to be reviewed twice per year.

He also said that those instructions are also subject to an internal audit, which is destined to be carried out once per year.

When we asked the director how did he rate the overall effectiveness of the internal control system implemented by his institute, he answered by ‘effective’, we can understand that the effectiveness of the ICS within the all services of HIBAG reflects the respect of rules and instructions and the minor corrections mentioned by ISO have been correctly. The director declares that there are rigorous mechanisms in place for reporting any concerns or anomalies such as that scientific assembly’s written records, formal communication, annual expected report, and annual reporting results. They are destined to the evaluation and even correction if needed and continuous enhancement.

The director shows that the ISO9001:2015 implementation did not add any extra work for the usual process. Such response shows that the direction manages all its establishment’s services and departments in according to the rules of the art. This is in full compliance with the responses and results of the various interviews with the above-mentioned services’ responsible. But, these good results continue to be, and even improve through the indices and the results achieved as well as the promotions and assured recruitments.

CONCLUSION

To sum up, the case study provides a valuable example of how quality and internal control measures can be used to enhance the performance of higher education institutions, and highlights the importance of continuous improvement and adaptability in a rapidly changing environment. In other words, by conducting a performance evaluation, examining the impact of quality, and analyzing the impact of internal control, we can identify areas for improvement and develop strategies to enhance every institution’s performance. The results of the study are pertinent to make evidence-based decisions to enhance for example the internal control system as well as to allocate resources effectively to improve the quality of education and outcomes for the institute’s students and all its different stakeholders.

Over the years, academic institutions have been constantly striving to achieve excellence in providing high-quality education to their students. The effectiveness of an academic institution is often measured by its performance, which includes various parameters such as student satisfaction, academic success, research output, financial stability, and social impact. Achieving and maintaining high levels of performance requires a systematic approach that involves a focus on quality management and internal control systems. The present study aimed to investigate the impact of quality management and internal control systems on the performance of academic institutions, with a case study of HIBAG. The study involved conducting a survey with students to assess the effect of quality management on their satisfaction and academic performance.

The study also involved analyzing the performance indicators and evolution of four services at HIBAG, including HR, financial and purchasing management service, library service, and 4C center, to assess the impact of internal control on the institution's overall performance. The findings of the study revealed that both quality management and internal control systems play a crucial role in enhancing the performance of academic institutions. The survey conducted with students revealed that quality management significantly influences their satisfaction and academic performance. The results of the survey indicated that students who perceived a high level of quality in their academic program were more likely to report higher levels of satisfaction and academic success. Furthermore, the analysis of the performance indicators and evolution of four services at HIBAG showed that an effective internal control system positively impacts the performance of the institution.

The interviews conducted with the managers and the institute director revealed that the internal control system has helped to enhance the efficiency and effectiveness of the institution's operations. In conclusion, the findings of the study highlight the importance of quality management and internal control systems in enhancing the performance of academic institutions. The study has shown that a focus on quality management and internal control systems can lead to better student satisfaction, academic success, research output, financial stability, and social impact. Academic institutions should prioritize quality management and internal control systems as part of their strategic planning and continuous improvement initiatives. To achieve sustainable growth and success, academic institutions should foster a culture of continuous improvement, regularly monitor performance indicators, and create an environment that supports innovation and creativity. Investing in quality management and internal control systems is crucial for academic institutions to remain competitive and provide high-quality education to their students.

Declaration of Conflicting Interests

Authors are very glad for the opportunity taken from the director of the HIBAG and all services responsible to do this study. The authors declared no potential conflicts of interest with respect to the research, authorship, and/or publication of this article.

Funding

The authors received no financial support for the research, authorship, and/or publication of this article.

REFERENCES

Blackmore, J. A. (2004). A critical evaluation of academic internal audit. *Quality Assurance in Education*, *12*(3), 128–135. doi:10.1108/09684880410548753

DeSimone, S., & Rich, K. (2020). Determinants and consequences of internal audit functions within colleges and universities. *Managerial Auditing Journal*, *35*(8), 1143–1166. doi:10.1108/MAJ-10-2019-2444

Forbes. (2021). Six Common Business Objectives. *Forbes.*

Investopedia. (2022). *Business Performance*. Author.

Primeum. (2021, April 6). *Business Performance: What is Business Performance.* Author.

Sari, N., Ghozali, I., & Achmad, T. (2017). The effect of internal audit and internal control system on public accountability: The empirical study in Indonesia state universities. *International Journal of Civil Engineering and Technology*, *8*(9), 157–166.

The National Association of State Budget Officers. (2016). *Budget processes and practices*. Author.

ENDNOTE

1 TQM is a comprehensive approach to management that involves all aspects of an entity.

Compilation of References

A methodology for creating intelligent wheelchair users' profiles(2012*Proceedings of the 4th International Conference on Agents and Artificial Intelligence*. doi:10.5220/0003749701710179

Accenture. (2016a). *Global FinTech investment growth continues in 2016 driven by Europe and Asia, Accenture study finds*. Available at https://newsroom.accenture.com/news/ global-FinTech-investment-growth-continues-in-2016- driven-by-europe-and-asia-accenture-study-finds.htm

Agarwal, S., & Zhang, J. (2020). FinTech, Lending and Payment Innovation: A Review. *Asia-Pacific Journal of Financial Studies*, *49*(7), 353–367. doi:10.1111/ajfs.12294

Aggarwal, K. K., & Aggarwal, S. (2021). Is Green banking an Adequate Initiative for Environment Sustainability. In New India: Emerging Trends in Indian Business Scenario (Vol. 1, pp. 87–97). Notion Press.

Ahmed, A. (2013). Perception of Life Insurance Policies in Rural India. *Kuwait Chapter of Arabian Journal of Business and Management Review, 2*, 17 – 24.

Ajeet Kumar Sahoo, P. R. (2019). Performance of Pradhan Mantri MUDRA Yojana (PMMY): A Case Study of Haryana. *International Journal of Research in Social Science*, *9*(5), 1–17.

Allegue, S., Abdellatif, T., & El Abed, H. (2023). SBM: A Smart Budget Manager in banking using machine learning, NLP, and NLU. *Concurrency and Computation*, *35*(11), e6673. doi:10.1002/cpe.6673

Almagsoosi, L., Abadi, M. T. E., Hasan, H. F., & Sharaf, H. K. (2022). Effect of the Volatility of the Crypto Currency and Its Effect on the Market Returns. *Industrial Engineering and Management Systems*, *21*(2), 238–243. doi:10.7232/iems.2022.21.2.238

Almansour, B. Y., Alshater, M. M., & Almansour, A. Y. (2021). Performance of ARCH and GARCH models in forecasting crypto currency market volatility. *Industrial Engineering and Management Systems*, *20*(2), 130–139. doi:10.7232/iems.2021.20.2.130

Anas, A Q., Azzouz, Z., & Mostafa, E. (2020). Does corruption adversely affect economic growth in Tunisia? ARDL approach. *Journal of Money Laundering Control, 23*(1), 38-54. doi:10.1108/JMLC-12-2018-0076

Aria, M., & Cuccurullo, C. (2017). bibliometrix: An R-tool for comprehensive science mapping analysis. *Journal of Informetrics, 11*(4), 959–975. doi:10.1016/j.joi.2017.08.007

Arner, D., Buckley, R., & Barberis, J. (2016). The Evolution of Fintech: A New Post-Crisis Paradigm? SSRN *Electronic Journal, 47*(4), 1271-1319. doi:10.2139/ssrn.2676553

Arulkumaran, K., Deisenroth, M. P., Brundage, M., & Bharath, A. A. (2017). Deep reinforcement learning: A brief survey. *IEEE Signal Processing Magazine, 34*(6), 26–38. doi:10.1109/MSP.2017.2743240

Auer, R., Haslhofer, B., Kitzler, S., Saggese, P., & Victor, F. (2023). *The Technology of Decentralized Finance (DeFi).* Bank for International Settlements, Monetary and Economic Department. doi:10.100742521-023-00088-8

Ayushman Bharat for a New India-2022, Announced. Press Information Bureau, Government of India, Department of Finance. (n.d.). Available from: http://www.pib.nic.in/newsite/PrintRelease.aspx?relid=176049

Ayushman Bharat Yojana. (n.d.). Available from: www.nap.gov.in

Bação, P., Gaspar, I., & Simões, M. (2019). Corruption and economic growth: The case of Portugal. *Notas Económicas*, (49), 11–33. doi:10.14195/2183-203X_49_2

Baliamoune-Lutz, M., & Ndikumana, L. (2009). Corruption and growth: Exploring the investment channel. *Economics Department Working Paper Series, 33.*

Bansal, N., Bhatnagar, M., & Taneja, S. (2023). Balancing Priorities Through Green Optim000ism: A Study Elucidating Initiatives, Approaches, and Strategies for Sustainable Supply Chain Management. In *Handbook of Research on Designing Sustainable Supply Chains to Achieve a Circular Economy* (pp. 60–81). IGI Global. doi:10.4018/978-1-6684-7664-2.ch004

Bansal, N., Taneja, S., & Ozen, E. (2023). Green Financing as a Bridge Between Green Banking Strategies and Environmental Performance in Punjab, India. *International Journal of Sustainable Development and Planning, 18*(10), 3155–3167. doi:10.18280/ijsdp.181017

Bao, Y., Hilary, G., & Ke, B. (2022). Artificial intelligence and fraud detection. Innovative Technology at the Interface of Finance and Operations, 1, 223-247.

Bardhan, P. (1997). Corruption and development: A review of issues. *Journal of Economic Literature, 35*(3), 1320–1346.

Barnes, R. (2017). Kahoot! in the Classroom: Student Engagement Technique. *Nurse Educator, 42*(6), 280. doi:10.1097/NNE.0000000000000419 PMID:29049160

Barro, R., & Sala-i-Martin, X. (2004). Economic growth (2nd ed.). Academic Press.

Barzykin, A., Bergault, P., & Guéant, O. (2023). Algorithmic market making in dealer markets with hedging and market impact. *Mathematical Finance, 33*(1), 41–79. doi:10.1111/mafi.12367

Beckert, J. (2016). *Imagined Futures: Fictional Expectations and Capitalist Dynamics*. Harvard University Press. doi:10.4159/9780674545878

Bellanova, R., & de Goede, M. (2022, January). The algorithmic regulation of security: An infrastructural perspective. *Regulation & Governance*, *16*(1), 102–118. doi:10.1111/rego.12338 PMID:35874795

Benmoussa, M. (2019). Api "Application Programming Interface" Banking: A Promising Future For Financial Institutions (International Experience). *Revue Des Sciences Commerciales*, *18*(2), 31–34.

Benuyenah, V. (2021). Theorising an organisational citizenship behaviour model for managerial decision-making: From history to contemporary application. *Management Research Review*, *44*(8), 1182–1198. doi:10.1108/MRR-07-2020-0422

Berensmann, K., & Lindenberg, N. (2019). *Green finance: actors, challenges and policy recommendations*. Briefing Paper 23. German Development Institute/ Deutsches Institut für Entwicklungspolitik (DIE).

Bergheim, S. (2005). *Human capital is the key to growth-success stories and policies for 2020*. Deutsche Bank Research Current Issues Working Paper.

Bhal, K. T. (2006). LMX-citizenship behavior relationship: Justice as a mediator. *Leadership and Organization Development Journal*, *27*(2), 106–117. doi:10.1108/01437730610646615

Bhatnagar, M., Özen, E., Taneja, S., Grima, S., & Rupeika-Apoga, R. (2022a). The Dynamic Connectedness between Risk and Return in the Fintech Market of India: Evidence Using the GARCH-M Approach. *Risks*, *10*(11), 209. doi:10.3390/risks10110209

Bhatnagar, M., Pathak, N., & Taneja, S. (2023). Tech-Optimists and Financial Education - A Research on the Efficacy of Communication Mediums of Government Economic Policies. *International Journal of Sustainable Development and Planning*, *18*(7), 2245–2252. doi:10.18280/ijsdp.180729

Bhatnagar, M., Taneja, S., Kumar, P., & Özen, E. (2023a). Does Financial Education Act as a Catalyst for SME Competitiveness. *International Journal of Education Economics and Development*, *1*(1), 1. doi:10.1504/IJEED.2023.10053629

Bhatnagar, M., Taneja, S., & Özen, E. (2022b). A wave of green start-ups in India—The study of green finance as a support system for sustainable entrepreneurship. *Green Finance*, *4*(2), 253–273. doi:10.3934/GF.2022012

Bhatnagar, M., Taneja, S., & Rupeika-Apoga, R. (2023). Demystifying the Effect of the News (Shocks) on Crypto Market Volatility. *Journal of Risk and Financial Management*, *16*(2), 136. Advance online publication. doi:10.3390/jrfm16020136

Bhatt, A. K., Verma, A. K., & Gaur, R. (2020). Consumer Cognizance about Forex Card in Digital Epoch. *2020 International Conference on Computation, Automation and Knowledge Management (ICCAKM)*, 493-498. 10.1109/ICCAKM46823.2020.9051547

Bindal, A., & Singh, R. (2022). A study and review of Pradhan Mantri Mudra Yojana. *Journal of Education: Rabindra Bharati University, 23*(1), 309-315.

Bizri, R. (2018). Diversity management and OCB: The connection evidence from the Lebanese banking sector. *Equality, Diversity and Inclusion, 37*(3), 233–253. doi:10.1108/EDI-03-2017-0059

Blackmore, J. A. (2004). A critical evaluation of academic internal audit. *Quality Assurance in Education, 12*(3), 128–135. doi:10.1108/09684880410548753

Bollaert, H., Lopez-de-Silanes, F., & Schwienbacher, A. (2021). Fintech and access to finance. *Journal of Corporate Finance, 68*(2), 1–14. doi:10.1016/j.jcorpfin.2021.101941

Bollerslev, T. (1986). Generalized autoregressive conditional heteroskedasticity. *Journal of Econometrics, 31*(3), 307–327. doi:10.1016/0304-4076(86)90063-1

Bose, I., Chen, X., & Wang, W. (2018). Enhancing credit scoring models with social network information: A survey and future directions. *European Journal of Operational Research, 268*(2), 626–637.

Brdnik, S., Heričko, T., & Šumak, B. (2022). Intelligent User Interfaces and Their Evaluation: A Systematic Mapping Study. *Sensors (Basel), 22*(15), 5830. doi:10.339022155830 PMID:35957387

Bruno, M., & Easterly, W. (1998). Inflation crises and long-run growth. *Journal of Monetary Economics, 41*(1), 3–26. doi:10.1016/S0304-3932(97)00063-9

Buczynski, W., Cuzzolin, F., & Sahakian, B. (2021). A review of machine learning experiments in equity investment decision-making: Why most published research findings do not live up to their promise in real life. *International Journal of Data Science and Analytics, 11*(3), 221–242. doi:10.100741060-021-00245-5 PMID:33842690

Bumin, M., & Ozcalici, M. (2023). Predicting the direction of financial dollarization movement with genetic algorithm and machine learning algorithms: The case of Turkey. *Expert Systems with Applications, 213*, 119301. doi:10.1016/j.eswa.2022.119301

Campos, N. F., Estrin, S., & Proto, E. (2010). *Corruption as a barrier to entry: Theory and evidence*. Academic Press.

Catania, L. J. (2021). The evolution of artificial intelligence (AI). Foundations of Artificial Intelligence in Healthcare and Bioscience. doi:10.1016/B978-0-12-824477-7.00002-X

Chakrabarty, K. C. (2012). *Financial Inclusion – Issues in Measurement and Analysis*. Reserve Bank of India at the BIS-BNM Workshop on Financial Inclusion Indicators at Kuala Lumpur. http://www.rbi.org.in/scripts/BSSpeechesView.aspx?id=749

Chakrabarty, B., & Pascual, R. (2023). Stock liquidity and algorithmic market making during the COVID-19 crisis. *Journal of Banking & Finance, 147*, 106415. doi:10.1016/j.jbankfin.2022.106415

Chandra, Y., & Mathur, K. (2021). Organization Citizenship Behaviour and Work-Life Interface Practices: Exploring Entrepreneurial and Intrapreneurial Mindset. *Vision: The Journal of Business Perspective*, *25*(3), 361–372. doi:10.1177/09722629211010980

Chen, X., Hui, C., & Sego, D. J. (1998). The role of Organizational Citizenship Behavior in Turnover. *The Journal of Applied Psychology*, *83*(December), 922–931. doi:10.1037/0021-9010.83.6.922

Chiu, H. (2016). Fintech and Disruptive Business Models in Financial Products, Intermediation and Markets- Policy Implications for Financial Regulators. *Journal of Technology Law and Policy*, *21*(1).

Chowdhary, T. U., Datta, R., & Mohajan, H. K. (2013). Green Finance is Essential for Economic Development and Sustainability. *International Journal of Research in Commerce, Economics and Management*, *3*(10), 104–108. https://mpra.ub.uni-muenchen.de/id/eprint/51169

Ch, R., Gadekallu, T. R., Abidi, M. H., & Al-Ahmari, A. (2020). Computational system to classify Cyber Crime offenses using machine learning. *Sustainability (Basel)*, *12*(10), 4087. Advance online publication. doi:10.3390u12104087

Christopher, A., Deniswara, K., & Handoko, B. L. (2022). Forecasting Crypto currency Volatility Using GARCH and ARCH Model. *ACM International Conference Proceeding Series*, 121–128. 10.1145/3537693.3537712

Cieślik, A., & Goczek, Ł. (2018). Control of corruption, international investment, and economic growth–Evidence from panel data. *World Development*, *103*, 323–335. doi:10.1016/j.worlddev.2017.10.028

CRISIL, (2018). *An index to measure India 's progress on Financial Inclusion.* Report of CRISIL Inclusix.

Cuervo-Cazurra, A. (2016). Corruption in international business. *Journal of World Business*, *51*(1), 35–49. doi:10.1016/j.jwb.2015.08.015

d'Agostino, G., Dunne, J. P., & Pieroni, L. (2012). Corruption, military spending and growth. *Defence and Peace Economics*, *23*(6), 591–604. doi:10.1080/10242694.2012.663579

D'Agostino, G., Dunne, J. P., & Pieroni, L. (2016). Government spending, corruption and economic growth. *World Development*, *84*, 190–205. doi:10.1016/j.worlddev.2016.03.011

Dabouis, B., Boccara, V., & Yannou, B. (2023). Retrospective coding of the ux design process for ux design enhancement in design agencies. *Proceedings of the Design Society*, *3*, 3105–3114. doi:10.1017/pds.2023.311

Dahiya, K., Taneja, S., & Özen, E. (2023). To Analyse the Impact of Multi-Media Technology on the Rural Entrepreneurship Development. In Contemporary Studies of Risks in Emerging Technology, Part A (pp. 221-240). Emerald Publishing Limited. doi:10.1108/978-1-80455-562-020231015

Dangwal, A., Kaur, S., Taneja, S., & Taneja, S. (2022a). A Bibliometric Analysis of Green Tourism Based on the Scopus Platform. In J. Kaur, P. Jindal, & A. Singh (Eds.), *Developing Relationships, Personalization, and Data Herald in Marketing 5.0* (Vol. 1, pp. 1–327). IGI Global. doi:10.4018/978-1-6684-4496-2.ch015

Dangwal, A., Taneja, S., Özen, E., Todorovic, I., & Grima, S. (2022b). Abridgement of Renewables: It's Potential and Contribution to India's GDP. *International Journal of Sustainable Development and Planning*, *17*(8), 2357–2363. doi:10.18280/ijsdp.170802

Dao, M. Q. (2012). Population and economic growth in developing countries. *International Journal of Academic Research in Business & Social Sciences*, *2*(1), 6.

Dash, S., & Pradhan, R. K. (2014). Determinants and consequences of Organizational Citizenship Behavior: A Theoretical Framework for Indian Manufacturing Organisations. *International Journal of Business and Management Invention*, *3*(1), 17–27.

Dedehayir, O., Ortt, J. R., & Seppänen, M. (2017). Disruptive change and the reconfiguration of innovation ecosystems. *Journal of Technology Management & Innovation*, *12*(3), 9–21. Advance online publication. doi:10.4067/S0718-27242017000300002

Deebak, B. D., & Al-Turjman, F. (2021). Digital-twin assisted: Fault diagnosis using deep transfer learning for machining tool condition. *International Journal of Intelligent Systems*, *37*(12), 10289–10316. doi:10.1002/int.22493

Deistler, M., & Scherrer, W. (2022). ARCH and GARCH Models. *Lecture Notes in Statistics*, *224*, 191–198. doi:10.1007/978-3-031-13213-1_11

Deotale, M. (2018). *Analytical study on impact of Organisational Citizenship Behaviour on Retention of employees working in IT industry*. Academic Press.

DeSimone, S., & Rich, K. (2020). Determinants and consequences of internal audit functions within colleges and universities. *Managerial Auditing Journal*, *35*(8), 1143–1166. doi:10.1108/MAJ-10-2019-2444

Dhoni, P. (2023). *Unleashing the Potential: Overcoming Hurdles and Embracing Generative AI in IT Workplaces: Advantages*. Guidelines, and Policies.

Dikau, S., & Volz, U. (2018). *Central Banking, Climate Change and Green Finance*. ADBI Working Paper 867. Tokyo: Asian Development Bank Institute.

Dipika. (2015). Green Banking in India: A Study of Various Strategies Adopted by Banks for Sustainable Development. *International Journal of Engineering Research & Technology.*

Doguc, O. (2021). Applications of Robotic Process Automation in Finance and Accounting. *Beykent Üniversitesi Fen ve Mühendislik Bilimleri Dergisi*, *14*(1), 51–59. Advance online publication. doi:10.20854/bujse.906795

Duncan, B. (2004). A theory of impact philanthropy. *Journal of Public Economics*, *88*(9–10), 2159–2180. doi:10.1016/S0047-2727(03)00037-9

Eichengreen, B. (2023). Financial regulation in the age of the platform economy. *Journal of Banking Regulation, 24*(1), 40–50.

Elshaer, I. A., Azazz, A. M. S., & Saad, S. K. (2022). Unethical Organization Behavior: Antecedents and Consequences in the Tourism Industry. *International Journal of Environmental Research and Public Health, 19*(9), 4972. doi:10.3390/ijerph19094972 PMID:35564367

Emilisa, N. (2019). *The Role of Altruism, Organizational Learning Capability and Organizational Trust: A Study from Online Motorcycle Drivers in Jakarta*. Available at: www.money.id

Erosa, V. E. (2018). Online Money Flows: Exploring the Nature of the Relation of Technology's New Creature to Money Supply—A Suggested Conceptual Framework and Research Propositions. *American Journal of Industrial and Business Management, 8*(02), 250–305. doi:10.4236/ajibm.2018.82017

Esmaeelinezhad, O., & Afrazeh, A. (2018). Linking personality traits and individuals' knowledge management behavior. *Aslib Journal of Information Management, 70*(3), 234–251. doi:10.1108/AJIM-01-2018-0019

Fajar, A. N., & Legowo, N. (2018). Services modeling based on soa and bpm for information system flexibility improvement. *Iranian Journal of Electrical and Computer Engineering, 8*(4), 2451. doi:10.11591/ijece.v8i4.pp2451-2455

Falcone, P. M., & Sica, E. (2019). Assessing the Opportunities and Challenges of Green Finance in Italy: An Analysis of the Biomass Production Sector. *Sustainability (Basel), 11*(2), 517. doi:10.3390u11020517

Farooq, K. (2015). Organization Citizenship Behaviour a Key for Employee Retention: An Empirical Investigation from Systematic Institutional Industry Pakistan. *Journal of Political Sciences & Public Affairs, 03*(02). Advance online publication. doi:10.4172/2332-0761.1000151

Farooq, R. (2021). Employee exit and its relationship with multidimensional knowledge retention: The moderating role of organizational structure. *VINE Journal of Information and Knowledge Management Systems*. Advance online publication. doi:10.1108/VJIKMS-06-2021-0093

Farrugia, M. (2020). *Imputation and anomaly detection for consumer load profiles* [Master's thesis]. University of Malta.

Fertani, O. (2023). *A Digital Marketing Toolbox Architecture For The Electronic Dance Music Industry: The Use Of Digital Marketing Tools To Reshape The Edm Scenery In The 21st Century* (Doctoral dissertation).

Financial Stability Board. (2017). *Artificial Intelligence and Machine Learning in Financial Services: Market Developments and Financial Stability Implications*. Retrieved from https://www.fsb.org/wp-content/uploads/P300117.pdf

Forbes. (2021). Six Common Business Objectives. *Forbes.*

Gandomi, A., & Haider, M. (2015). Beyond the hype: Big data concepts, methods, and analytics. *International Journal of Information Management*, *35*(2), 137–144. doi:10.1016/j.ijinfomgt.2014.10.007

Garcia, D., Hu, X., & Rohrer, M. (2023). The colour of finance words. *Journal of Financial Economics*, *147*(3), 525–549. doi:10.1016/j.jfineco.2022.11.006

Geddes, A., Schmidt, T. S., & Steffen, B. (2018). The multiple roles of state investment banks in low-carbon energy finance: An analysis of Australia, the UK and Germany. *Energy Policy*, *115*, 158–170. doi:10.1016/j.enpol.2018.01.009

Germana, C., & Luisa, C. (2017). Inclusive finance for inclusive growth and development. *Current Opinion in Environmental Sustainability, 24*, 19-23. doi:10.1016/j.cosust.2017.01.013

Ghoneim, A. F., & Ezzat, A. M. (2016). Growth and Corruption in Arab Countries: What Type of Relationship Connects Them? *Journal of Economics and International Finance*, *8*(5), 44–55. doi:10.5897/JEIF2015.0675

Gibson, A., & Martínez-Maldonado, R. (2017). That dashboard looks nice, but what does it mean? *Proceedings of the 29th Australian Conference on Computer-Human Interaction.* 10.1145/3152771.3156171

Gold, A. H., Malhotra, A., & Segars, A. H. (2001). Knowledge management: An organizational capabilities perspective. *Journal of Management Information Systems*, *18*(1), 185–214. doi:10.1080/07421222.2001.11045669

Goldstein, I., Jiang, W., & Andrew Karolyi, G. (2019). To FinTech and Beyond. *Review of Financial Studies, 32*(5), 1647-1661. doi:10.1093/rfs/hhz025

Gomez, P., & Lambertz, M. (2023). *Leading by Weak Signals: Using Small Data to Master Complexity* (Vol. 5). Walter de Gruyter GmbH & Co KG. doi:10.1515/9783110797886

Group of Twenty. (2016). *G20 Green Finance Synthesis Report 2016*. https://unepinquiry.org/wpcontent/uploads/2016/09/Synthesis_Report_Full_EN.pdf

Gründler, K., & Potrafke, N. (2019). Corruption and economic growth: New empirical evidence. *European Journal of Political Economy*, *60*, 101810. doi:10.1016/j.ejpoleco.2019.08.001

Guinot, J., Chiva, R., & Mallén, F. (2015). The effects of altruism and relationship conflict on organizational learning. *International Journal of Conflict Management*, *26*(1), 85–112.

Gupta, M., Arora, R., & Taneja, S. (2023). Bibliometric Analysis on Employee Engagement and Human Resource Management. In *Enhancing Customer Engagement Through Location-Based Marketing* (pp. 185–205). IGI Global. doi:10.4018/978-1-6684-8177-6.ch013

Gupta, S., & Arora, N. (2022). Quality Management Practices and Organisational Performance A Study of Indian Manufacturing Organisations. *International Journal of Business and Globalisation*, *1*(1), 1. doi:10.1504/IJBG.2022.10044486

Gupta, S., Davoodi, H., & Alonso-Terme, R. (2002). Does Corruption Affect Income Inequality and Poverty? *Economics of Governance*, *3*(1), 23–45. doi:10.1007101010100039

Gupta, V., & Agarwal, U. A. (2018). Relationships between job characteristics, work engagement, conscientiousness and managers' turnover intentions: A moderated-mediation analysis. *Personnel Review*.

Gyimah-Brempong, K., & de Gyimah-Brempong, S. M. (2006). Corruption, growth, and income distribution: Are there regional differences? *Economics of Governance*, *7*(3), 245–269. doi:10.100710101-005-0008-2

Hair, J.F., Howard, M.C., & Nitzl, C. (2020). Assessing measurement model quality in PLS-SEM using confirmatory composite analysis. *Journal of Business Research*, *109*, 101–110.

Hair, J.F., Risher, J.J., Sarstedt, M., & Ringle, C.M. (2019). When to use and how to report the results of PLS-SEM. *European Business Review*.

Hair, J. F., Hult, G. T. M., Ringle, C. M., & Sarstedt, M. (2017). *A Primer on Partial Least Squares Structural Equation Modeling (PLS-SEM)*. Sage.

Hair, J. F., Sarstedt, M., Hopkins, L., & Kuppelwieser, V. G. (2014). Partial least squares structural equation modeling (PLS-SEM): An emerging tool in business research. *European Business Review*, *26*(2), 106–121. doi:10.1108/EBR-10-2013-0128

Haitian, L., Bingzhong, W., Qing, W., & Jing, Y. (2020). Fintech and the Future of Financial Service: A Literature Review and Research Agenda. *China Accounting and Finance Review*, *22*(3), 107–136.

Hall, P., Cox, B., Dickerson, S., Kannan, A. R., Kulkarni, R., & Schmidt, N. (2021). A United States fair lending perspective on machine learning. *Frontiers in Artificial Intelligence*, *4*, 695301. doi:10.3389/frai.2021.695301 PMID:34164616

Hambly, B., Xu, R., & Yang, H. (2023). Recent advances in reinforcement learning in finance. *Mathematical Finance*, *33*(3), 437–503. doi:10.1111/mafi.12382

Harvey, J., Bolino, M. C., & Kelemen, T. K. (2018). Organizational Citizenship Behavior in the 21 st Century: How Might Going the Extra Mile Look Different at the Start of the New Millennium? Academic Press.

Hasan, M., Le, T., & Hoque, A. (2021). How does financial literacy impact on inclusive finance? *Financial Innovation*, *7*(1), 40. doi:10.118640854-021-00259-9

Haseeb, M., & Azam, M. (2021). Dynamic nexus among tourism, corruption, democracy and environmental degradation: A panel data investigation. *Environment, Development and Sustainability*, *23*(4), 5557–5575. doi:10.100710668-020-00832-9

Hazzi, O. A. (2018). Organizational Citizenship Behavior: A Holistic Review. Global Encyclopedia of Public Administration, Public Policy, and Governance, 1–12.

Headey, D. D., & Hodge, A. (2009). The effect of population growth on economic growth: A meta-regression analysis of the macroeconomic literature. *Population and Development Review*, *35*(2), 221–248. doi:10.1111/j.1728-4457.2009.00274.x

Henseler, J., Ringle, C. M., & Sarstedt, M. (2015). A new criterion for assessing discriminant validity in variance-based structural equation modeling. *Journal of the Academy of Marketing Science*, *43*(1), 115–135. doi:10.100711747-014-0403-8

Hickey, A. J., & Conway, J. (2021). Historical perspective - Disruptive technologies and strategies. Inhaled Medicines: Optimizing Development through Integration of In Silico, In Vitro and In Vivo Approaches. doi:10.1016/B978-0-12-814974-4.00003-1

Holland FinTech. (2015, March 20). *The future of finance: The socialization of finance*. Available at http://hollandFinTech. com/the-future-of-finance-the-socialization-of-finance

Hou, M., Zhu, H., Zhou, M., & Arrabito, G. G. (2011). Optimizing operator–agent interaction in intelligent adaptive interface design: A conceptual framework. *IEEE Transactions on Systems, Man, and Cybernetics. Part C, Applications and Reviews*, *41*(2), 161–178. doi:10.1109/TSMCC.2010.2052041

Hout, K., Itkin, A., von Sydow, L., & Toivanen, J. (2018). Special issue—Computational and algorithmic finance. *Journal of Computational Science*, *24*, 180–181. doi:10.1016/j.jocs.2017.12.009

Howitt, P. (2005). Health, human capital, and economic growth: A Schumpeterian perspective. *Health and economic growth: Findings and policy implications, 1*, 19-40.

Huang, A. H., Wang, H., & Yang, Y. (2023). FinBERT: A large language model for extracting information from financial text. *Contemporary Accounting Research*, *40*(2), 806–841. doi:10.1111/1911-3846.12832

Huang, C. J. (2016). Is corruption bad for economic growth? Evidence from Asia-Pacific countries. *The North American Journal of Economics and Finance*, *35*, 247–256. doi:10.1016/j.najef.2015.10.013

Hu, L. T., & Bentler, P. M. (1999). Cutoff criteria for fit indexes in covariance structure analysis: Conventional criteria versus new alternatives. *Structural Equation Modeling*, *6*(1), 1–55. doi:10.1080/10705519909540118

Hussain, A. (2015). Pradhan Mantri Jan Dhan Yojana: A SWOT Analysis. *Journal for Advanced Research in Commerce and Management Studies*, *2*(2), 84–94.

Iandoli, L. (2023). *When solutions are in search of problems: New venture creation in the booming market of digital speech recognition*. SAGE Publications.

Investopedia. (2022). *Business Performance*. Author.

IraniL. (2023). Algorithms of Suspicion: Authentication and Distrust on the Amazon Mechanical Turk Platform. Available at SSRN 4482508. doi:10.2139/ssrn.4482508

Jahangir, N., Akbar, M. M., & Haq, M. (2004). *Organizational citizenship behavior: Its nature and antecedents. BRAC University Journal, 1.*

Jain, N. R., & Rizvi, I. A. (2020). Impact of Corporate Citizenship on Organizational Citizenship Behaviour of Managers: A Study from Selected Indian Banks. *Global Business Review*, *21*(1), 294–311. doi:10.1177/0972150917749289

Jain, S. (2020). *Financing India's green transition. ORF Issue Brief No. 338.* Observer Research Foundation.

Januszewski, A., & Kujawski, J. (2021). Best practices in robotic process automation in global business services. *27th Annual Americas Conference on Information Systems, AMCIS 2021.*

Jayasubramanian, P., & Shanthi, M. (2014). Green Finance. *Indian Journal of Applied Research*, *4*(8). doi:10.15373/2249555X/August2014/161

Jenkins, M. (2021). Altruism in the Workplace. In *Expert Humans: Critical Leadership Skills for a Disrupted World* (pp. 85–100). Emerald Publishing Limited. doi:10.1108/978-1-80071-260-720211009

Jiang, Z., & Liang, J. (2017). *Cryptocurrency portfolio management with deep reinforcement learning. In 2017 Intelligent Systems Conference (IntelliSys) (pp. 905-913).* IEEE.

JoshiM.RajpurohitV. (2016), Pradhan Mantri Jan Dhan Yojana (The Financial Inclusion): A Study of Awareness doi:10.2139/ssrn.2816493

Kanasro, H. A., Rohra, C. L., & Junejo, M. A. (2009). Measurement of stock market volatility through ARCH and GARCH models: A case study of Karachi stock exchange. *Australian Journal of Basic and Applied Sciences*, *3*(4), 3123–3127.

Kantar, L. (2021). ARCH models and an application on exchange rate volatility: ARCH and GARCH models. In *Handbook of Research on Emerging Theories, Models, and Applications of Financial Econometrics*. Springer. doi:10.1007/978-3-030-54108-8_12

Kari, R., & Steinert, M. (2021). Human factor issues in remote ship operations: Lesson learned by studying different domains. *Journal of Marine Science and Engineering*, *9*(4), 385. doi:10.3390/jmse9040385

Karthik, K., Ranjithkumar, V., Kiran, S., & Kumar, S. P. (2023). A Survey of Price Prediction using Deep Learning Classifier for Multiple Stock Datasets. In *2023 Second International Conference on Electronics and Renewable Systems (ICEARS)* (pp. 1268-1275). IEEE.

Kasinathan, S., & Rajee, M. (2017). Interrelationship among factors of OCB in Service industry with respect to Information Technology. *An Empirical Study*, *6*(4), 120–126.

Katsiampa, P. (2017). Volatility estimation for Bitcoin: A comparison of GARCH models. *Economics Letters*, *158*, 3–6. doi:10.1016/j.econlet.2017.06.023

Kaur, H., & Singh, K. N. (2015). Pradhan Mantri Jan Dhan Yojana (PMJDY): A Leap towards Financial Inclusion in India. *International Journal of Emerging Research in Management &Technology, 4*(1), 26-27.

Keerthi, B. S. (2013). A Study on Emerging Green Finance in India: Its challenges and Opportunities. *International Journal of Management and Social Sciences Research, 2*(2), 49–53.

Kim, J., Shah, P., Gaskell, J. C., Prasann, A., & Luthra, A. (2020). Scaling Up Disruptive Agricultural Technologies in Africa. Scaling Up Disruptive Agricultural Technologies in Africa. doi:10.1596/978-1-4648-1522-5

Kim, A., Trimborn, S., & Haerdle, W. K. (2021). VCRIX - A volatility index for crypto-currencies. *International Review of Financial Analysis, 78*, 101915. Advance online publication. doi:10.1016/j.irfa.2021.101915

Kour, M. (2023). Blockchain Technology Changing Landscape of Banking Industry. In *2023 2nd International Conference on Applied Artificial Intelligence and Computing (ICAAIC)* (pp. 1212-1216). IEEE. 10.1109/ICAAIC56838.2023.10140854

Kour, M., & Sharma, N. (2023). Security Issues in e-Banking. In *2023 2nd International Conference on Applied Artificial Intelligence and Computing (ICAAIC)* (pp. 1291-1294). IEEE. 10.1109/ICAAIC56838.2023.10140397

Koys, D. J. (2001). The Effects of Employee Satisfaction, Organizational Citizenship Behavior, and a Unit-Level, Longitudinal Study. *Performance Improvement, 54*, 101–114.

KPMG. (2015, December 14). *H2 Ventures KPMG FinTech 100: Announcing the world's leading FinTech innovators for 2015.* Available at https://home.kpmg.com/xx/en/home/ insights/2015/12/ventures-kpmg-FinTech-fs.html

Kremer, S., Bick, A., & Nautz, D. (2013). Inflation and growth: New evidence from a dynamic panel threshold analysis. *Empirical Economics, 44*(2), 861–878. doi:10.100700181-012-0553-9

Kroll, J. A., Davey, I., & Felten, E. W. (2017). The economics of Bitcoin mining, or Bitcoin in the presence of adversaries. *Proceedings of WEIS.*

Kumar, P., Taneja, S. M., & Ozen, E. (2023). Digital transformation of the insurance industry - a case of the Indian insurance sector. In *The Impact of Climate Change and Sustainability Standards on the Insurance Market.* Wiley. https://www.scopus.com/inward/record.uri?eid=2-s2.0-85168611885&partnerID=40&md5=6c2fb77610b1390b55b6945d955c0955

Kumar, P., Taneja, S., Özen, E., & Singh, S. (2023b). Artificial Intelligence and Machine Learning in Insurance: A Bibliometric Analysis. In Smart Analytics, Artificial Intelligence and Sustainable Performance Management in a Global Digitalised Economy (pp. 191-202). Emerald Publishing Limited. doi:10.1108/S1569-37592023000110A010

Kumar, R. (2018). A study on Pradhan Mantri Jan Dhan Yojana awareness and its satisfaction – A Financial inclusion initiative (With special reference to Coimbatore district). *International Journal of Research and Analytical Reviews, 5*(3).

Kumar, A. S., & Anandarao, S. (2019). Volatility spillover in crypto-currency markets: Some evidences from GARCH and wavelet analysis. *Physica A*, *524*, 448–458. doi:10.1016/j.physa.2019.04.154

Kumarathunga, M., Calheiros, R., & Ginige, A. (2020, May). Towards Trust Enabled Commodity Market for Farmers with Blockchain Smart Contracts. In *Proceedings of the 2020 Asia Service Sciences and Software Engineering Conference* (pp. 75-82). 10.1145/3399871.3399891

Kumar, P., Verma, P., Bhatnagar, M., Taneja, S., Seychel, S., Todorović, I., & Grim, S. (2023). The financial performance and solvency status of the Indian public sector banks: A CAMELS rating and Z index approach. *International Journal of Sustainable Development and Planning*, *18*(2), 367–376. doi:10.18280/ijsdp.180204

Kundu, S. C., & Lata, K. (2017). Effects of supportive work environment on employee retention. *The International Journal of Organizational Analysis*, *25*(4), 703–722. doi:10.1108/IJOA-12-2016-1100

Lahmiri, S., & Bekiros, S. (2019). Decomposing the persistence structure of Islamic and green crypto-currencies with nonlinear stepwise filtering. *Chaos, Solitons, and Fractals*, *127*, 334–341. doi:10.1016/j.chaos.2019.07.012

Lau, P. Y. Y., McLean, G. N., Lien, B. Y.-H., & Hsu, Y.-C. (2016). Self-rated and peer-rated organizational citizenship behavior, affective commitment, and intention to leave in a Malaysian context. *Personnel Review*, *45*(3), 569–592. doi:10.1108/PR-04-2014-0083

Lee, I., & Shin, Y. J. (2020). Machine learning for enterprises: Applications, algorithm selection, and challenges. *Business Horizons*, *63*(2), 157–170. doi:10.1016/j.bushor.2019.10.005

Legowo, M. B., Subanidja, S., & Sorongan, F. A. (2021). Fintech and bank: Past, present, and future. *Jurnal Teknik Komputer AMIK BSI*, *7*(1), 94–99. doi:10.31294/jtk.v7i1.9726

Legowo, M. B., Subanija, S., & Sorongan, F. A. (2020). Role of FinTech mechanism to technological innovation: A conceptual framework. *International Journal of Innovative Science and Research Technology*, *5*(5), 1–6.

Lehoux, P. (2004). Patients' perspectives on high-tech home care: A qualitative inquiry into the user-friendliness of four technologies. *BMC Health Services Research*, *4*(1), 28. Advance online publication. doi:10.1186/1472-6963-4-28 PMID:15462682

Lestari, E. P., Prajanti, S. D. W., Wibawanto, W., & Adzim, F. (2022). ARCH-GARCH Analysis: An Approach to Determine The Price Volatility of Red Chili. *Agraris*, *8*(1), 90–105. doi:10.18196/agraris.v8i1.12060

Li, W., Bao, R., Harimoto, K., Chen, D., Xu, J., & Su, Q. (2021, January). Modeling the stock relation with graph network for overnight stock movement prediction. In *Proceedings of the twenty-ninth international conference on international joint conferences on artificial intelligence* (pp. 4541-4547). Academic Press.

Liao, B., Huang, Z., Cao, X., & Li, J. (2022). Adopting Nonlinear Activated Beetle Antennae Search Algorithm for Fraud Detection of Public Trading Companies: A Computational Finance Approach. *Mathematics*, *10*(13), 2160. Advance online publication. doi:10.3390/math10132160

Li, H.-F., Xing, D.-Z., Huang, Q., & Li, J.-C. (2021). Roles of GARCH and ARCH effects on the stability in stock market crash. *Europhysics Letters*, *136*(4), 48003. Advance online publication. doi:10.1209/0295-5075/ac4527

Liu, J., & Wu, Y. (2022). Green Human Resource Management, Employee Work Values, and Enterprise Environmental Performance. *Journal of Environmental and Public Health*, *2022*, 1–6. Advance online publication. doi:10.1155/2022/8129359 PMID:35795538

Liu, P., Zhang, Y., Bao, F., Yao, X., & Zhang, C. (2023). Multi-type data fusion framework based on deep reinforcement learning for algorithmic trading. *Applied Intelligence*, *53*(2), 1683–1706. doi:10.100710489-022-03321-w

Li, Y., Jiang, W., Yang, L., & Wu, T. (2018). On neural networks and learning systems for business computing. *Neurocomputing*, *275*, 1150–1159. doi:10.1016/j.neucom.2017.09.054

Li, Y., Ni, P., & Chang, V. (2020). Application of deep reinforcement learning in stock trading strategies and stock forecasting. *Computing*, *102*(6), 1305–1322. doi:10.100700607-019-00773-w

Locatelli, R., Schena, C., & Tanda, A. (2021). *A Historical Perspective on Disruptive Technologies*. doi:10.1007/978-3-030-81835-7_2

Lorde, T., & Joseph, T. S. D. (2019). Airbnb, technological change and disruption in Barbadian tourism: A theoretical framework. *Third World Quarterly*, *40*(12), 2190–2209. Advance online publication. doi:10.1080/01436597.2019.1633913

Lucas, R. E. Jr. (1988). On the mechanics of economic development. *Journal of Monetary Economics*, *22*(1), 3–42. doi:10.1016/0304-3932(88)90168-7

Mahesh, B. (2020). Machine learning algorithms—A review. *International Journal of Scientific Research*, *9*, 381–386.

Makhlouf, A. (2023). *Workshop Report: Cryptos: Distinguishing Hype and Realities in Islamic Finance*. Academic Press.

Malhotra, Y. (2015). Cybersecurity & Cyber-Finance Risk Management: Strategies, Tactics, Operations, &, Intelligence: Enterprise Risk Management to Model Risk Management: Understanding Vulnerabilities, Threats, & Risk Mitigation (Presentation Slides). SSRN *Electronic Journal*. doi:10.2139/ssrn.2693886

Mallén, F., Domínguez-Escrig, E., Lapiedra, R., & Chiva, R. (2019). Does leader humility matter? Effects on altruism and innovation. *Management Decision*, *58*(5), 967–981. doi:10.1108/MD-11-2018-1180

Mallick, E., Pradhan, R. K., Tewari, H. R., & Jena, L. K. (2014). Organizational Citizenship Behaviour, Job Performance and HR Practices: A Relational Perspective. *Management and Labour Studies*, *39*(4), 449–460. doi:10.1177/0258042X15578023

Mallik, G., & Saha, S. (2016). Corruption and growth: A complex relationship. *International Journal of Development Issues*, *15*(2), 113–129. doi:10.1108/IJDI-01-2016-0001

Marevac, E., Patković, S., & Žunić, E. (2023). Decision-making AI for customer worthiness and viability. In *2023 22nd International Symposium INFOTEH-JAHORINA (INFOTEH)* (pp. 1-6). IEEE. 10.1109/INFOTEH57020.2023.10094207

Marquering, W. A., & de Goeij, P. (2005). Modeling the Conditional Covariance Between Stock and Bond Returns: A Multivariate Garch Approach. SSRN *Electronic Journal, 2*(4), 1–58. doi:10.2139/ssrn.302335

Martínez-Plumed, F., Gómez, E., & Hernández-Orallo, J. (2021). Futures of artificial intelligence through technology readiness levels. *Telematics and Informatics*, *58*, 101525. doi:10.1016/j.tele.2020.101525

Mathis, F. J., & Almarzoqi, R. M. (2022). Global innovation, finance, and international commerce. In *Global Innovation*. Finance, and International Commerce. doi:10.4324/9781003024675

Mauro, P. (1995). Corruption and growth». *The Quarterly Journal of Economics*, *110*(3), 681–712. doi:10.2307/2946696

McAfee, A., Brynjolfsson, E., & Davenport, T. H. (2017). Big data. *MIT Sloan Management Review*, *55*(2), 1–4.

Méon, P. G., & Sekkat, K. (2005). Does corruption grease or sand the wheels of growth? *Public Choice*, *122*(1), 69–97. doi:10.100711127-005-3988-0

Mnif, E., Mouakhar, K., & Jarboui, A. (2023). Energy-conserving crypto currency response during the COVID-19 pandemic and amid the Russia–Ukraine conflict. *The Journal of Risk Finance*, *24*(2), 169–185. doi:10.1108/JRF-06-2022-0161

Mohd, S., & V K, K. (2018). Green Finance: A Step towards Sustainable Development. *MUDRA Journal of Finance and Accounting*, *5*(1), 59–74. doi:10.17492/mudra.v5i01.13036

Morales, L., Gray, G., & Rajmil, D. (2022). Emerging Risks in the FinTech Industry–Insights from Data Science and Financial Econometrics Analysis. *Economics, Management & Financial Markets, 17*(2).

Moser, C. (2008). Poverty reduction, patronage or vote-buying? The allocation of public goods and the 2001 election in Madagascar. *Economic Development and Cultural Change*, *57*(1), 137–162. doi:10.1086/590458

Mossholder, K. W. (2005). A Relational Perspective on Turnover Examing Strucutal. *Pdf*, *48*(4), 607–618.

Mougayar, W. (2016). *The business blockchain: Promise, practice, and application of the next internet technology*. Wiley.

Murphy, K. M., Shleifer, A., & Vishny, R. W. (1991). The allocation of talent: Implications for growth. *The Quarterly Journal of Economics*, *106*(2), 503–530. doi:10.2307/2937945

Naimy, V., Haddad, O., Fernandez-Aviles, G., & El Khoury, R. (2021). The predictive capacity of GARCH-type models in measuring the volatility of crypto and world currencies. *PLoS One*, *16*(1), e0245904. Advance online publication. doi:10.1371/journal.pone.0245904 PMID:33513150

Nasir, A., Shaukat, K., Hameed, I. A., Luo, S., Alam, T. M., & Iqbal, F. (2020). A bibliometric analysis of corona pandemic in social sciences: A review of influential aspects and conceptual structure. *IEEE Access : Practical Innovations, Open Solutions*, *8*, 133377–133402. doi:10.1109/ACCESS.2020.3008733 PMID:34812340

Nassiry, D. (2018). *Green Bond Experiences in Nordic Countries*. ADBI Working Paper No. 816.

Nielsen, J. F. (2002). Internet technology and customer linking in Nordic banking. *Internal Journal of Service Banking*, *13*(2), 475–496.

Njoya, N., & Aman, N. (2017). *Corruption et croissance économique au Cameroun: de l'effet direct et des effets indirects à travers la répartition des dépenses publiques* (Doctoral dissertation, Rennes 1).

Nsor-Ambala, R., & Coffie, C. P. K. (2021). Non-linear ADRL estimation of corruption and FDI inflow to Ghana. *Journal of Financial Crime*.

Nüesch, R., Alt, R., & Puschmann, T. (2015). Hybrid customer interaction. *Business & Information Systems Engineering*, *57*(1), 73–78. doi:10.100712599-014-0366-9

Nur Laily, V. O., Warsito, B., & Maruddani, I. D. A. (2018). Comparison of ARCH / GARCH model and Elman Recurrent Neural Network on data return of closing price stock. In Journal of Physics: Conference Series (Vol. 1025, Issue 1). Institute of Physics Publishing. doi:10.1088/1742-6596/1025/1/012103

OECD INFE. (2011). *Measuring Financial Literacy: Core Questionnaire in Measuring Financial Literacy: Questionnaire and Guidance Notes for conducting an Internationally Comparable Survey of Financial literacy*. OECD.

Oktaviani, F., Miftahuddin, & Setiawan, I. (2021). Forecasting sea surface temperature anomalies using the SARIMA ARCH/GARCH model. In Journal of Physics: Conference Series (Vol. 1882, Issue 1). IOP Publishing Ltd. doi:10.1088/1742-6596/1882/1/012020

Olendo, O. P., & Muindi, F. (2017). The Perceived Relationship between Employee Retention Practices and Organization Citizenship Behaviour at D.T.Dobie (K) Ltd. *International Journal of Scientific and Research Publications*, *7*(2), 320.

Olga, B., & Smorodinov, O. (2017). Challenges to green finance in G20 countries. *Mirovaya ekonomika i mezhdunarodnye otnosheniya*, *61*(10), 16-24.

Omidvar, O., Safavi, M., & Glaser, V. L. (2023). Algorithmic routines and dynamic inertia: How organizations avoid adapting to changes in the environment. *Journal of Management Studies*, *60*(2), 313–345. doi:10.1111/joms.12819

Oprea, S. V., Bâra, A., & Andreescu, A. I. (2020). Two novel blockchain-based market settlement mechanisms embedded into smart contracts for securely trading renewable energy. *IEEE Access : Practical Innovations, Open Solutions*, *8*, 212548–212556. doi:10.1109/ACCESS.2020.3040764

Organ. (2005). *OCB in the Context of Organization Theory*. Author.

Örtqvist, D. (2020). Performance outcomes from reciprocal altruism: A multi-level model. *Journal of Small Business and Entrepreneurship*, *32*(3), 227–240. doi:10.1080/08276331.2019.1661616

Othman, A. H. A., Alhabshi, S. M., & Haron, R. (2019). The effect of symmetric and asymmetric information on volatility structure of crypto-currency markets A case study of bitcoin currency. *Journal of Financial Economic Policy*, *11*(3), 432–450. doi:10.1108/JFEP-10-2018-0147

Othmani, A., Bakari, S., & Slimani, S. (2015). *Impact Direct et Indirect de la Corruption sur le Commerce Extérieur en Tunisie: Étude Descriptive*. Academic Press.

Ouadah, A., Zemmouchi-Ghomari, L., & Salhi, N. (2022). Selecting an appropriate supervised machine learning algorithm for predictive maintenance. *International Journal of Advanced Manufacturing Technology*, *119*(7-8), 4277–4301. doi:10.100700170-021-08551-9

Ouattara, W. (2011). Corruption, investissements et croissance économique en Côte d'Ivoire. *Savings and Development*, *35*(1), 55–73. doi:10.2307avideve.35.1.55

Özen, E., & Sanjay, T. (2022a). Empirical Analysis of the Effect of Foreign Trade in Computer and Communication Services on Economic Growth in India. *Journal of Economics and Business Issues*, *2*(2), 24–34. https://doi.org/https://jebi-academic.org/index.php/jebi/article/view/41

Padhan, H., Behera, D. K., Sahu, S. K., & Dash, U. (2022). Does Corruption Hinderance Economic Growth Despite Surge of Remittance and Capital Inflows Since Economic Liberalization in an Emerging Economy, India. *Journal of the Knowledge Economy*, 1–24.

Paillé, P. (2013). Organizational citizenship behaviour and employee retention: How important are turnover cognitions? *International Journal of Human Resource Management*, *24*(4), 768–790. doi:10.1080/09585192.2012.697477

Paillé, P., Raineri, N., & Valeau, P. J. (2015). Retention : Examining The Relationships. *Journal of Applied Business Research*, *31*(4), 1437–1452. doi:10.19030/jabr.v31i4.9329

Paillé, P., & Valéau, P. (2019). I don't complain, but I am ready for any eventuality. *The International Journal of Organizational Analysis*, *27*(3), 566–581. doi:10.1108/IJOA-02-2018-1351

Paldam, M. (2002). The cross-country pattern of corruption: Economics, culture and the seesaw dynamics. *European Journal of Political Economy*, *18*(2), 215–240. doi:10.1016/S0176-2680(02)00078-2

Pallathadka, H., Ramirez-Asis, E. H., Loli-Poma, T. P., Kaliyaperumal, K., Ventayen, R. J. M., & Naved, M. (2023). Applications of artificial intelligence in business management, e-commerce and finance. *Materials Today: Proceedings*, *80*, 2610–2613. doi:10.1016/j.matpr.2021.06.419

Pandey, N., Jha, S., & Rai, V. (2021). Ayushman Bharat: Service Adoption Challenges in Universal Healthcare System. *South Asian Journal of Business and Management Cases*, *10*(1), 35–49. doi:10.1177/2277977921991915

Parry, J. (2008). Intention to leave the profession: Antecedents and role in nurse turnover. *Journal of Advanced Nursing*, *64*(2), 157–167. doi:10.1111/j.1365-2648.2008.04771.x PMID:18990096

Paulson-Luna, M., & Reily, K. (2020, May). The Financial Derivative Ecosystem is Old-Decentralized Ledger Technology is its Fountain of Youth. In *Proceedings of the 2020 Asia Service Sciences and Software Engineering Conference* (pp. 105-112). 10.1145/3399871.3399904

Pediredla, V. K., Chandrasekaran, K., Annamraju, S., & Thondiyath, A. (2021). Design, analysis, and control of a 3-dof novel haptic device displaying stiffness, texture, shape, and shear. *IEEE Access : Practical Innovations, Open Solutions*, *9*, 72055–72065. doi:10.1109/ACCESS.2021.3079175

Pellegrini, L., & Gerlagh, R. (2004). Corruption's effect on growth and its transmission channels. *Kyklos*, *57*(3), 429–456. doi:10.1111/j.0023-5962.2004.00261.x

Pesaran, M. H., Shin, Y., & Smith, R. J. (2001). Bounds testing approaches to the analysis of level relationships. *Journal of Applied Econometrics*, *16*(3), 289–326. doi:10.1002/jae.616

Poonam, & Aggarwal, K. K. (2023). Analysis of the impact of COVID-19 on the stock market and capability of investing strategies. *AIP Conference Proceedings, 2782*(1), 20112. doi:10.1063/5.0154174

Popescu, A. M., Deaconu, A., & Popescu, T. (2015). Organization's Age and Organizational Citizenship Behavior (OCB), Performance Criteria at SMEs Level. Case Study – Bucharest – Ilfov Development Region. *Procedia Economics and Finance*, *22*(October), 645–654.

Postolea, I. D., & Bodea, C. N. (2022). Building RPA solutions for customer-oriented processes automation. *Issues in Information Systems*, *23*(2). Advance online publication. doi:10.48009/2_iis_2022_108

Primeum. (2021, April 6). *Business Performance: What is Business Performance*. Author.

Pujari, B. (2019). *Promoting standard of living through Financial Inclusion: A study on Bargarh and Sambalpur districts of western Odisha* (Doctoral dissertation). Retrieved from http://hdl.handle.net/10603/284279

Puschmann, T. (2017). Fintech. *Business & Information Systems Engineering*, *59*(1), 69–76. doi:10.100712599-017-0464-6

Rabhi, F. A., Mehandjiev, N., & Baghdadi, A. (2020). State-of-the-art in applying machine learning to electronic trading. In *Enterprise Applications, Markets and Services in the Finance Industry: 10th International Workshop, FinanceCom 2020, Helsinki, Finland, August 18, 2020, Revised Selected Papers 10* (pp. 3-20). Springer International Publishing. 10.1007/978-3-030-64466-6_1

Rakshit, S., Clement, N., & Vajjhala, N. R. (2022). Exploratory review of applications of machine learning in finance sector. In *Advances in Data Science and Management. Proceedings of ICDSM, 2021*, 119–125.

Rao, N. D. (2013). *Status of Financial Inclusion Among Rural Households in Andhra Pradesh. From Andhra University* (Doctoral dissertation).

Rasoolimanesh, S. M., Taheri, B., Gannon, M., Vafaei-Zadeh, A., & Hanifah, H. (2019). Does living in the vicinity of heritage tourism sites influence residents' perceptions and attitudes? *Journal of Sustainable Tourism*, *27*(9), 1295–1317. doi:10.1080/09669582.2019.1618863

Reddy, A. S. (2018). Green Finance- Financial Support for Sustainable Development. *International Journal of Pure and Applied Mathematics*, *118*(20), 645–650.

Reepu, T. S., & Singh, A. (2023). *Context aware computing. In Big Data: A Road-Map for Successful Digital Marketing*. Nova Science Publishers, Inc. https://www.scopus.com/inward/record.uri?eid=2-s2.0-85172698675&partnerID=40&md5=dfe437743a3d43d55acac9e4849f23f7

Reepu, R., Taneja, S., Ozen, E., & Singh, A. (2023). A Globetrotter to the Future of Marketing: Metaverse. In *Cultural Marketing and Metaverse for Consumer Engagement* (pp. 1–11). IGI Global. doi:10.4018/978-1-6684-8312-1.ch001

Reppen, A. M., Soner, H. M., & Tissot-Daguette, V. (2023). Deep stochastic optimization in finance. *Digital Finance*, *5*(1), 91–111. doi:10.100742521-022-00074-6

Romer, P. M. (1987). Growth based on increasing returns due to specialization. *The American Economic Review*, *77*(2), 56–62.

Rosario Núñez, A., Marquez, E., Zayas, M., & López, E. (2020). Relationship between organizational citizenship and commitment in Puerto Rico banks. *The International Journal of Sociology and Social Policy*, *40*(7/8), 643–658. doi:10.1108/IJSSP-02-2020-0028

Sachs, J. D., Woo, N., Yoshino, N., & Hesary, T. (2019). *Hesary; Why is Green Finance Important?* ADBI working paper 917. https://www.adb.org/publications/why-green-finance-important

Sachs, J. D. (2008). The African green revolution. *Scientific American*, *298*(5), 42–43. doi:10.1038cientificamerican0508-42 PMID:18444321

Saef, D., Wang, Y., & Aste, T. (2023). Regime-based Implied Stochastic Volatility Model for Crypto Option Pricing. *ACM Web Conference 2023 - Companion of the World Wide Web Conference, WWW 2023*, 1103–1110. 10.1145/3543873.3587621

Saksa, J. (2015), *An Investigation of Research on Altruism in Recent Literature of the Three Sectors: Public, Private, and Non-Profit*. Available at: https://scholarworks.gvsu.edu/honorsprojects/556

Salameh, A., & Bass, J. M. (2020, April). Heterogeneous tailoring approach using the spotify model. In *Proceedings of the 24th International Conference on Evaluation and Assessment in Software Engineering* (pp. 293-298). 10.1145/3383219.3383251

Sari, N., Ghozali, I., & Achmad, T. (2017). The effect of internal audit and internal control system on public accountability: The empirical study in Indonesia state universities. *International Journal of Civil Engineering and Technology*, *8*(9), 157–166.

Sathye, M. (1999). Adoption of internet banking by Australian consumers: An empirical investigation. *International Journal of Bank Marketing*, *17*(7), 324–339. doi:10.1108/02652329910305689

Schwartz, R. A., Byrne, J. A., & Schnee, G. (2013). The quality of our financial markets: Taking stock of where we stand. In *The Quality of Our Financial Markets*. Taking Stock of Where We Stand. doi:10.1007/978-1-4614-5592-9

Scott, E. D. (2002). Organizational Moral Values. Business Ethics Quarterly, 12(1), 33–55. doi:10.2307/3857647

Seka, P. (2013). Corruption, croissance et capital humain: Quels rapports? *Africa Development. Afrique et Developpement*, *XXXVIII*(1&2), 133–150.

Serov, E. R., & Vasiliev, S. A. (2023). Application of quantum technologies in banking. *Economics and Management*, *29*(3), 248–255. Advance online publication. doi:10.35854/1998-1627-2023-3-248-255

Setiawati, I., Ardiansyah, & Taufikurohman, R. (2021). Price volatility of staple food using ARCH-GARCH model. *IOP Conference Series. Earth and Environmental Science*, *653*(1), 012146. Advance online publication. doi:10.1088/1755-1315/653/1/012146

Shen, C., Zhao, K., & Ge, J. (2020). An Overview of Green Building Performance Database. *Journal of Engineering*, *2020*, 1–9. doi:10.1155/2020/3780595

Shleifer, A., & Vishny, R. W. (1993). Corruption. *The Quarterly Journal of Economics*, *108*(3), 599–617. doi:10.2307/2118402

Singh, V., Taneja, S., Singh, V., Singh, A., & Paul, H. L. (2021). Online advertising strategies in Indian and Australian e-commerce companies:: A comparative study. *Big Data Analytics for Improved Accuracy, Efficiency, and Decision Making in Digital Marketing*, 124–138. doi:10.4018/978-1-7998-7231-3.ch009

Singh, A., Sharma, S., Singh, A., Unanoğlu, M., & Taneja, S. (2023). Cultural Marketing and Metaverse for Consumer Engagement. In *Cultural Marketing and Metaverse for Consumer Engagement*. IGI Global. doi:10.4018/978-1-6684-8312-1

Singh, D. (2019). A Literature Review on Employee Retention with Focus on Recent Trends. *International Journal of Scientific Research in Science, Engineering and Technology*, 425–431. doi:10.32628/IJSRST195463

Singh, K. R. (2018). Development of Micro, Small and Medium Enterprises through MUDRA Loans with Special Reference to Manipur. *Abhinav National Monthly Refereed Journals of Research in Commerce & Management*, *7*(1), 55–61.

Song, C. Q., Chang, C. P., & Gong, Q. (2021). Economic growth, corruption, and financial development: Global evidence. *Economic Modelling*, *94*, 822–830. doi:10.1016/j.econmod.2020.02.022

Soundarrajan, P., & Vivek, N. (2016). Green finance for sustainable green economic growth in India. *Zemedelská Ekonomika*, *62*(1), 35–44. doi:10.17221/174/2014-AGRICECON

Sriboonlue, P., & Peemanee, J. (2014). Personal-organizational factors, OCB, and job performance: The governance bank employees. *International Journal of Strategic Management*, *14*(2), 101–110. doi:10.18374/IJSM-14-2.9

Sriee G V VP, & Maiya GR. (2021). Coverage, utilization, and impact of Ayushman Bharat scheme among the rural field practice area of Saveetha Medical College and Hospital, Chennai. *J Family Med Prim Care*, *10*(3), 1171-1176. . doi:10.4103/jfmpc.jfmpc_1789_20

Sun, W., Dedahanov, A. T., Shin, H. Y., & Li, W. P. (2021). Factors affecting institutional investors to add crypto-currency to asset portfolios. *The North American Journal of Economics and Finance*, *58*, 101499. Advance online publication. doi:10.1016/j.najef.2021.101499

Swaleheen, M. (2011). Economic growth with endogenous corruption: An empirical study. *Public Choice*, *146*(1), 23–41. doi:10.100711127-009-9581-1

Taneja, S., Dangwal, A., Kaur, S., Ozen, E., & Kukreti, M. (2023). An evaluation of the operational and regulatory aspects of using blockchain in the insurance industry. In *The Application of Emerging Technology and Blockchain in the Insurance Industry*. River Publishers. https://www.scopus.com/inward/record.uri?eid=2-s2.0-85175665567&partnerID=40&md5=fa6499e497e6fb8a5f1510ffccd27bb6

Taneja, S., Bhatnagar, M., Kumar, P., & Grima, S. (2023c). A panel analysis of the effectiveness of the asset management in Indian agricultural companies. *International Journal of Sustainable Development and Planning*, *18*(3), 653–660. doi:10.18280/ijsdp.180301

Taneja, S., Bhatnagar, M., Kumar, P., & Rupeika-apoga, R. (2023b). India ' s Total Natural Resource Rents (NRR) and GDP : An Augmented Autoregressive Distributed Lag (ARDL) Bound Test. *Journal of Risk and Financial Management*, *16*(2), 91. doi:10.3390/jrfm16020091

Taneja, S., Grima, S., Kumar, P., & Ozen, E. (2023). Special Issue: 'Green Asset and Risk Management for Promoting Sustainable Entrepreneurship in the Building of the Green Economy.'. *International Journal of Technology Management & Sustainable Development*, *22*(2), 127–130. doi:10.1386/tmsd_00071_7

Taneja, S., Gupta, M., Bhushan, P., Bhatnagar, M., & Singh, A. (2023f). Cultural Marketing in the Digital Era. In *Cultural Marketing and Metaverse for Consumer Engagement* (pp. 109–122). IGI Global. doi:10.4018/978-1-6684-8312-1.ch008

Taneja, S., Jaggi, P., Jewandah, S., & Ozen, E. (2022b). Role of Social Inclusion in Sustainable Urban Developments: An Analyse by PRISMA Technique. *International Journal of Design & Nature and Ecodynamics*, *17*(6), 937–942. doi:10.18280/ijdne.170615

Taneja, S., Kaur, S., & Özen, E. (2022a). Using green finance to promote global growth in a sustainable way. *International Journal of Green Economics*, *16*(3), 246–257. doi:10.1504/IJGE.2022.128930

Taneja, S., Kumar, P., Grima, S., Ozen, E., & Sood, K. (2023). *Sustainable investments in Green Finance*. IGI Global. doi:10.4018/979-8-3693-1388-6

Taneja, S., & Ozen, E. (2023). Impact of the European Green Deal (EDG) on the agricultural carbon (CO2) emission in Turkey. *International Journal of Sustainable Development and Planning*, *18*(3), 715–727. doi:10.18280/ijsdp.180307

Taneja, S., & Özen, E. (2023). To analyse the relationship between bank's green financing and environmental performance. *International Journal of Electronic Finance*, *12*(2), 163–175. doi:10.1504/IJEF.2023.129919

Taneja, S., & Sharma, V. (2023e). Role of Beaconing Marketing in Improving Customer Buying Experience. In *Enhancing Customer Engagement Through Location-Based Marketing* (pp. 176–184). IGI Global. doi:10.4018/978-1-6684-8177-6.ch012

Tanzi, V., & Davoodi, H. (1997). *Corruption, Public Investment, and Growth.* IMF Working Papers 97/139, International Monetary Fund.

Tanzi, V., & Davoodi, H. R. (2000). *Corruption, growth, and public finances*. Academic Press.

Thacker, J. (2020). The Age of AI: Artificial Intelligence and the Future of Humanity. *Perspectives on Science and Christian Faith*, *72*(4), 252–254. Advance online publication. doi:10.56315/PSCF12-20Thacker

The National Association of State Budget Officers. (2016). *Budget processes and practices*. Author.

Théate, T., & Ernst, D. (2021). An application of deep reinforcement learning to algorithmic trading. *Expert Systems with Applications*, *173*, 114632. doi:10.1016/j.eswa.2021.114632

Thekkethil, M. S., Shukla, V. K., Beena, F., & Chopra, A. (2021). Robotic Process Automation in Banking and Finance Sector for Loan Processing and Fraud Detection. *2021 9th International Conference on Reliability, Infocom Technologies and Optimization (Trends and Future Directions), ICRITO 2021*. 10.1109/ICRITO51393.2021.9596076

Thorat, U. (2007). *Financial Inclusion – The Indian experience Speech.* Academic Press.

Tian, H., Iqbal, S., Akhtar, S., Qalati, S. A., Anwar, F., & Khan, M. A. S. (2020). The Impact of Transformational Leadership on Employee Retention: Mediation and Moderation Through Organizational Citizenship Behavior and Communication. *Frontiers in Psychology*, *11*(March), 1–11. doi:10.3389/fpsyg.2020.00314 PMID:32256424

Transparency International. (2018). *Indice de perception de la corruption 2018.* https://www.transparency.org/cpi

Transparency International. (2019). *Indice de perception de la corruption 2019.* https://www.transparency.org/cpi

Trapletti, A., & Hornik, K. (2017). tseries: Time Series Analysis and Computational Finance. *R Package Version 0.10-42.*

Tsanana, E., Chapsa, X., & Katrakilidis, C. (2016). Is growth corrupted or bureaucratic? Panel evidence from the enlarged EU. *Applied Economics*, *48*(33), 3131–3147. doi:10.1080/00036846.2015.1136395

Tulchinsky, I., & Mason, C. E. (2023). *The Age of Prediction: Algorithms, AI, and the Shifting Shadows of Risk.* MIT Press. doi:10.7551/mitpress/13872.001.0001

Usman, M., Wardhana, M. Y., & Istiqamah, M. (2022). Analysis of the Risk of Rubber Prices Using the ARCH-GARCH and VaR Methods on Farm Income in West Aceh District. *International Journal on Advanced Science, Engineering and Information Technology*, *12*(3), 1018–1022. doi:10.18517/ijaseit.12.3.13637

Utpal Kalita. (n.d.). *Social Awareness Scale, 781 P, (SESS(R)–DSDV) Hindi/English.* National Psychological Corp.

Vedder, R., Welters, M., Mints, A., & Ramkhelawan, A. (2016). *Robotic process automation in the Finance function of the future.* Ernst & Young.

Veilleux, M., Sénécal, S., Demolin, B., Bouvier, F., Di Fabio, M. L., Coursaris, C., & Léger, P. M. (2020). Visualizing a user's cognitive and emotional journeys: A fintech case. *Design, User Experience, and Usability. Interaction Design: 9th International Conference, DUXU 2020, Held as Part of the 22nd HCI International Conference, HCII 2020, Copenhagen, Denmark, July 19–24, 2020 Proceedings*, *22*(Part I), 549–566.

Verma, Y., & Garg, P. (2016). Pradhan Mantri Jan Dhan Yojana (PMJDY): A step towards eradicating financial untouchability. *Indian Journal of Finance*, *10*(1), 56–64. doi:10.17010/ijf/2016/v10i1/85845

Volz, U. (2018). *Fostering green finance for sustainable development in Asia.* ADBI Working Paper Series (814).

Walz, S. M., & Niehoff, B. P. (1996). Organizational Citizenship Behaviors and Their Effect on Organizational Effectiveness in Limited-Menu Restaurants. *Proceedings - Academy of Management*, *1996*(1), 307–311. doi:10.5465/ambpp.1996.4980770

Wang, K., Tsai, S.-B., Du, X., & Bi, D. (2019). Internet Finance, Green Finance, and Sustainability. *Sustainability (Basel), 11*(14), 3856. doi:10.3390u11143856

Weber, P., Carl, K. V., & Hinz, O. (2023). Applications of Explainable Artificial Intelligence in Finance—a systematic review of finance, information systems, and computer science literature. *Management Review Quarterly*, 1-41.

Woodhead, R., Stephenson, P., & Morrey, D. (2018). Digital construction: From point solutions to IoT ecosystem. *Automation in Construction, 93*, 35–46. Advance online publication. doi:10.1016/j.autcon.2018.05.004

World Economic Forum Boston Consulting Group (BCG). (2018). *Towards a reskilling revolution: A future of jobs for all.* World Economic Forum.

Yadav, N., Taneja, S., Özen, E., Singh, A. B., & Vida, I. (2023). A Bibliometric Survey on Sustainable Finance: Research Patterns and Trends. *Acta Polytechnica Hungarica, 20*(10), 109–125. doi:10.12700/APH.20.10.2023.10.7

Yi, J., Meng, S., Macaulay, C. D., & Peng, M. W. (2019). Corruption and foreign direct investment phases: The moderating role of institutions. *Journal of International Business Policy, 2*(2), 167–181. doi:10.105742214-019-00024-x

Yuniawan, A., Udin, U., Abdurrahman, A., & Suci, R. P. (2018). *A Systematic Literature Review of Altruism: Challenges* (Vol. 21). Outcomes and Future Research Directions, European Research Studies Journal.

Zabalo, E. A., Erle, G. L., & Gerrikagoitia, J. K. (2018). *Evaluating the human machine interface experience in industrial workplaces.* Electronic Workshops in Computing. doi:10.14236/ewic/HCI2018.93

Zakharov, N. (2019). Does corruption hinder investment? Evidence from Russian regions. *European Journal of Political Economy, 56*, 39–61. doi:10.1016/j.ejpoleco.2018.06.005

Zangina, S., & Hassan, S. (2020). Corruption and FDI inflow to Nigeria: A nonlinear ARDL approach. *Journal of Financial Crime, 27*(2), 635–650. doi:10.1108/JFC-09-2019-0116

Zhou, J. Q., & Peng, M. W. (2012). Does bribery help or hurt firm growth around the world? *Asia Pacific Journal of Management, 29*(4), 907–921. doi:10.100710490-011-9274-4

Zhu, L., Xu, X., Lu, Q., Governatori, G., & Whittle, J. (2022). AI and ethics—Operationalizing responsible AI. In *Humanity Driven AI* (pp. 15–33). Productivity, Well-being, Sustainability and Partnership. doi:10.1007/978-3-030-72188-6_2

Ziritt Trejo, G., Taboada Hernandez, R., Moreno, Z., & Isabel Castellano, M. (2018). Public Management and Sustainable Development: Expression of Social Responsibility. Innovation Management and Education Excellence Through Vision 2020, Vols I -Xi.

About the Contributors

Amandeep Singh holds a Doctorate in Management specializing in Marketing and he is also UGC-NET qualified. He holds more than 16 years of teaching experience. His main area of research is Consumer Sciences and Business Innovations. Currently, he is working as Professor at Chitkara Business School, Chitkara University, Punjab, India. He has published 48 research papers in various journals and conferences which are indexed in Scopus, Web of Science and Google Scholar. He has edited 7 books published by IGI Global, De Gruyter and Wiley. He has also chaired many National and International Conferences. He is on the editorial board of 3 International Journals. He was awarded the Best Teacher in 2008. He is also part of the Board of Studies of various B-Schools and leading universities in Northern India.

Sanjay Taneja is currently an Associate Professor at Graphic Era Deemed to be University, Dehradun, India. His significant thrust areas are Banking Regulations, Banking and Finance (Fin Tech, Green Finance), Risks, Insurance Management, Green Economics and Management of Innovation in Insurance. He holds a double master's degree (MBA &M.Com.) in management with a specialization in Finance and Marketing. He received his PG degrees in Management (Gold Medalist) from Chaudhary Devi University, Sirsa, India in 2012. He earned his Doctor of Philosophy (Sponsored By ICSSR) in Banking and Finance entitled "An Appraisal of financial performance of Indian Banking Sector: A Comparative study of Public, Private and Foreign banks in 2016 from Chaudhary Devi University, Sirsa, India. He received his Post Doctoral Degree from faculty of Social Sciences, Department of Banking and Insurance, Usak University, Turkey entitled "Impact of the European Green Deal on Carbon (CO2) Emission in Turkey" in 2023. He has published research papers in reputed SCOPUS/Web of Science/SCI/ABDC/UGC Care Journals. Prof. Taneja has more than fifty publications in total (Scopus/ABDC/Web of Science- 27). He also has 2 e-books/1 text book/12 edited books (Emerald Publishing House/Nova Science/IGI and four book chapters to his credit (all are Scopus indexed). He has three Indian patents published and two more patents filed for a grant in India. He has handled various Scopus/ABDC/Web of Science journals in the capacity of Special Issue Editor. He is also reviewer in several Scopus/ABDC/ABS journals. He received several academic awards/recognitions- Best Researcher, Best Teacher, award etc. Overall, he is a very dynamic, creative, and positive individual. His motto in life is to grow and help others in growth.

Pawan Kumar is having academic experience of 15 years and have done his PhD from Kurukshetra university, Kurukshetra. He have done 20 publications in national and international journals and had presented papers in 15 National & International seminars and conferences.

* * *

Nilesh Arora is an academician with 21 years of Industry, teaching, and research experience. He has MBA in Marketing and Ph.D. in Management. He has been in academic leadership roles for the last 10 years and has 6 years of experience in the industry. He is presently working as Professor in Marketing area and Director, University School of Business, Chandigarh University, Mohali, Punjab, India. He has been teaching courses like Marketing Management, Consumer Behavior and Advertising. He is an avid researcher, prolific writer, and an academician of repute. He has attended and presented research papers in various National and International Conferences and Seminars in leading Universities and has several publications in national and international journals of repute. He has published research papers in various journals like Journal of Consumer Marketing, Marketing Intelligence and Planning, Journal of Global Scholars of Marketing Science, Journal of Global Marketing, Asian Academy of Management Journal, Decision, International Journal of Business and Globalisation. Dr. Arora's research interests include Consumer Behavior, Celebrity Endorsement, Social Media Advertising, and Retail.

Shaina Arora is a Research Scholar at University School of Business, Chandigarh University, Mohali, India.

Arvind Kumar Bhatt is an Associate Professor in the area of Marketing. He is having more than having more than 20 years of teaching and industrial experience. He has worked as Head of Marketing, Fiji National University, Fiji and also worked as Associate Professor, School of Business & Management, Addis Ababa Science & Technology University, Addis Ababa, Ethiopia, East Africa, Under United Nations Development Program. He is the author of books titled 'Innovation & Entrepreneurship". He has published several research papers in international and national journals.

Mohammad Kashif is a distinguished academician and researcher in the area of finance, economics and international business at Graphic Era Deemed to be University, Dehradun, India . He has several publications indexed in WoS, Scopus and ABDC. He authored a book titled Financial Management for undergraduate students. He is guiding PhD scholars in his area of expertise. Besides he is a member of several professional bodies at university level. He has been awarded many academic and research awards by reputed organizations.

Jaspreet Kaur is currently working as an Assistant Professor in University Business School, Chandigarh University, Mohali, Punjab. She is a post graduate (MBA-H.R) from Panjab University, Chandigarh. She has also qualified UGC NET JRF in Human Resource Management/Labour and Social Welfare and is currently pursuing PhD in Business Management from Chandigarh University, Mohali. She has over 8 years of experience in academic and administrative assignments. She also received Best Teacher of the Department Award in the year 2019 and 2021 in the field of imparting quality education. Her research interests include Employee Engagement, Management of Organizational Change and Organization Development. She has published several research papers and articles in reputed international and national journals and has presented papers in various national and international conferences. She also contributed one edited book and 10 book chapters on various topics.

Rumit Kaur is a Research Scholar of Management at Chandigarh University, Mohali. She holds a Master's Degree in MBA (Finance and Marketing) from Punjabi University, Patiala. With almost 4 years 9 Months experience in Industrial Sector and 5 years 2 Months of teaching experience at an A+ Accredited(NAAC) Institute, her research interest include (but not limited to) Finance and Marketing.

Manjit Kour is working as a Professor at University Business School at Chandigarh University. She holds a PhD in Business Management from IK Gujral Punjab Technical University, India. She has a good research record with several research papers published in reputed journals. She has presented numerous papers at international/national conferences and seminars. She has two books to her credit as well. She is an editorial board member and reviewer of many reputed journals including ABDC and Web of Science indexed journals. She has acted as a resource person in many seminars and workshops. She has also received International Researcher Award 2021 from the International Institute of Organized Research (I2OR). Her areas of interest include sustainability, green practices, Fintech, online marketing trends and business ethics.

Kaushal Mishra is working as a Professor of Marketing at the University School of Business, Chandigarh University, Mohali, Punjab. He has published 26 national and international research papers including three in Scopus-indexed journals and presented 26 papers at national and international conferences. He has 24 years of teaching and research experience. He did his PhD in Strategy formulation for marketing of services in rural Uttar Pradesh from Uttar Pradesh Rajarshi Tandon University, Allahabad. He has qualified for UGC – NET in Management twice.

Harvinder Singh is working as an Assistant Professor of Finance at the University School of Business, Chandigarh University, Mohali, Punjab. He has published 7 national and international research papers including one in web of science indexed journals and presented 5 papers at national and international conferences. He has 12 years of teaching and research experience. He did his PhD in Financial Inclusion from CT University, Ludhiana, Punjab. He has qualified for UGC–NET in Management as well as in Commerce.

Index

www.ingramcontent.com/pod-product-compliance
Lightning Source LLC
LaVergne TN
LVHW080647011026
849160LV00014B/1348
* 9 7 9 8 3 6 9 3 4 4 8 9 7 *